# Information Theory and Coding

## RIVER PUBLISHERS SERIES IN COMPUTING AND INFORMATION SCIENCE AND TECHNOLOGY

*Series Editors:*

**K. C. CHEN**
*National Taiwan University, Taipei, Taiwan*
*University of South Florida, USA*

**SANDEEP SHUKLA**
*Virginia Tech, USA*
*Indian Institute of Technology Kanpur, India*

The "River Publishers Series in Computing and Information Science and Technology" covers research which ushers the 21st Century into an Internet and multimedia era. Networking suggests transportation of such multimedia contents among nodes in communication and/or computer networks, to facilitate the ultimate Internet.

Theory, technologies, protocols and standards, applications/services, practice and implementation of wired/wireless networking are all within the scope of this series. Based on network and communication science, we further extend the scope for 21st Century life through the knowledge in machine learning, embedded systems, cognitive science, pattern recognition, quantum/biological/molecular computation and information processing, user behaviors and interface, and applications across healthcare and society.

Books published in the series include research monographs, edited volumes, handbooks and textbooks. The books provide professionals, researchers, educators, and advanced students in the field with an invaluable insight into the latest research and developments.

Topics included in the series are as follows:-

- Artificial intelligence
- Cognitive Science and Brian Science
- Communication/Computer Networking Technologies and Applications
- Computation and Information Processing
- Computer Architectures
- Computer networks
- Computer Science
- Embedded Systems
- Evolutionary computation
- Information Modelling
- Information Theory
- Machine Intelligence
- Neural computing and machine learning
- Parallel and Distributed Systems
- Programming Languages
- Reconfigurable Computing
- Research Informatics
- Soft computing techniques
- Software Development
- Software Engineering
- Software Maintenance

For a list of other books in this series, visit www.riverpublishers.com

# Information Theory and Coding

**Marcelo Sampaio de Alencar**
Institute for Advanced Studies in Communications (Iecom)
Federal University of Paraíba (UFPB), Brazil

River Publishers

Routledge
Taylor & Francis Group
NEW YORK AND LONDON

**Published 2026 by River Publishers**
River Publishers
Broagervej 10, 9260 Gistrup, Denmark
www.riverpublishers.com

**Distributed exclusively by Routledge**
605 Third Avenue, New York, NY 10017, USA
4 Park Square, Milton Park, Abingdon, Oxon OX14 4RN

*Information Theory and Coding* / by Marcelo Sampaio de Alencar.



Routledge is an imprint of the Taylor & Francis Group, an informa business

ISBN 978-87-4381-359-0 (hardback)
ISBN 978-87-4381-365-1 (paperback)
ISBN 978-87-4381-362-0 (online)
ISBN 978-87-4381-361-3 (master ebook)
ISBN 978-87-4381-364-4 (ePub)

DOI: 10.1201/9788743813613

*This book is dedicated to my family*

# Contents

# Preface

Information Theory and Coding is a classic topic in the educational market, that evolved from the amalgamation of different areas of Mathematics and Probability, which includes set theory, developed by Georg Cantor, and measure theory, fostered by Henri Lebesgue, as well as the axiomatic treatment of probability by Andrei Kolmogorov, in 1931, and finally the beautiful development of Communication Theory by Claude Shannon, in 1948.

Information Theory and Coding is fundamental to several areas of knowledge, including the Engineering, Computer Science, Mathematics, Physics, Sciences, Economics, Social Sciences and Social Communication. It is part of the syllabus for most courses in Computer Science, Mathematics and Engineering.

For Electrical Engineering courses it is a pre-requisite to some disciplines, including communication systems, transmission techniques, error control coding, estimation and digital signal processing. This book is self-contained, it is a reference and an introduction for graduate students who did not have information theory before. It could also be used for as and undergraduate textbook. It is addressed to a large audience in Electrical and Computer Engineering or Mathematics and Applied Physics. The book target graduate students in these areas, who may not have taken basic courses in specific topics, which can find a quick and concise way to obtain the knowledge they need to succeed in advanced courses.

According to a study by the Institute of Electrical and Electronics Engineers (IEEE), the companies, enterprises and industry are in need of professionals with a solid background on mathematics and sciences, instead of the specialized professional of the previous century. The employment market in this area is in demand of information technology professionals and engineers who could afford to change and learn, as the market changes. The market needs professionals who can model and design.

Few books have been published covering the subjects needed to understand the very fundamental concepts of Information Theory. Most books which deal with the subject are destined to very specific audiences.

The more mathematically oriented books are seldom used by people with engineering, economics or statistical background, because the authors are more interested in theorems and related conditions than in fundamental concepts and applications. The books written for engineers usually lack the required rigour, or skip some important points in favour of simplicity and conciseness.

The idea is to present a seamless connection between the more abstract advanced set theory, the fundamental concepts from measure theory and integration and probability, filling in the gaps from previous books and leading to an interesting, robust and, hopefully, self-contained exposition of the Information Theory.

The book begins with the historical evolution of Information Theory. Chapter 1 deals with the basic concepts of information theory, and how to measure information. The information associated to a certain source is discussed in Chapter 2. The usual types of source codes are presented in Chapter 3. Information transmission, joint information, conditional entropy, mutual information and channel capacity are the subject of Chapter 4. Error ccorrecting codes are discussed in Chapter 5. Chapter 6 presents the some of the main decoding algorithms, including the decoding of cyclic and algrabraic codes, and soft decision decoding.

Chapter 7 presents spread spectrum and code division multiple access, the basic block of most cellular and personal communication systems in operation. The information theoretical aspects of cryptography, including network security and hash functions, are presented in Chapter 8. The appendices include a review of probability theory and a glossary of terms on information and coding theory. Illustrations and graphics help the reader understand the theory.

**Marcelo S. Alencar**

# Acknowledgments

The author is grateful to all the members of the Communications Research Group, certified by the Brazilian Council for Scientific and Technological Development (CNPq), and the colleagues from the Federal University of Rio Grande do Norte, for their collaboration in many ways, helpful discussions and friendship, as well as our colleagues at the Institute for Advanced Studies in Communications (Iecom).

The author wishes to acknowledge the contribution of professors Francisco Madeiro, from the State University of Pernambuco, and Waslon T. A. Lopes, from the Federal University of Paraíba, Brazil, to the chapter on source coding.

The author is also grateful to professor Valdemar Cardoso da Rocha Jr., from the Federal University of Pernambuco, Brazil, for contributions to the chapters on coding theory, and also for the long term cooperation and useful discussions related to information theory and coding.

The author is indebted to Silvana, Thiago, Raissa, Marcella, Raphael, Vicente, Cora and Maria Isabela for their patience and support during the course of the preparation of this book.

Finally, the author registers the support of Junko Nakajima from River Publishers, in the book preparation process.

# List of Figures

# List of Tables

# 1

# Information Theory

*"Information is not knowledge."*
Albert Einstein

Information Theory is a branch of Probability Theory which has application and correlation with many areas, including communication systems, communication theory, Physics, language and meaning, cybernetics, psychology, art and complexity theory (Pierce, 1980). The basis for the theory was established by Harry Theodor Nyqvist (1889-1976) (Nyquist, 1924), also known as Harry Nyquist, and Ralph Vinton Lyon Hartley (1888-1970), who invented the Hartley oscillator (Hartley, 1928). They published the first articles on the subject, in which the factors that influenced the transmission of information were discussed.

The seminal article by Claude E. Shannon (1916-2001) extended the theory to include new factors, such as the noise effect in the channel and the savings that could be obtained as a function of the statistical structure of the original message and the information receiver characteristics (Shannon, 1948a). Shannon defined the fundamental communication problem as the possibility of, exactly or approximately, reproducing, at a certain point, a message that has been chosen at another one.

In his classical paper, Shannon provided a precise mathematical definition for the intuitive notion of information. In terms of this definition it was possible to state precisely the notion of a communication channel and its capacity. By a communication channel one means, in simple terms, an apparatus for signaling from one point to another.

A communication channel is meant, in basic words, a set of devices for signaling from one point to another. The abstract properties of a channel that are of concern to the information theorist are: a finite set of signals that may be transmitted; a set, not necessarily finite, of signals that may be received; and the probability, or probability density, of the reception of any particular signal when the transmitted signal is specified (Feinstein, 1954).

DOI: 10.1201/9788743813613-1

The main semantic aspects of the communication, initially established by Charles Sanders Peirce (1839-1914), a philosopher and creator of Semiotic Theory, are not relevant for the development of the Shannon information theory. What is important is to consider that a particular message is selected from a set of possible messages.

Of course, as mentioned by John Robinson Pierce (1910-2002), quoting the philosopher Alfred Jules Ayer (1910-1989, it is possible to communicate not only information, but knowledge, errors, opinions, ideas, experiences, desires, commands, emotions, feelings. Heat and movement can be communicated, as well as, force, weakness and disease (Pierce, 1980).

Hartley has found several reasons why the natural information measure should be the logarithm:

- It is a practical metric in Engineering, considering that various parameters, such as time and bandwidth, are proportional to the logarithm of the number of possibilities.
- From a mathematical point of view, it is an adequate measure, because several limit operations are simply stated in terms of logarithms.
- It has an intuitive appeal, as an adequate metric, because, for instance, two binary symbols have four possibilities of occurrence.

The choice of the logarithm base defines the information unit. If base 2 is used, the unit is the bit, an acronym suggested by John W. Tukey for binary digit, that is also a play or words, that can also mean a piece of information.

The information transmission is informally given in bit/s, but a unit has been proposed to pay tribute to the scientist who developed the concept, it is called the shannon, or [Sh] for short. This has a direct correspondence with the unit for frequency, hertz or [Hz], for cycles per second, which was adopted by the International System of Units (SI)[1].

Aleksandr Yakovlevich Khinchin (1894-1959) (Khinchin, 1957) put the Information Theory in solid basis, with a more precise and unified mathematical discussion about the entropy concept, which supported Shannon's intuitive and practical view.

The books by Robert B. Ash (1935-2015), and American mathematician who worked in various areas, including Information Theory and Discrete Mathematics (Ash, 1965), and Amiel Feinstein (Feinstein, 1958) give the mathematical reasons for the choice of the logarithm to measure information, and the book by J. Aczél e Z. Daróczy (Aczél and Daróczy, 1975) presents several Shannon information measures and their characterization, as well as Alfréd Rényi (1921-1970) entropy metric.

A discussion on generalized entropies can be found in the book edited by Luigi M. Ricciardi (Ricciardi, 1990). Lotfi Asker Zadeh introduced the concept of fuzzy set, and efficient tool to represent the behavior of systems that depend on the perception and judgement of human beings, and applied it to information measurement (Zadeh, 1965).

## 1.1 Information Measurement

The objective of this section is to establish a measure for the information content of a discrete system, using Probability Theory. Consider a discrete random experiment, such as the occurrence of a symbol, and its associated sample space $\Omega$, in which $X$ a real random variable (Reza, 1961).

The random variable $X$ can assume the following values

$$X = \{x_1, x_2, \ldots, x_n\},$$
$$\text{in which } \bigcup_{k=1}^{N} x_k = \Omega, \tag{1.1}$$

with probabilities in the set $P$

$$P = \{p_1, p_2, \ldots, p_n\},$$
$$\text{in which } \sum_{k=1}^{N} p_k = 1. \tag{1.2}$$

The information, or surprise, associated to a particular event is based on the information measure proposed by Hartley. Shannon generalized the concept of information and proposed the following formula

$$I(x_i) = \log\left(\frac{1}{p_i}\right), \tag{1.3}$$

that is meaningful, because the sure event has probability one and zero information, by a property of the logarithm, and the impossible event has zero probability and infinite information.

**Example:** Suppose the sample space is partitioned into two equally probable spaces. Then

$$I(x_1) = I(x_2) = -\log\tfrac{1}{2} = 1 \text{ bit}, \tag{1.4}$$

that is, the choice between two equally probable events requires one unit of information, when a base 2 logarithm is used.

Considering the occurrence of $2^N$ equiprobable symbols, then the self-information of each event is given by

$$I(x_k) = -\log p_k = -\log 2^{-N} = N \text{ bits}. \tag{1.5}$$

It is possible to define the source entropy, $H(X)$, as the average information, obtained by weighing of all the occurrences

$$H(X) = E[I(x_i)] = -\sum_{i=1}^{N} p_i \log p_i. \tag{1.6}$$

Observe that Equation 1.6 is the weighing average of the logarithms of the probabilities, in which the weights are the real values of the probabilities of the random variable $X$, and this indicates that $H(X)$ can be interpreted as the expected value of the random variable that assumes the value $-\log p_i$, with probability $p_i$ (Ash, 1965).

**Example:** Consider a source that emits two symbols, with unequal probabilities, given in Table 1.1.

**Table 1.1** Symbol probabilities of a two-symbol source.

| Symbol | Probability |
|---|---|
| $x_1$ | $\frac{1}{4}$ |
| $x_2$ | $\frac{3}{4}$ |

The source entropy is calculated as

$$H(X) = -\frac{1}{4}\log\frac{1}{4} - \frac{3}{4}\log\frac{3}{4} = 0,81 \text{ bits per symbol}.$$

## 1.2 Requirements for an Information Metric

A few fundamental properties are necessary for the entropy, in order to obtain an axiomatic approach to base the information measurement (Reza, 1961).

- If the event probabilities suffer a small change, the associated measure must change in accordance, in a continuous manner, which provides a physical meaning to the metric.

$$H(p_1, p_2, \ldots, p_N) \text{ is continuous in } p_k, k = 1, 2, \ldots, N, \quad 0 \leq p_k \leq 1. \tag{1.7}$$

- The information measure must be symmetric in relation to the probability set $P$. That is, the entropy is invariant to the order of events.

$$H(p_1, p_2, p_3, \ldots, p_N) = H(p_1, p_3, p_2, \ldots, p_N). \tag{1.8}$$

- The maximum of the entropy is obtained when the events are equally probable. That is, when nothing is known about the set of events, or about what message has been produced, the assumption of a uniform distribution gives the highest information quantity, that corresponds to the highest level of uncertainty.

$$\text{Maximum of } H(p_1, p_2, \ldots, p_N) = H\left(\frac{1}{N}, \frac{1}{N}, \ldots, \frac{1}{N}\right). \tag{1.9}$$

**Example:** Consider two sources that emit four symbols The first source symbols, shown in Table 1.2, have equal probabilities, and the second source symbols, shown in Table 1.3, are produced with unequal probabilities.

**Table 1.2** Identically distributed symbol probabilities.

| Symbol | Probability |
|---|---|
| $x_1$ | $\frac{1}{4}$ |
| $x_2$ | $\frac{1}{4}$ |
| $x_3$ | $\frac{1}{4}$ |
| $x_4$ | $\frac{1}{4}$ |

**Table 1.3** Unequal symbol probabilities.

| Symbol | Probability |
|---|---|
| $x_1$ | $\frac{1}{2}$ |
| $x_2$ | $\frac{1}{4}$ |
| $x_3$ | $\frac{1}{8}$ |
| $x_4$ | $\frac{1}{8}$ |

The mentioned property indicates that the first source attains the highest level of uncertainty, regardless of the probability values of the second source, as long as they are different.

- Consider that and adequate measure for average uncertainty was found $H(p_1, p_2, \ \dots \ , p_N)$ associated to a set of events. Assume that event $\{x_N\}$ is divided into $M$ disjoint sets, with probabilities $q_k$, such that

$$p_N = \sum_{k=1}^{M} q_k, \tag{1.10}$$

and the probabilities associated to the new events can be normalized in such a way that

$$\frac{q_1}{p_n} + \frac{q_2}{p_n} + \cdots + \frac{q_m}{p_n} = 1. \tag{1.11}$$

Then, the creation of new events from the original set modifies the entropy to

$$\begin{aligned} H(p_1, p_2, \ \dots \ , p_{N-1}, q_1, q_2, \ \dots \ , q_M) &= H(p_1, \dots, p_{N-1}, p_N) \\ + \ p_N H\left(\frac{q_1}{p_N}, \frac{q_2}{p_N}, \ \dots \ , \frac{q_M}{p_N}\right), \end{aligned} \tag{1.12}$$

with

$$p_N = \sum_{k=1}^{M} q_k.$$

It is possible to show that the function defined by Equation 1.6 satisfies all requirements. To demonstrate the continuity, is suffices to do (Reza, 1961)

$$\begin{aligned} H(p_1, p_2, \dots, p_N) &= -\left[p_1 \log p_1 + p_2 \log p_2 + \cdots + p_N \log p_N\right] \\ &= -\left[p_1 \log p_1 + p_2 \log p_2 + \cdots p_{N-1} \log p_{N-1}\right. \\ &+ \ (1 - p_1 - p_2 - \cdots - p_{N-1}) \\ &\cdot \ \left.\log(1 - p_1 - p_2 - \cdots - p_{N-1})\right]. \end{aligned} \tag{1.13}$$

Notice that, for all independent random variables, the set of probabilities $p_1, p_2, \ \dots \ , p_{N-1}$ and also $(1 - p_1 - p_2 - \ \dots \ - p_{N-1})$ are contiguous in $[0, 1]$, and that the logarithm of a continuous function is also continuous. The entropy is clearly symmetric.

The maximum value property can be demonstrated, if one considers that all probabilities are equal and that the entropy is maximized by that condition

$$p_1 = p_2 = \cdots = p_N. \tag{1.14}$$

Taking into account, according to intuition, that the uncertainty is maximum for a system of equiprobable states, it is possible to arbitrarily choose a random variable with probability $p_N$ depending on $p_k$, and $k = 1, 2, \ldots, N-1$. Taking the derivative of the entropy in terms of each probability

$$\begin{aligned}\frac{dH}{dp_k} &= \sum_{i=1}^{N} \frac{\partial H}{\partial p_i}\frac{\partial p_i}{\partial p_k} \\ &= -\frac{d}{dp_k}(p_k \log p_k) - \frac{d}{dp_N}(p_N \log p_N)\frac{\partial p_N}{\partial p_k}. \qquad (1.15)\end{aligned}$$

But, probability $p_N$ can be written as

$$p_N = 1 - (p_1 + p_2 + \cdots + p_k + \cdots + p_{N-1}). \qquad (1.16)$$

Therefore, the derivative of the entropy is

$$\frac{dH}{dp_k} = -(\log_2 e + \log p_k) + (\log_2 e + \log p_n), \qquad (1.17)$$

that, using a property of logarithms, simplifies to,

$$\frac{dH}{dp_k} = -\log\frac{p_k}{p_n}. \qquad (1.18)$$

But,

$$\frac{dH}{dp_k} = 0, \text{ which gives } p_k = p_N. \qquad (1.19)$$

As $p_k$ was chosen in an arbitrarily manner, one concludes that, to obtain a maximum for the entropy function, one must have

$$p_1 = p_2 = \cdots = p_N = \frac{1}{N}. \qquad (1.20)$$

The maximum is guaranteed, because

$$H(1, 0, 0, \ldots, 0) = 0. \qquad (1.21)$$

On the other hand, for equiprobable events, it is possible to verify that the entropy is always positive, for it attains its maximum at (Csiszár and Kórner, 1981)

$$H\left(\frac{1}{N}, \frac{1}{N}, \ldots, \frac{1}{N}\right) = \log N > 0. \qquad (1.22)$$

To prove additivity, is suffices to use the definition of entropy, computed for a two set partition, with probabilities $\{p_1, p_2, \ldots, p_{N-1}\}$ e $\{q_1, q_2, \ldots, q_M\}$,

$$
\begin{aligned}
H(p_1, p_2, \ldots, p_{N-1}, q_1, q_2, \ldots, q_M) \\
&= -\sum_{k=1}^{N-1} p_k \log p_k - \sum_{k=1}^{M} q_k \log q_k \\
&= -\sum_{k=1}^{N} p_k \log p_k + p_N \log p_N - \sum_{k=1}^{M} q_k \log q_k \\
&= H(p_1, p_2, \ldots, p_N) + p_N \log p_N \\
&- \sum_{k=1}^{M} q_k \log q_k .
\end{aligned} \tag{1.23}
$$

But, the second part of the last term can be written in a way to display the importance of the entropy in the derivation

$$
\begin{aligned}
p_N \log p_N - \sum_{k=1}^{M} q_k \log q_k &= p_N \sum_{k=1}^{M} \frac{q_k}{p_N} \log p_N - \sum_{k=1}^{M} q_k \log q_k \\
&= -p_N \sum_{k=1}^{M} \frac{q_k}{p_N} \log \frac{q_k}{p_N} \\
&= p_N H\left(\frac{q_1}{p_N}, \frac{q_2}{p_N}, \ldots, \frac{q_M}{p_N}\right),
\end{aligned} \tag{1.24}
$$

and this demonstrates the mentioned property.

The entropy is non-negative, which guarantees that the partitioning of one event into several other events does not reduce the system entropy, as shown in the following

$$
H(p_1, \ldots, p_{N-1}, q_1, q_2, \ldots, q_M) \geq H(p_1, \ldots, p_{N-1}, p_N), \tag{1.25}
$$

that is, is one splits a symbol into two or more, the entropy always increases, and that is the physical origin of the word.

**Example:** A binary source, $X$, emits symbols 0 and 1 with probabilities $p$ and $q = 1 - p$. The average information per symbol is given by $H(X) = -p \log p - q \log q$, that is known as entropy function.

$$
H(p) = -p \log p - (1 - p) \log (1 - p). \tag{1.26}
$$

**Example:** For the binary source, consider that the symbol probabilities are $p = 1/8$ and $q = 7/8$, and compute the entropy of the source.

The average information per symbol is given by

$$H(X) \;=\; -\,1/8 \log 1/8 \;-\; 7/8 \log 7/8,$$

which gives $H(X) = 0.544$.

Note that even though 1 bit is produced for each symbol, the actual average information is 0.544 bits due to the unequal probabilities.

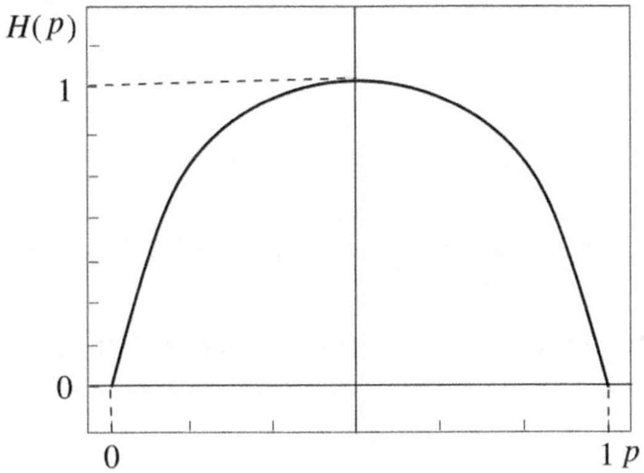


**Figure 1.1** Graph of an information function.

The entropy function is illustrated in Figure 1.1, in which it is possible to notice the symmetry, concavity and the maximum for equiprobable symbols. As as consequence of the symmetry the sample spaces, with probability distributions obtained from permutations of a common distribution provide the same information quantity (van der Lubbe, 1997).

The entropy function has a maximum when all symbols are equiprobable, for $p = q = 1/2$, for which the entropy is 1 bit/symbol. The function attains a minimum for $p = 0$ or $p = 1$.

This function plays an essential role in determining the capacity of a binary symmetric channel. Observe that the entropy function is concave, that is

$$H(p_1) \,+\, H(p_2) \,\leq\, 2H\left(\frac{p_1 \,+\, p_2}{2}\right). \tag{1.27}$$

**Example:** A source emits symbols from an alphabet $X = \{x_1, x_2, x_3, x_4\}$, with probabilities given in Table 1.4. Calculate the entropy of this source?

**Table 1.4** Symbol probabilities of a certain source.

| Symbol | Probability |
|---|---|
| $x_1$ | $\frac{1}{2}$ |
| $x_2$ | $\frac{1}{4}$ |
| $x_3$ | $\frac{1}{8}$ |
| $x_4$ | $\frac{1}{8}$ |

The entropy is computed using Formula 1.6, for $N = 4$ symbols, as

$$H(X) = -\sum_{i=1}^{4} p_i \log p_i,$$

or

$$H(X) = -\frac{1}{2}\log\frac{1}{2} - \frac{1}{4}\log\frac{1}{4} - \frac{2}{8}\log\frac{1}{8} = 1.75 \text{ bits per symbol.}$$

**Example:** Compute the following important limit, which appears frequently in information theory.

$$\lim_{x\to 0} x \log x.$$

As can be noted, the previous operation is indeterminate. Therefore, it is possible to use L'Hopital's Rule to calculate the limit. But first, observe that

$$f(x) = x \log x = \frac{\log x}{1/x}.$$

Taking the limit as $x \to 0$, one obtains

$$\lim_{x\to 0} f(x) = \lim_{x\to 0} x \log x = \lim_{x\to 0} \frac{\log x}{1/x}.$$

Applying L'Hopital's Rule, one finally obtains the required limit,

$$\lim_{x\to 0} f(x) = \lim_{x\to 0} \frac{1/x}{-1/x^2} = \lim_{x\to 0} \frac{-x^2}{x} = \lim_{x\to 0} -x = 0.$$

## Notes

[1]The author of this book proposed the adoption of the shannon [Sh] unit during the IEEE International Conference on Communications (ICC'2001), in Helsinki, Finland, shortly after Shannon's death.

# 2

# Sources of Information

*"The control of information is something the elite always does, particularly in a despotic form of government. Information, knowledge, is power. If you can control information, you can control people."*
Tom Clancy

## 2.1 Source Coding

The efficient representation of data produced by a discrete source is called source coding. For a source coder to obtain a good performance it is necessary to take the symbol statistics into account. If the symbol probabilities are different, it is useful to assign short codewords to probable symbols and long ones to infrequent symbols. This produces a variable length code, such as the Morse code.

Two usual requirements to build an efficient code are:

1. The codewords generated by the coder are binary.
2. The codewords are unequivocally decodable, and the original message sequence can be reconstructed from the binary coded sequence.

Consider Figure 2.1, that shows a discrete memoryless source (DMS), whose output $x_k$ is converted by the source coder into a sequence of 0's e 1's, denoted $b_k$. Assume that the source alphabet has $K$ different symbols, and that the $k$-ary symbol, $x_k$, occurs with probability $p_k$, $k = 0, 1, \ldots, K-1$.

Let $l_k$ be the average length, measured in bits, of the binary word assigned to symbol $x_k$. The average length of the words produced by the source encoder is defined as (Haykin, 1988)

$$\overline{L} = \sum_{k=1}^{K} p_k l_k. \tag{2.1}$$

DOI: 10.1201/9788743813613-2

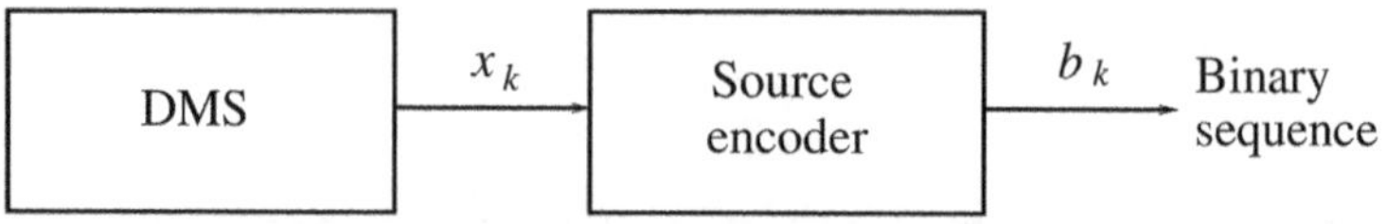


**Figure 2.1** Discrete memoryless source (DMS) encoder.

The parameter $\overline{L}$ represents the average number of bits per symbol from that are used in the source coding process. Let $L_{\text{min}}$ be the smallest possible value of $\overline{L}$. The source coding efficiency is defined as (Haykin, 1988)

$$\eta = \frac{L_{\text{min}}}{\overline{L}}. \tag{2.2}$$

Because $\overline{L} \geq L_{\text{min}}$, then $\eta \leq 1$. The source coding efficiency increases as $\eta$ approaches 1.

Shanon's first Theorem, or source coding theorem, provides a means to determine $L_{\text{min}}$ (Haykin, 1988),

> Given a memoryless discrete source with entropy $H(X)$, the average length of the codewords is limited by
>
> $$\overline{L} \geq H(X).$$

Entropy $H(X)$, therefore, represents a fundamental limit for the average number of bits per source symbol $\overline{L}$, that are needed to represent a memoryless discrete source, and this number can be as small as, but never smaller, than the source entropy $H(X)$. Therefore, for $L_{\text{min}} = H(X)$, the source coding efficiency can be written as (Haykin, 1988)

$$\eta = \frac{H(X)}{\overline{L}}. \tag{2.3}$$

The code redundancy is given by (Abramson, N., 1963).

$$1 - \eta = \frac{\overline{L} - H(X)}{\overline{L}}. \tag{2.4}$$

## 2.2 Extension of a Memoryless Discrete Source

It is useful to consider the encoding of blocks of $N$ successive symbols from the source, instead of individual symbols. Each bloc can be seen as a product of an extended source, with an alphabet $X^N$ that has $K^N$ distinct blocks. The symbols are statistically independent, therefore, the probability of an extended symbol is the product of the probabilities of the original symbols, and it can be shown that

$$H(X^N) = NH(X). \tag{2.5}$$

**Example**: consider the discrete memoryless source with alphabet

$$X = \{x_1, x_2, x_3\}.$$

The second order extended source has an alphabet

$$X^2 = \{x_1x_1, x_1x_2, x_1x_3, x_2x_1, x_2x_2, x_2x_3, x_3x_1, x_3x_2, x_3x_3\}.$$

For the second order extended source of the example, $p(x_ix_j) = p(x_i)p(x_j)$. In particular, if all original source symbols are equiprobable, then $H(X) = \log_2 3$ bits. The second order extended source has nine equiprobable symbols, therefore, $H(X^2) = \log_2 9$ bits. It can be noticed that $H(X^2) = 2H(X)$.

### 2.2.1 Improving the Coding Efficiency

The following example illustrates how to improve the coding efficiency using extensions of a source (Abramson, N., 1963).

**Example**: consider a memoryless source $S = \{x_1, x_2\}$, with $p(x_1) = \frac{3}{4}$ and $p(x_2) = \frac{1}{4}$. The source entropy is given by $\frac{1}{4}\log_2 4 + \frac{3}{4}\log_2 \frac{4}{3} = 0,811$ bit.

A compact code for the source is presented in Table 2.1.

**Table 2.1** A compact code.

| $x_i$ | $p(x_i)$ | Compact code |
|---|---|---|
| $x_1$ | $\frac{3}{4}$ | 0 |
| $x_2$ | $\frac{1}{4}$ | 1 |

The average codeword length is one bit, and the efficiency is

$$\eta_1 = 0,811.$$

**Table 2.2** A compact code for an extension of a source.

| Symbol | Probability | Compact code |
|---|---|---|
| $x_1x_1$ | 9/16 | 0 |
| $x_1x_2$ | 3/16 | 10 |
| $x_2x_1$ | 3/16 | 110 |
| $x_2x_2$ | 1/16 | 111 |

**Example**: to improve the efficiency, the second extension of the source is encoded, as shown in Table 2.2.

The average codeword length is $\frac{27}{16}$ bits. The extended source entropy is $2 \times 0,811$ bits, and the efficiency is

$$\eta_2 = \frac{2 \times 0,811 \times 16}{27} = 0,961.$$

The efficiency improves for each new extension of the original source but, of course, the codes get longer, which implies that they take more time to transmit or process.

**Example**: the efficiencies associated to the third and fourth extensions of the source are

$$\eta_3 = 0,985.$$

and

$$\eta_4 = 0,991.$$

As higher order extensions of the source are encoded, the efficiency approaches 1, a result that is proved in the next section.

## 2.3 Prefix Codes

For a prefix code, no codeword is a prefix, of the first part, of another codeword. Therefore, the code shown in Table 2.3 is prefix. On the other hand, code shown in Table 2.4 is not prefix, because the binary word 10, for instance, is a prefix for the codeword 100.

To decode a sequence of binary words produced by a prefix encoder, the decoder begins at the first binary digit of the sequence, and decodes a codeword at a time. It is similar to a decision tree, which is a representation of the codewords of a given source code.

**Table 2.3** A prefix code for given a source.

| Symbol | Code |
|---|---|
| $x_1$ | 1 |
| $x_2$ | 01 |
| $x_3$ | 001 |
| $x_4$ | 000 |

**Table 2.4** A source code that is nor prefix.

| Symbol | Code |
|---|---|
| $x_1$ | 1 |
| $x_2$ | 10 |
| $x_3$ | 100 |
| $x_4$ | 1000 |

Figure 2.2 illustrates the decision tree for the prefix code pointed in Table 2.5.

The tree has one initial state and four final states, which correspond to the symbols $x_1$, $x_2$, and $x_3$. From the initial state, for each received bit, the decoder searches the tree until a final state is found.

The decoder, then, emits a corresponding decoded symbol and returns to the initial state. Therefore, from the initial state, after receiving a 1, the source decoder decodes symbol $x_1$ and returns to the initial state. If it receives a 0, the decoder moves to the lower part of the tree, in the following, after receiving another 0, the decoder moves further to the lower part of the tree and, after receiving a 1, the decoder retrieves $x_2$ and returns to the initial state.

Considering the code from Table 2.5, with the decoding tree from Figure 2.5, the binary sequence 011100010010100101 is decoded into the output sequence $x_1 x_0 x_0 x_3 x_0 x_2 x_1 x_2 x_1$.

By construction, a prefix code is always unequivocally decodable, which is important to avoid any confusion at the receiver.

Consider a code that has been constructed for a discrete source with alphabet $\{x_1, x_2, \ldots, x_K\}$. Let $\{p_1, p_1, \ldots, p_K\}$ be the source statistics, and $l_k$ be the codeword length for symbol $x_k$, $k = 1, \ldots, K$. If the binary code constructed for the source is a prefix one, then one can use the Kraft-McMillan inequality

**Table 2.5** Example of a prefix code.

| Source symbol | Probability of occurrence | Code |
|---|---|---|
| $x_0$ | 0,5 | 1 |
| $x_1$ | 0,25 | 01 |
| $x_2$ | 0,125 | 001 |
| $x_3$ | 0,125 | 000 |

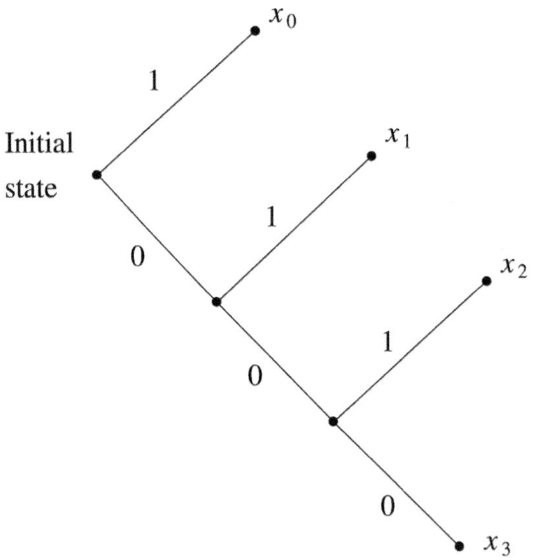


**Figure 2.2** Decision tree for the code in Table 2.5.

$$\sum_{k=1}^{K} 2^{-l_k} \leq 1, \tag{2.6}$$

in which factor 2 is the radix, or number of symbols, of the binary alphabet.

For a memoryless discrete source with entropy $H(X)$, the codeword average length of a prefix code is limited to

$$H(X) \leq \overline{L} < H(X) + 1. \tag{2.7}$$

The left hand side equality is obtained on the condition that symbol $x_k$ be emitted from the source with probability $p_k = 2^{-l_k}$, in which $l_k$ is the length of the codeword assigned to symbol $x_k$.

Consider the $N$-th order extension of a memoryless discrete source. For the $N$-th order extension of a code the encoder operates on blocks of $N$

symbols from the original source, instead of individual ones, and the source alphabet $X^N$ has an entropy that is $N$ times the entropy of the original source.

Let $\overline{L}_N$ be the average length for the extended prefix code. For an unequivocally decodable code, $\overline{L}_N$ is as small as possible, From Equation 2.7, it follows that

$$H(X^N) \leq \overline{L}_N < H(X^N) + 1, \tag{2.8}$$

therefore,

$$NH(X) \leq \overline{L}_N < NH(X) + 1, \tag{2.9}$$

or, in an equivalent way,

$$H(X) \leq \frac{\overline{L}_N}{N} < H(X) + \frac{1}{N}. \tag{2.10}$$

In the limit, as $N$ goes to infinity, the inferior and superior limitants converge, and therefore,

$$\lim_{N \to \infty} \frac{1}{N} \overline{L}_N = H(X). \tag{2.11}$$

Therefore, for a prefix extended encoder, as the order $N$ increases, the code represents the source as efficiently as desired, and the average codeword length can be as close to the source entropy as possible, according to Shannon's source coding theorem. On the other hand, there is a compromise between the reduction on the average codeword length and the increase in complexity of the decoding process (Haykin, 1988).

## 2.4 The Information Unit

There is some confusion between the binary digit, abbreviated as bit, and the information particle, also baptized as bit by John Tukey and Claude Shannon.

In a meeting of the Institute of Electrical and Electronics Engineers (IEEE) the largest scientific institution in the World, the author of this book proposed the shannon [Sh] as a unit of information transmission, equivalent to bit per second. It is instructive to say that the bit, as used today, is not a unit of information, because it is not approved by the International System of Units (SI).

What is curious about that meeting was the misunderstanding that surrounded the units, in particular regarding the difference between the concepts of information unit and digital logic unit (Alencar, 2007).

To make things clear the binary digit is associated to a certain state of a digital system, and not to information. A binary digit "1" can refer to 5 volts, in TTL logic, or 12 volts, for CMOS logic.

The information bit exists independent of any association to a particular voltage level. It can be associated, for example, to a discrete information or to the quantization of an analog information.

For instance, the information bits recorded on the surface of a compact disk are stored as a series of depressions on the plastic material, which are read by an optical beam, generated by a semiconductor laser. But, obviously, the depressions are not the information. They represent a means for the transmission of information, a material substrate that carries the data.

In the same way, the information can exist, even if it is not associated to light or other electromagnetic radiation. It can be transported by several means, including paper, and materializes itself when is processed by a computer of by a human being.

# 3

# Source Coding

*"Information technology and business are becoming inextricably interwoven. I don't think anybody can talk meaningfully about one without the talking about the other."*
Bill Gates

## 3.1 Types of Source Codes

Source coding represents a mapping from a sequence of symbols of an information source to a sequence of alphabet symbols, usually binary. This is done such that the source symbols can be exactly recovered from the binary symbols, in case of lossless source coding, or can be recovered within some distortion, which is considered lossy source coding.

It is usual that messages that appear frequently be represented with shorter codes, while infrequent messages be represented with longer codes, resulting in compressed data length. This chapter presents the classification of source codes, block codes, non-singular codes, uniquely decodable codes and instantaneous codes.

After introducing the encoding techniques, it is possible to evaluate the coding efficiency to determine if the encoding method is efficient. In order to discuss coding efficiency, it is important to understand the concept of entropy.

### 3.1.1 Block Codes

Let $S = \{x_0, x_1, \ldots, x_{K-1}\}$ be a set of symbols of a given source alphabet. A code is defined as a mapping of all possible symbol sequences from $S$ into sequences of another set $X = \{x_0, x_1, \ldots, x_{M-1}\}$, called the code alphabet.

A block code maps each of the symbols from the source set into a sequence of the code alphabet. The fixed sequences of symbols $x_j$ are called

DOI: 10.1201/9788743813613-3

codewords $X_i$. Note that $X_i$ denotes a sequence of $x_j$'s (Abramson, N., 1963).

**Example**: A binary block code is presented in Table 3.1, and a ternary block code is shown in Table 3.2

**Table 3.1** A binary block code.

| Source symbols | Code |
|---|---|
| $x_0$ | 0 |
| $x_1$ | 11 |
| $x_2$ | 00 |
| $x_3$ | 1 |

**Table 3.2** A ternary block code.

| Source symbols | Code |
|---|---|
| $x_0$ | 0 |
| $x_1$ | 1 |
| $x_2$ | 2 |
| $x_3$ | 01 |

### 3.1.2 Non-Singular Codes

A block code is said to be non-singular if all codewords are distinct (Abramson, N., 1963). Table 3.2 shows an example of a non-singular code. The code shown in Table 3.3 is also non-singular, but although the codewords are distinct there is certain ambiguity between some symbol sequences of the code regarding the source symbol sequences.

**Example**: The sequence 1111 can correspond to $x_2x_2x_2x_2$, or $x_2x_3x_2$, or even $x_3x_3$. Which indicates that it is necessary to define a more strict condition than non-singularity for a code, to guarantee that it can be used in a practical situation.

### 3.1.3 Uniquely Decodable Codes

Let a block code map symbols from a source alphabet $S$ into fixed symbol sequences of a code alphabet $X$. The source can be an extension of another

**Table 3.3** A non-singular block code.

| Source symbols | Code |
|---|---|
| $x_0$ | 0 |
| $x_1$ | 01 |
| $x_2$ | 1 |
| $x_3$ | 11 |

source, which is composed of symbols from the original alphabet. The $n$-ary extension of a block code that maps symbols $x_i$ into codewords $X_i$ is the block code that maps symbol sequences from the source $(x_{i1}x_{i2} \; \ldots \; x_{in})$ into the codeword sequences $(X_{i1}X_{i2} \; \ldots \; X_{in})$ (Abramson, N., 1963).

From the previous definition, the $n$-ary extension of a block code is also a block code. The second order extension of the block code presented in Table 3.4 is the block code of Table 3.5.

**Table 3.4** A non-singular block code.

| Source symbols | Code |
|---|---|
| $x_0$ | 1 |
| $x_1$ | 00 |
| $x_2$ | 11 |
| $x_3$ | 10 |

**Table 3.5** The second extension of a block code.

| Source symbols | Code | Source symbols | Code |
|---|---|---|---|
| $x_0x_0$ | 11 | $x_2x_0$ | 111 |
| $x_0x_1$ | 100 | $x_2x_1$ | 1100 |
| $x_0x_2$ | 111 | $x_2x_2$ | 1111 |
| $x_0x_3$ | 110 | $x_2x_3$ | 1110 |
| $x_1x_0$ | 001 | $x_3x_0$ | 101 |
| $x_1x_1$ | 0000 | $x_3x_1$ | 1000 |
| $x_1x_2$ | 0011 | $x_3x_2$ | 1011 |
| $x_1x_3$ | 0010 | $x_3x_3$ | 1010 |

A block code is said to be uniquely decodable if and only if the $n$-ary extension of the code is non-singular for all finite $n$.

### 3.1.4 Instantaneous Codes

Table 3.6 presents two examples of uniquely decodable codes. Code $\mathcal{A}$ is a simpler method to construct a uniquely decodable set of sequences, because all codewords have the same length and it is a non-singular code.

Code $\mathcal{B}$ is also uniquely decodable. It is also called a comma code, because the digit zero is used to separate the codewords (Abramson, N., 1963).

**Table 3.6** Uniquely decodable codes.

| Source symbols | Code $\mathcal{A}$ | Code $\mathcal{B}$ |
|---|---|---|
| $x_0$ | 000 | 0 |
| $x_1$ | 001 | 10 |
| $x_2$ | 010 | 110 |
| $x_3$ | 011 | 1110 |
| $x_4$ | 100 | 11110 |
| $x_5$ | 101 | 111110 |
| $x_6$ | 110 | 1111110 |
| $x_7$ | 111 | 11111110 |

Consider the code shown in Table 3.7. Code $\mathcal{C}$ differ from $\mathcal{A}$ and $\mathcal{B}$ from Table 3.6 in an important aspect. If a binary sequence composed of codewords from code $\mathcal{C}$ occurs, it is not possible to decode the sequence.

**Example**: If the bit stream 100000 is received, for example, it is not possible to decide if is corresponds to symbol $x_5$, unless the next symbol is available. If the next symbol is 1, then the sequence is 100000, but if it is 0, then it is necessary to inspect one more symbol to know if the sequence corresponds to $x_6$ (1000000) or $x_7$ (10000000).

A uniquely decodable code is instantaneous if it is possible to decode each codeword in a sequence with no reference to subsequent symbols (Abramson, N., 1963). Code $\mathcal{A}$ and $\mathcal{B}$ are instantaneous, and $\mathcal{C}$ is not.

It is possible to devise a test to indicate when a code is instantaneous. Let $X_i = x_{i1}x_{i2} \ \ldots \ x_{im}$ be a word from a certain code. The sequence of symbols $(x_{i1}x_{i2} \ \ldots \ x_{ij})$, with $j \leq m$, is called the prefix of the codeword $X_i$.

**Example**: The codeword 10000 has five prefixes: 1, 10, 100, 1000 and 10000. A necessary condition for a code to be instantaneous is that no codeword is a prefix of another codeword.

**Table 3.7** Another uniquely decodable code.

| Source symbols | Code $C$ |
|---|---|
| $x_0$ | 1 |
| $x_1$ | 10 |
| $x_2$ | 100 |
| $x_3$ | 1000 |
| $x_4$ | 10000 |
| $x_5$ | 100000 |
| $x_6$ | 1000000 |
| $x_7$ | 10000000 |

The various classes of codes presented in this section are summarized in Figure 3.1.

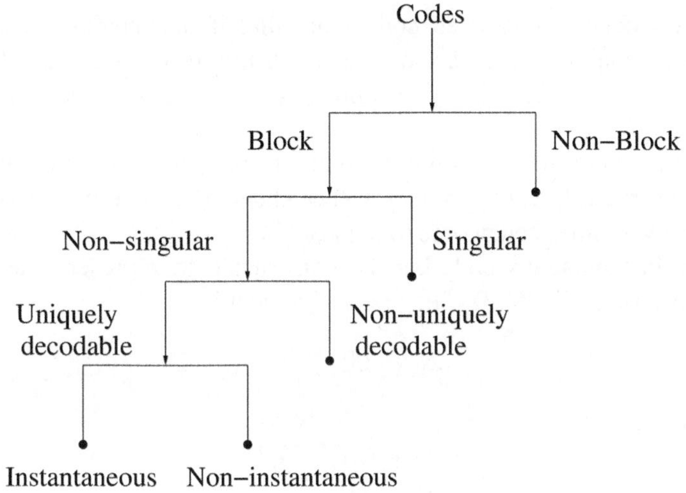


**Figure 3.1** Classes of source codes.

## 3.2 Construction of Instantaneous Codes

In order to construct a binary instantaneous code for a source with five symbols, one can begin by attributing the digit 0 to symbol $s_0$ (Abramson, N., 1963)

$$x_0 \leftarrow 0.$$

In this case, the remaining source symbols should correspond to the codewords that begin with the digit 1. Otherwise, it is not a prefix code. It is not possible to associate $x_1$ to the codeword 1, because no other symbol would remain to begin the other codewords.

Therefore,

$$x_1 \leftarrow 10.$$

This codeword assignment requires that the remaining codewords begin with 11. If

$$x_2 \leftarrow 110$$

then, the only unused prefix with three bits is 111, which implies that

$$x_3 \leftarrow 1110$$

and

$$x_4 \leftarrow 1111.$$

In the previously constructed code, note that if one begins the code construction by making $x_0$ to correspond to 0, this restricts the available number of codewords, because the remaining codewords had to, necessarily, begin with 1.

On the other hand, if a two-digit word had been chosen to represent $x_0$, there would be more freedom to choose the others, and there would be no need to assign very long codewords to the last ones.

A binary instantaneous code can be constructed to represent the five symbols (Abramson, N., 1963). The first assignment is

$$x_0 \leftarrow 00.$$

Then, one can assign

$$x_1 \leftarrow 01$$

and two unused prefixes of length two are saved to the following codeword assignment:

$$x_2 \leftarrow 10$$

$$x_3 \leftarrow 110$$

$$x_4 \leftarrow 111$$

The question of which code is the best is postponed for the next section, because it requires the notion of average length of a code, that depends on the symbol probability distribution.

## 3.3 Kraft Inequality

The Kraft inequality gives a necessary and sufficient condition for the existence of a prefix code. The inequality was developed by Leon G. Kraft Jr, in 1949, as a result of his doctorate, obtained from the Electrical Engineering Department, Massachusetts Institute of Technology.

Later on, in 1956, Brockway McMillan (1915-2016) independently developed an analogous inequality that provides a necessary and sufficient condition for the existence of a uniquely decodable code, for a given set of codeword lengths. It is frequently called the Kraft-McMillan inequality.

Consider an instantaneous code with source alphabet given by

$$S = \{x_0, x_1, \ldots, x_{K-1}\}$$

and code alphabet

$$X = \{x_0, x_1, \ldots, x_{M-1}\}.$$

Let $X_0, X_1, \ldots, X_{K-1}$ be the codewords, and let $l_i$ be the length of the word $X_i$. The Kraft inequality establishes that a necessary and sufficient condition for the existence of an instantaneous code of length $l_0, l_1, \ldots, l_{K-1}$ is

$$\sum_{i=0}^{K-1} r^{-l_i} \leq 1, \tag{3.1}$$

in which $r$ is the number of different symbols of the code.

For the binary case,

$$\sum_{i=0}^{K-1} 2^{-l_i} \leq 1. \tag{3.2}$$

The Kraft inequality can be used to determine if a given sequence of length $l_i$ is acceptable for a codeword of an instantaneous code.

Consider an information source, with four possible symbols, $x_0$, $x_1$, $x_2$ e $x_3$. Table 3.8 presents five possible codes to represent the original symbols, using a binary alphabet.

**Example**: Consider the previously discussed codes. For code $\mathcal{A}$, one obtains

$$\sum_{i=0}^{3} 2^{-l_i} = 2^{-2} + 2^{-2} + 2^{-2} + 2^{-2} = 1.$$

Therefore, the codeword lengths of this code are acceptable for an instantaneous code. But, the Kraft inequality does not tell if $\mathcal{A}$ is an instantaneous code. It is only a necessary condition that has to be fulfilled by the lengths.

For the example, the inequality states that there is an instantaneous code with four codewords of length 2. In this case, it is clear that the binary codewords of code $\mathcal{A}$ satisfy the Kraft inequality and also form an instantaneous code.

For code $\mathcal{B}$, on the other hand, the application of the Kraft inequality gives the following result

$$\sum_{i=0}^{3} 2^{-l_i} = 2^{-1} + 2^{-3} + 2^{-3} + 2^{-3} = 7/8 \leq 1.$$

In this case, the lengths of the codewords are suitable to compose an instantaneous code. Code $\mathcal{B}$ is also a prefix code.

Code $\mathcal{C}$ is similar to code $\mathcal{B}$, except for a discarded bit in the second codeword. For this code, one obtains

$$\sum_{i=0}^{3} 2^{-l_i} = 2^{-1} + 2^{-2} + 2^{-3} + 2^{-3} = 1.$$

The codeword lengths satisfy the Kraft inequality and, by inspection, one observes that this code is instantaneous.

Code $\mathcal{D}$ is obtained from $\mathcal{B}$, discarding a bit in the fourth codeword. Although the lengths satisfy the Kraft inequality, code $\mathcal{D}$ is not instantaneous, because it is not a prefix code. The fourth codeword is a prefix of the third one.

Finally, for code $\mathcal{E}$,

$$\sum_{i=0}^{3} 2^{-l_i} = \frac{9}{8},$$

and the codeword lengths do not satisfy the Kraft inequality. Therefore, code $\mathcal{E}$ is not instantaneous.

Consider a source with eight symbols to be encoded into an instantaneous ternary code, whose codeword lengths are $1, 2, 2, 2, 2, 3, 3, 3$. Using the Kraft inequality,

$$\sum_{i=0}^{9} 3^{-l_i} = \frac{1}{3} + 4\frac{1}{9} + 3\frac{1}{27} = \frac{24}{27} < 1,$$

which indicates that this code is possible, as follows:

$$x_0 \leftarrow 0$$

**Table 3.8** Selected binary codes.

| Source symbols | Code $\mathcal{A}$ | Code $\mathcal{B}$ | Code $\mathcal{C}$ | Code $\mathcal{D}$ | Code $\mathcal{E}$ |
|---|---|---|---|---|---|
| $x_0$ | 11 | 1 | 1 | 1 | 1 |
| $x_1$ | 10 | 011 | 01 | 011 | 01 |
| $x_2$ | 01 | 001 | 001 | 001 | 001 |
| $x_3$ | 00 | 000 | 000 | 00 | 00 |

$$x_1 \leftarrow 10$$
$$x_2 \leftarrow 11$$
$$x_3 \leftarrow 20$$
$$x_4 \leftarrow 21$$
$$x_5 \leftarrow 220$$
$$x_6 \leftarrow 221$$
$$x_7 \leftarrow 222$$

For a source with eleven symbols, if the codeword lengths are 1, 2, 2, 2, 2, 2, 2, 3, 3, 3, 3; it is not possible to obtain a ternary instantaneous code, because

$$\sum_{i=0}^{10} 3^{-l_i} = \frac{1}{3} + 6\frac{1}{9} + 4\frac{1}{27} = \frac{31}{27} > 1.$$

## 3.4 Huffman Code

The Huffman coding algorithm is discussed in the following, along with a procedure to construct the Huffman code when the source statistics are known.

The technique was developed by David Albert Huffman (1925-1999), in a paper for a course on Information Theory taught by Robert Mario Fano (1917-), at the Massachusetts Institute of Technology (MIT). The obtained sequences are called Huffman codes, and they are prefix codes.

Huffman procedure is based on two assumptions regarding the optimum prefix codes:

1. The most frequent symbols, those with higher probability, are represented by shorter codewords.

2. The least frequent symbols are assigned codewords of same length.

According with the first assumption, as the most probable symbols are also the most frequent, they must be as short as possible to decrease the average length of the code. The second assumption is also true, because for a prefix code a shorter codeword could not be a prefix of another one. The least probable symbols must be distinct and have same length (Sayood, K., 2006).

Furthermore, the Huffman process is completed by the addition of a simple requisite. The longer codewords that correspond to the least frequent symbols differ only on the last digit.

### 3.4.1 Constructing a Binary Huffman Code

Consider a discrete binary source of information, it is possible to construct a binary Huffman code according to the following steps:

1. The source symbols are arranged in decreasing order of probability. The least probable symbols receive the assignments 0 and 1.
2. Both symbols are combined to create a new source symbol, whose probability is the sum of the original ones. The list is then reduced by one symbol. The new symbol is positioned in the list according to its probability.
3. This procedure continues until the list has only two symbols, which receive the assignments 0 and 1.
4. Finally, the binary codeword for each symbol is obtained by a reverse reading process.

In order to explain the algorithm, consider the source of Table 3.9.

**Table 3.9** Discrete source with five symbols and their probabilities.

| Symbols | Probabilities |
|---|---|
| $x_0$ | 0,4 |
| $x_1$ | 0,2 |
| $x_2$ | 0,2 |
| $x_3$ | 0,1 |
| $x_4$ | 0,1 |

The first phase is to arrange the symbols in a decreasing order of probability. Assign the values 0 and 1 to the symbols with the smallest probabilities. They are, then, combined to create a new symbol. The probability associated to the new symbol is the sum of the previous probabilities. The new symbol is repositioned in the list, to maintain the same decreasing order for the probabilities. The procedure is shown in Figure 3.2.

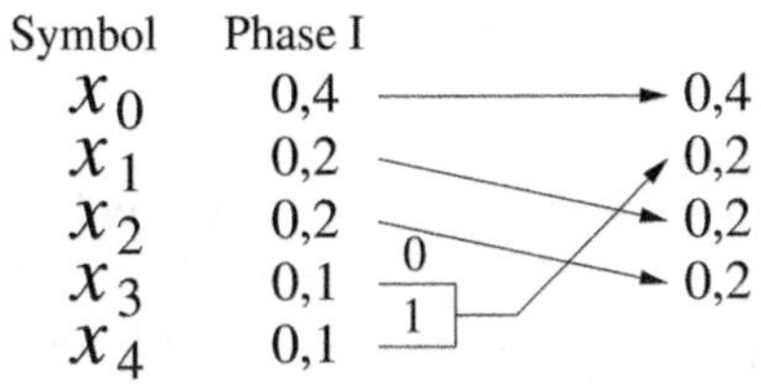


**Figure 3.2** Probabilities in descending order for the Huffman code.

The procedure is repeated until only two symbols remain, which are assigned to 0 and 1, as shown in Figure 3.3.

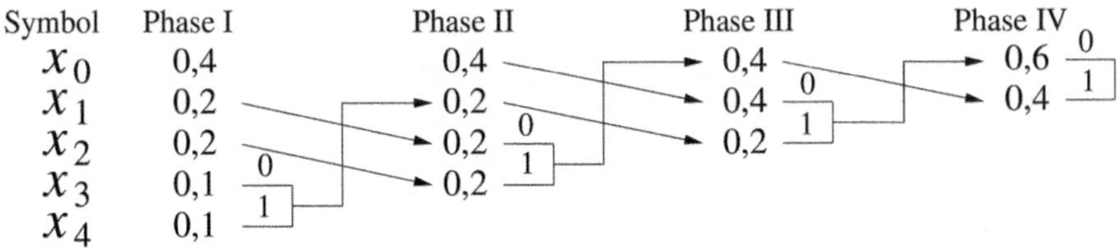


**Figure 3.3** Huffman code. At each phase, the two least probable symbols are combined.

The procedure is repeated to obtain all codewords, by reading the digits in inverse order, from Phase IV to Phase I, as illustrated in Figure 3.4. Following the arrows, for symbol $x_4$ one finds the codeword 011.

For the example, the average codeword length for the Huffman code is given by

$$\overline{L} = \sum_{i=0}^{4} p_k l_k = 0,4(2) + 0,2(2) + 0,2(2) + 0,1(3) + 0,1(3) = 2,2 \text{ bits.}$$

The source entropy is calculated as

$$\begin{aligned} H(X) &= \sum_{i=0}^{4} p_k \log_2 \left(\frac{1}{p_k}\right) \\ H(X) &= 0,4 \log_2 \left(\frac{1}{0,4}\right) + 0,2 \log_2 \left(\frac{1}{0,2}\right) + 0,2 \log_2 \left(\frac{1}{0,2}\right) \\ &+ 0,1 \log_2 \left(\frac{1}{0,1}\right) + 0,1 \log_2 \left(\frac{1}{0,1}\right), \end{aligned}$$

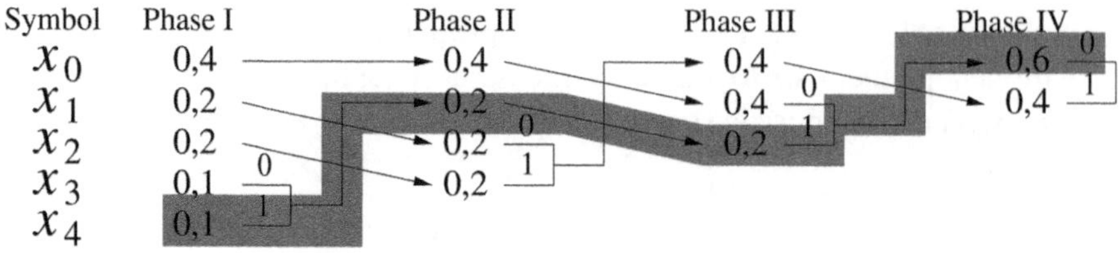


(a)

| Symbol | Probability | Codeword |
|---|---|---|
| $x_0$ | 0,4 | 00 |
| $x_1$ | 0,2 | 10 |
| $x_2$ | 0,2 | 11 |
| $x_3$ | 0,1 | 010 |
| $x_4$ | 0,1 | 011 |

(b)

**Figure 3.4** (a) Example of the Huffman coding algorithm to obtain the codewords. (b) Resulting code.

or,

$$H(X) = 2,12193 \text{ bits.}$$

The code efficiency is

$$\eta = \frac{H(X)}{\overline{L}} = \frac{2,12193}{2,2},$$

which is equal to 96,45%.

It is important to say that the Huffman procedure is not unique, and several variations cam be obtained for the final set of codewords, depending on the way the bits are assigned. But, in spite of how the probabilities are positioned, the average length is always the same, if the rules are followed.

The difference is the variance of the codeword lengths, defined as

$$\text{V}[L] = \sum_{k=0}^{K-1} p_k (l_k - \overline{L})^2, \tag{3.3}$$

in which $p_k$ and $l_k$ denote the probability of occurrence of the $k$-th source symbol, and length of the respective codeword.

Usually, the procedure of displacing the probability of the new symbol to the highest position in the list produces smaller values for $\text{V}[L]$, as compared to the displacement of the probability to the lowest position of the list.

Table 3.10 presents four Huffman codes obtained for the source of Table 3.9. Codes 1 and 2 were obtained shifting the new symbol to the highest position in the list of decreasing probabilities.

Codes 3 and 4 were produced by shifting the new symbol to the lowest position in the list. Codes 1 and 3 used the systematic assignment of 0 followed by 1 to the least frequent symbols. Codes 2 and 4 used the systematic assignment of 1 followed by 0 to the least frequent symbols.

For all codes the average codeword length is 2,2 bits. For codes 1 and 2, the variance of the codeword lengths is 0,16. For codes 3 and 4, the variance is 1,36.

**Table 3.10** Four distinct Huffman codes obtained for the source of Table 3.9.

| Symbols | Code 1 | Code 2 | Code 3 | Code 4 |
|---|---|---|---|---|
| $x_0$ | 00 | 11 | 1 | 0 |
| $x_1$ | 10 | 01 | 01 | 10 |
| $x_2$ | 11 | 00 | 000 | 111 |
| $x_3$ | 010 | 101 | 0010 | 1101 |
| $x_4$ | 011 | 100 | 0011 | 1100 |

# 4

# Information Transmission

*"The two words 'information' and 'communication' are often used interchangeably, but they signify quite different things. Information is giving out; communication is getting through."*
Sydney J. Harris

Claude Elwood Shannon (1916-2001) is considered the father of Information Theory. In 1948, he published a seminal article on the mathematical concept of information, which is one of the most cited for decades. Information left the Journalism field to occupy a more formal area, as part of Probability Theory.

The entropy, in the context of information theory, was initially defined by Ralph Vinton Lyon Hartley (1888-1970), in the article "Transmission of Information", published the Bell System Technical Journal, in July, 1928, twenty years before the formalization of the concept by Claude Shannon.

Shannon's development was also based on Harry Nyquist's work (Harry Theodor Nyqvist, 1889-1976), which determined the sampling rate, as a function of frequency, necessary to reconstruct an analog signal using a set of discrete samples.

In an independent way, Andrei N. Kolmogorov developed his Complexity Theory, during the 1960 decade. I was a new information theory, based on the length of an algorithm developed to describe a certain data sequence. He used the concept of Alan Turing's machine for this new definition. Under certain conditions, Kolmogorov's and Shannon's definitions are equivalent.

The idea of relating the number of states of a system with a physical measure, although, dates back to the XIX century. Rudolph Clausius proposed the term entropy for such a measure, in 1895.

Entropy comes from the Greek word for transformation and, in Physics, is related to the logarithm of the ratio between the final and initial temperature of a system, or to the ratio of the heat variation and the temperature of the same system.

DOI: 10.1201/9788743813613-4

Shannon defined the entropy of an alphabet at the negative of the mean value of the logarithm of the symbols' probability. This way, when the symbols are equiprobable, the definition is equivalent to Nyquist's.

But, as a more generic definition, Shannon's entropy can be used to compute the capacity of communication channels. Most part the the researchers' work is devoted to either compute the capacity or to develop error correcting codes to attained that capacity.

Shannon died on February 24, 2001, as a victim of a disease named after the physician Aloysius Alzheimer. According to his wife, who represented him during the 1994 IEEE Information Theory Symposium, at the end, he lived a quiet and retired life, but had lost his capacity to retain information.

## 4.1 The Concept of Information Theory

According to Shannon's definition, the concept of information transmission is associated with the existence of a communication channel that links the source and destination of the message. This can imply the occurrence of transmission errors, caused by the probabilistic nature of the channel.

Figure 4.1 illustrates the canonical model for a communication channel, proposed by Shannon in his seminal paper of 1948 (Shannon, 1948a). This is a simplified model of reality, but contains the basic blocks upon which the mathematical structure is built.

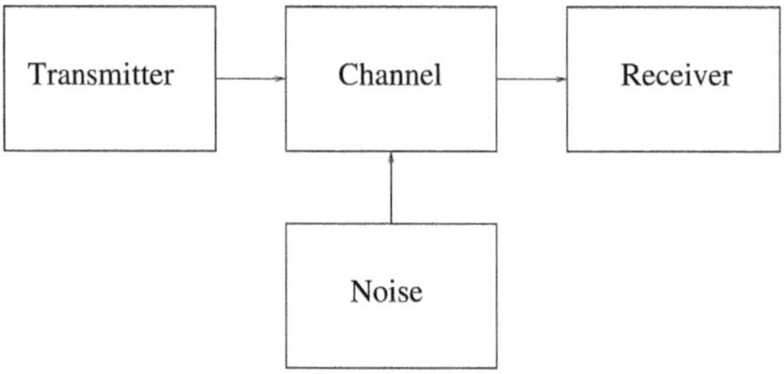


**Figure 4.1** Model for a communication channel.

## 4.2 Joint Information Measurement

Consider two discrete and finite sample spaces, $\Omega$ e $\Psi$, with the associated random variables $X$ e $Y$,

$$X = x_1, x_2, \ldots, x_N,$$
$$Y = y_1, y_2, \ldots, y_M. \quad (4.1)$$

The events from $\Omega$ may jointly occur with events from $\Psi$. Therefore, the following matrix contains the whole set of events in the product space $\Omega\Psi$,

$$[XY] = \begin{bmatrix} x_1y_1 & x_1y_2 & \cdots & x_1y_M \\ x_2y_1 & x_2y_2 & \cdots & x_2y_M \\ \cdots & \cdots & \cdots & \cdots \\ x_Ny_1 & x_Ny_2 & \cdots & x_Ny_M \end{bmatrix} \quad (4.2)$$

The joint probability matrix is given in the following, in which no restriction is assumed regarding the dependence between the random variables.

$$[\mathrm{P}(X,Y)] = \begin{bmatrix} p_{1,1} & p_{1,2} & \cdots & p_{1,M} \\ p_{2,1} & p_{2,2} & \cdots & p_{2,M} \\ \cdots & \cdots & \cdots & \cdots \\ p_{N,1} & p_{N,2} & \cdots & p_{N,M} \end{bmatrix} \quad (4.3)$$

Figure 4.2 shows the relation between the input and output alphabets, which are connected by the joint probability distribution matrix $[\mathrm{P}(X,Y)]$.

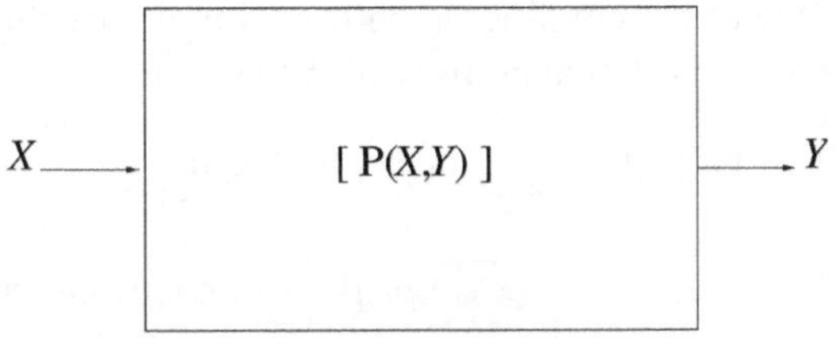


**Figure 4.2** A probabilistic communication channel.

The joint entropy between the random variables from sources $X$ and $Y$ is given by

$$H(X,Y) = -\sum_{k=1}^{N}\sum_{j=1}^{M} p_{k,j} \log p_{k,j}, \quad (4.4)$$

which may be simplified to

$$H(X,Y) = -\sum_{X}\sum_{Y} p(x,y) \log p(x,y). \quad (4.5)$$

The marginal entropies may be written in terms of the marginal probabilities, $p(x)$ e $p(y)$

$$H(X) = -\sum_{X} p(x) \log p(x) \tag{4.6}$$

and

$$H(Y) = -\sum_{Y} p(y) \log p(y). \tag{4.7}$$

## 4.3 Conditional Entropy

The concept of conditional entropy is essential to model, and understand, the operation of the communication channel, cause it provides information about a particular symbol, given that another symbol has occurred The entropy of alphabet $X$ conditioned to the occurrence of a particular symbol $y$ is given by

$$\begin{aligned} H(X|y) &= -\sum_{X} \frac{p(x,y)}{p(y)} \log \frac{p(x,y)}{p(y)} \\ &= -\sum_{X} p(x|y) \log p(x|y). \end{aligned} \tag{4.8}$$

The expected value of the conditional entropy, for all possibles values of $y$, provides the average conditional entropy of the system,

$$\begin{aligned} H(X|Y) = E[H(X|y)] &= \sum_{Y} p(y) \, [H(X|y)] \\ &= -\sum_{Y} p(y) \sum_{X} p(x|y) \log p(x|y), \end{aligned} \tag{4.9}$$

which can be written as

$$H(X|Y) = -\sum_{Y}\sum_{X} p(y)p(x|y) \log p(x|y), \tag{4.10}$$

or

$$H(X|Y) = -\sum_{Y}\sum_{X} p(x,y) \log p(x|y). \tag{4.11}$$

In the same way, the mean conditional entropy of source $Y$, given the information about source $X$, is

$$H(Y|X) = -\sum_{X}\sum_{Y} p(x)p(y|x) \log p(y|x), \tag{4.12}$$

or

$$H(Y|X) = -\sum_X \sum_Y p(x, y) \log p(y|x). \tag{4.13}$$

## 4.4 Model for a Communication Channel

A communication channel can be modeled based on the previous developments. Consider a source that has the given alphabet $X$. The source transmits the information to the destiny using a certain channel. The system maybe described by a joint probability matrix, which gives the joint probability of occurrence of a transmitted symbol and a received one,

$$[P(X, Y)] = \begin{bmatrix} p(x_1, y_1) & p(x_1, y_2) & \cdots & p(x_1, y_N) \\ p(x_2, y_1) & p(x_2, y_2) & \cdots & p(x_2, y_N) \\ \cdots & \cdots & \cdots & \cdots \\ p(x_M, y_1) & p(x_M, y_2) & \cdots & p(x_M, y_N) \end{bmatrix} \tag{4.14}$$

There are five probability schemes to analyse:

1. $[P(X, Y)]$, joint probability matrix,
2. $[P(X)]$, marginal probability matrix of $X$,
3. $[P(Y)]$, marginal probability matrix of $Y$,
4. $[P(X|Y)]$, probability matrix conditioned on $Y$,
5. $[P(Y|X)]$, probability matrix conditioned on $X$.

Those probability schemes produce five entropy functions, associated to the communication channel, whose interpretations are given as follows:

1. $H(X)$ – Average information per source symbol, or source entropy,
2. $H(Y)$ – Average information per received symbol, or receiver entropy.
3. $H(X, Y)$ – Average information associated to pairs of transmitted and received symbols, or average uncertainty of the communication system.
4. $H(Y|X)$ – Average information measurement of the received symbol, given that $X$ was transmitted, or conditional entropy of $Y$ given $X$. The conditional entropy quantifies the amount of information needed to describe the outcome of a random variable $Y$, given that the value of another random variable $X$ is known.
5. $H(X|Y)$ – Average information measurement of the source, given that $Y$ was received, or conditional entropy of $X$ given $Y$. It is also called equivocation.

Some important properties of the conditional information are listed in the following:

1. The conditional entropy equals zero, that is $H(Y|X) = 0$, if and only if the value of $Y$ is completely determined by the value of $X$.
2. The conditional entropy of independent random variables $Y$ and $X$ results in $H(Y|X) = H(Y)$.
3. The chain rule of conditional entropy is given by $H(Y|X) = H(X,Y) - H(X)$, which is the quantity of information needed to describe the system once $X$ is known.
4. For a noiseless channel one must have zero equivocation, or $H(X|Y) = 0$.

## 4.5 Noiseless Channel

For the noiseless discrete channel, each symbol from the input alphabet has a one to one correspondence with the output. The joint probability matrix, as well as, the transition probability matrix, have the same diagonal format,

$$[P(X,Y)] = \begin{bmatrix} p(x_1,y_1) & 0 & \cdots & 0 \\ 0 & p(x_2,y_2) & \cdots & 0 \\ \cdots & \cdots & \cdots & \cdots \\ 0 & 0 & \cdots & p(x_N,y_N) \end{bmatrix} \quad (4.15)$$

$$[P(X|Y)] = [P(Y|X)] = \begin{bmatrix} 1 & 0 & \cdots & 0 \\ 0 & 1 & \cdots & 0 \\ \cdots & \cdots & \cdots & \cdots \\ 0 & 0 & \cdots & 1 \end{bmatrix} \quad (4.16)$$

The joint entropy equals the marginal entropies

$$H(X,Y) = H(X) = H(Y) = -\sum_{i=1}^{N} p(x_i,y_i) \log p(x_i,y_i), \quad (4.17)$$

and the conditional entropies are null

$$H(Y|X) = H(X|Y) = 0. \quad (4.18)$$

As a consequence, the receiver uncertainty is equal to the source entropy, and there is no ambiguity at the reception, which indicates that the conditional entropies are all zero.

## 4.6 Channel with Independent Output and Input

For the channel with independent input and output there is no relation between the transmitted and received symbols, that is, given that a given symbol has been transmitted, any symbol can received, with no connection whatsoever with it. The joint probability matrix has $N$ identical columns

$$[P(X,Y)] = \begin{bmatrix} p & p_1 & \cdots & p_1 \\ p_2 & p_2 & \cdots & p_2 \\ \cdots & \cdots & \cdots & \cdots \\ p_M & p_M & \cdots & p_M \end{bmatrix}, \qquad \sum_i^M p_i = \frac{1}{N}. \tag{4.19}$$

The input and output symbol probabilities are statistically independent, that is,

$$p(x,y) = p(x)p(y). \tag{4.20}$$

Computing the entropy gives

$$H(X,Y) = -N \left( \sum_{i=1}^{M} p_i \log p_i \right), \tag{4.21}$$

$$H(X) = -\sum_{i=1}^{M} Np_i \log Np_i = -N \left( \sum_{i=1}^{M} p_i \log p_i \right) - \log N, \tag{4.22}$$

$$H(Y) = -N \left( \frac{1}{N} \log \frac{1}{N} \right) = \log N, \tag{4.23}$$

$$H(X|Y) = -\sum_{i=1}^{M} Np_i \log Np_i = H(X), \tag{4.24}$$

$$H(Y|X) = -\sum_{i=1}^{M} Np_i \log \frac{1}{N} = \log N = H(Y). \tag{4.25}$$

As a consequence, the channel with independent input and output does not provides information, that is, has the highest possible loss, contrasting with the noiseless channel.

## 4.7 Relations Between the Entropies

It is possible to show, using Bayes rule for the conditional probability, that the joint entropy can be written in terms of the conditional entropy, in the following way

$$H(X,Y) = H(X|Y) + H(Y), \tag{4.26}$$
$$H(X,Y) = H(Y|X) + H(X). \tag{4.27}$$

Shannon has shown the fundamental inequality

$$H(X) \geq H(X|Y), \tag{4.28}$$

whose demonstration is given in the following.

The logarithm concavity property can be used to demonstrate the inequality, $\ln x \leq x - 1$, as follows,

$$\begin{aligned} H(X|Y) - H(X) &= \sum_Y \sum_X p(x,y) \log \frac{p(x)}{p(x|y)} \\ &\leq \sum_Y \sum_X p(x,y) \left( \frac{p(x)}{p(x|y)} - 1 \right) \log e. \end{aligned} \tag{4.29}$$

But, the right hand side of the inequality is zero, as shown in the following

$$\begin{aligned} \sum_Y \sum_X (p(x) \cdot p(y) - p(x,y)) \log e &= \sum_Y (p(y) - p(y)) \log e \\ &= 0. \end{aligned} \tag{4.30}$$

Therefore,

$$H(X) \geq H(X|Y), \tag{4.31}$$

In a similar manner, is can be shown that

$$H(Y) \geq H(Y|X). \tag{4.32}$$

The equality is attained if and only if $X$ and $Y$ are statistically independent.

## 4.8 Mutual Information

A measure of mutual information provided by two symbols $(x_i, y_i)$ can be written as

$$\begin{aligned} I(x_i; y_j) &= \log_2 p(x_i|y_j) - \log_2 p(x_i) \\ &= \log_2 \frac{p(x_i|y_j)}{p(x_i)} = \log \frac{p(x_i, y_j)}{p(x_i)p(y_j)}. \end{aligned} \tag{4.33}$$

It can be noticed that the *a priori* information of symbol $x_i$ is contained in the marginal probability $p(x_i)$. The *a posteriori* probability that symbol $x_i$ has been transmitted, given that $y_i$ was received is $p(x_i|y_i)$. Therefore, in an informal way, the information gain for the observed symbol equals the difference between the initial information, or uncertainty, and the final one.

The mutual information is continuous in $p(x_i|y_i)$, and also symmetric, or

$$I(x_i; y_j) = I(y_j; x_i), \tag{4.34}$$

which indicates that the information provided by $x_i$ about $y_i$ is the same provided by $y_i$ about $x_i$.

The function $I(x_i; x_i)$ can be called the auto-information of $x_i$, or

$$I(x_i) = I(x_i; x_i) = \log \frac{1}{p(x_i)}, \tag{4.35}$$

because, for an observer of the source alphabet, the *a priori* knowledge of the situation is that $x_i$ will be transmitted with probability $p(x_i)$, and the *a posteriori* knowledge is the certainty that $x_i$ transmitted.

In conclusion,

$$I(x_i; y_j) \leq I(x_i; x_i) = I(x_i), \tag{4.36}$$

$$I(x_i; y_j) \leq I(y_j; y_j) = I(y_j). \tag{4.37}$$

The statistical mean of the mutual information per pairs of symbols provides an interesting interpretation of the mutual information concept,

$$I(X; Y) = E[I(x_i; y_j)] = \sum_i \sum_j p(x_i, y_j)\, I(x_i; y_j), \tag{4.38}$$

which can be written as

$$I(X; Y) = \sum_i \sum_j p(x_i, y_j) \log \frac{p(x_i|y_j)}{p(x_i)}. \tag{4.39}$$

The average mutual information can be interpreted as a reduction on the uncertainty about the input $X$, when the output $Y$ is observed (MacKay, 2003). This definition provides an adequate metric for the average mutual information of all pairs of symbols, and can be put in terms of the entropy, such as

$$I(X; Y) = H(X) + H(Y) - H(X, Y), \tag{4.40}$$

$$I(X; Y) = H(X) - H(X|Y), \tag{4.41}$$

$$I(X; Y) = H(Y) - H(Y|X). \tag{4.42}$$

Put that way, the average mutual information gives a measure of the information that is transmitted by the channel. Because of this, it is called transinformation, or information transferred by the channel. It is always non-negative, even if the individual information quantities are negative for certain pairs of symbols.

For a noiseless channel, the average mutual information equals the joint entropy.

$$I(X;Y) = H(X) = H(Y), \tag{4.43}$$
$$I(X;Y) = H(X,Y). \tag{4.44}$$

On the other hand, for a channel in which the output is independent of the input, the average mutual information is null, implying that no information is transmitted by the channel.

$$\begin{aligned} I(X;Y) &= H(X) - H(X|Y), \\ &= H(X) - H(X) = 0. \end{aligned} \tag{4.45}$$

It is possible to use the set theory, presented in the Appendix, to obtain a pictorial interpretation of the fundamental inequalities discovered by Shannon. Consider, the set of events $A$ and $B$, associated to the set of symbols $X$ and $Y$, and a Lebesgue measure $m$. It is possible to associate, unambiguously, the measures of $A$ and $B$ with the entropies of $X$ and $Y$ (Reza, 1961),

$$m(A) \longleftrightarrow H(X), \tag{4.46}$$
$$m(B) \longleftrightarrow H(Y). \tag{4.47}$$

In the same way, one can associate the joint and conditional entropies the the union and intersection of sets, respectively,

$$m(A \cup B) \longleftrightarrow H(X,Y), \tag{4.48}$$
$$m(A\overline{B}) \longleftrightarrow H(X|Y), \tag{4.49}$$
$$m(B\overline{A}) \longleftrightarrow H(Y|X). \tag{4.50}$$

The average mutual information is, therefore, associated to the measure of the intersection of the sets,

$$m(A \cap B) \longleftrightarrow I(X;Y). \tag{4.51}$$

Those relations can be seen in Figure 4.3, which also serve as a means to memorize the entropy and mutual information properties.

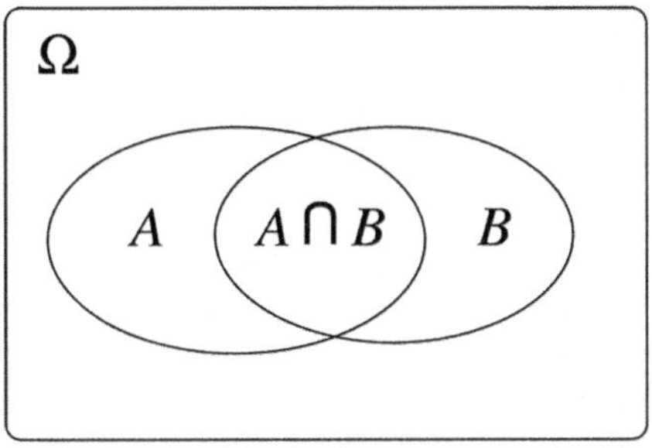


**Figure 4.3** Venn diagram corresponding to the relation between the entropies.

Therefore, the fundamental inequalities can be written as a result of set operations (Reza, 1961),

$$m(A \cup B) \leq m(A) + m(B) \longleftrightarrow H(X,Y) \leq H(X) + H(Y), \quad (4.52)$$
$$m(A\overline{B}) \leq m(A) \longleftrightarrow H(X|Y) \leq H(X), \quad (4.53)$$
$$m(B\overline{A}) \leq m(B) \longleftrightarrow H(Y|X) \leq H(Y), \quad (4.54)$$

and, finally,

$$m(A \cup B) = m(A\overline{B}) + m(B\overline{A}) + m(A \cap B), \quad (4.55)$$

which is equivalent to

$$H(X,Y) = H(X|Y) + H(Y|X) + I(X;Y). \quad (4.56)$$

For a noiseless channel, the two sets coincide, and the relations can be written as:

$$m(A) = m(B) \longleftrightarrow H(X) = H(Y), \quad (4.57)$$
$$m(A \cup B) = m(A) = m(B) \longleftrightarrow H(X,Y) = H(X) = H(Y) \quad (4.58)$$
$$m(A\overline{B}) = 0 \longleftrightarrow H(X|Y) = 0, \quad (4.59)$$
$$m(B\overline{A}) = 0 \longleftrightarrow H(Y|X) = 0, \quad (4.60)$$

and, finally,

$$m(A \cap B) = m(A) = m(B) = m(A \cup B) \longleftrightarrow I(X;Y) = H(X) = H(Y) = H(X,Y). \quad (4.61)$$

For a channel with output symbols independent from the input symbols, the sets $A$ and $B$ are considered mutually exclusive, therefore:

$$m(A \cup B) = m(A) + m(B) \longleftrightarrow H(X,Y) = H(X) + H(Y) \quad (4.62)$$
$$m(A\overline{B}) = m(A) \longleftrightarrow H(X|Y) = H(X) \quad (4.63)$$
$$m(A \cap B) = 0 \longleftrightarrow I(X;Y) = 0. \quad (4.64)$$

The same procedure can be applied to a multiple port channel. For a three port channel, one can obtain the following relations for the entropies:

$$H(X,Y,Z) \leq H(X) + H(Y) + H(Z), \quad (4.65)$$
$$H(Z|X,Y) \leq H(Z|Y). \quad (4.66)$$

In the same reasoning, it is possible to obtains the following relations for the average mutual information for a three-port channel:

$$I(X;Y,Z) = I(X;Y) + I(X;Z|Y), \quad (4.67)$$
$$I(Y,Z;X) = I(Y;X) + I(Z;X|Y). \quad (4.68)$$

## 4.9 Channel Capacity

Shannon defined the discrete channel capacity as the maximum of the average mutual information, computed for all possible probability sets that can be associated to the input symbol alphabet, that is, for all memoryless sources,

$$C = \max I(X;Y) = \max\,[H(X) - H(X|Y)]. \quad (4.69)$$

### 4.9.1 Capacity of the Memoryless Discrete Channel

Consider $X$ as the alphabet of a source with $N$ symbols. Because the transition probability matrix is diagonal, then one obtains

$$C = \max I(X;Y) = \max[H(X)] = \max\left[-\sum_{i=1}^{N} p(x_i)\log p(x_i)\right]. \quad (4.70)$$

**Example**: The entropy attains a maximum when all symbols are equiprobable. Therefore, for the memoryless discrete channel, the capacity is

$$C = \max\left[-\sum_{i=1}^{N} \frac{1}{N}\log\frac{1}{N}\right],$$

which gives

$$C = \log N \qquad \text{bits per symbol.} \quad (4.71)$$

The channel capacity can also be expressed in bits per second, or shannon (Sh), and corresponds to the information transmission rate of the channel, for symbols with duration $T$ seconds,

$$C_T = \frac{C}{T} \quad \text{bits per second, or Sh.} \tag{4.72}$$

Therefore, for the noiseless channel,

$$C_T = \frac{C}{T} = \frac{1}{T} \log N \quad \text{bits per second, or Sh.} \tag{4.73}$$

### 4.9.2 Relative Redundancy and Efficiency

The absolute redundancy for a noisy channel, $A$, is the difference between the actual information transmission rate and $I(X;Y)$ and the maximum possible value,

$$\begin{aligned} A &= C - I(X;Y) \\ &= \log N - H(X). \end{aligned} \tag{4.74}$$

The ratio between the absolute redundancy and the channel capacity is defined as the system relative redundancy, $D$,

$$\begin{aligned} D &= \frac{\log N - H(X)}{\log N} \\ &= 1 - \frac{H(X)}{\log N}. \end{aligned} \tag{4.75}$$

The system efficiency, or the efficiency of the noiseless channel, $E$, is defined as the complement of the relative redundancy,

$$\begin{aligned} E &= \frac{I(X;Y)}{\log N} = \frac{H(X)}{\log N} \\ &= 1 - D. \end{aligned} \tag{4.76}$$

When the transmitted symbols do not occupy the same time interval, it is still possible to define the average information transmission rate for the noiseless channel, as

$$R_T = \frac{-\sum_{i=1}^{N} p(x_i) \log p(x_i)}{\sum_{i=1}^{N} p(x_i) T_i}, \tag{4.77}$$

in which $T_i$ represent the symbol intervals.

For a discrete noisy channel the capacity is the maximum of the average mutual information, when the noise characteristic $p(y_i|x_i)$ is specified.

$$C = \max \left( \sum_{i=1}^{N} \sum_{j=1}^{M} p(x_i)\, p(y_j|x_i) \log \frac{p(y_j|x_i)}{p(y_j)} \right), \tag{4.78}$$

in which the maximum is over $p(x_i)$. It must be noticed that the maximization in relation to the input probabilities do not always leads to an admissible set of source probabilities.

Bayes' rule defines the relation between the marginal probabilities $p(y_j)$ and the *a priori* probabilities $p(x_i)$,

$$p(y_j) = \sum_{i=1}^{N} p_1(x_i)\, p(y_j|x_i), \tag{4.79}$$

in which the variable are restricted to the following conditions:

$$p(x_i) \geq 0 \qquad i = 1, 2, \ldots, N, \tag{4.80}$$

$$\sum_{i=1}^{N} p_1(x_i) = 1.$$

**Example**: Determine the capacity of the memoryless Binary Symmetric Channel (BSC) (Blake, 1987).

The channel is illustrated in Figure 4.4, in which the error probability, or the probability of transmitting a symbol and receiving another one, is indicated as $p$.

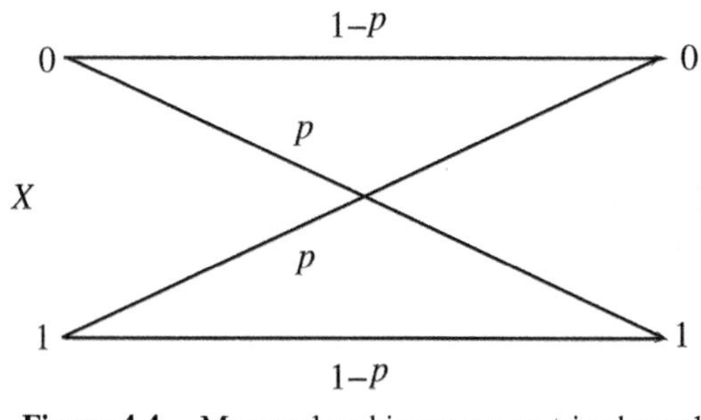


**Figure 4.4** Memoryless binary symmetric channel.

The channel capacity is given by Formula 4.69,

$$C = \max I(X;Y),$$

in which the average mutual information can be written as

$$I(X;Y) = \sum_{i=0}^{1}\sum_{j=0}^{1} p_{ij} \log \frac{p_{ij}}{p_i q_j}. \tag{4.81}$$

Assume that the symbol *a priori* probabilities are $p_0 = r$ and $p_1 = v$, with $r + v = 1$. Probabilities $r$ and $v$ are chosen in such a manner that, for each channel use, the maximum quantity of information is transferred.

The joint probabilities are $p_{00} = r(1-p)$, $p_{01} = rp$, $p_{10} = (1-r)p$, $p_{11} = (1-r)(1-p)$. and the average mutual information can be written as

$$\begin{aligned} I(X;Y) &= [(1-p)r] \log \left( \frac{(1-p)r}{r[(1-p)r + (1-r)p]} \right) \\ &+ [rp] \log \left( \frac{rp}{r[(rp + (1-r)(1-p)]} \right) \\ &+ [(1-r)p] \log \left( \frac{(1-r)p}{(1-r)[r(1-p) + (1-r)p]} \right) \\ &+ [(1-p)(1-r)] \log \left( \frac{(1-p)(1-r)}{(1-r)[(rp + (1-r)(1-p)]} \right), \end{aligned}$$

that can be put in the following way, after the simplification with logarithm properties,

$$\begin{aligned} I(X;Y) &= p \log p + (1-p) \log (1-p) \\ &- [r(1-p) + (1-r)p] \log [r(1-p) + (1-r)p] \\ &+ [rp + (1-r)(1-p)] \log [rp + (1-r)(1-p). \end{aligned}$$

The objective is to determine the value of $r$ that maximizes the expression, taking into account that the logarithms are base two. The obtained expression for $r$ is a complicated one, but the maximum that the average mutual information attains is given by

$$C = \max I(X;Y) = 1 - p \log p + (1-p) \log (1-p), \tag{4.82}$$

that represents the memoryless binary symmetric channel capacity. The graph for the capacity $C(p)$, as a function of the channel error probability, is shown in Figure 4.5.

**Example**: Determine the capacity of the Binary Erasure Channel (BEC), shown in Figure 4.6, in which the parameter $E$ represents the erasure and $1 - p$ the occurrence probability (Blake, 1987).

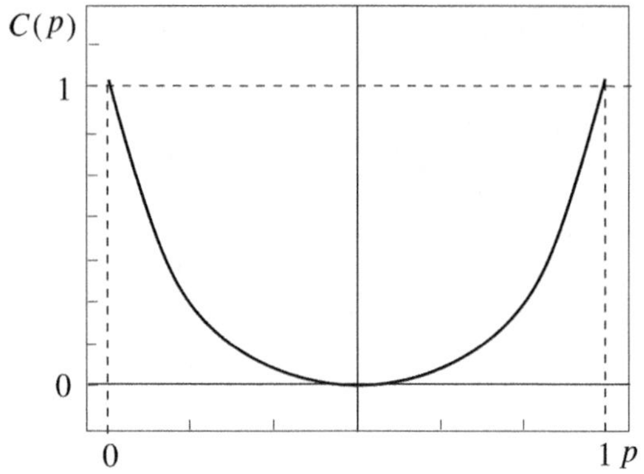


**Figure 4.5** Graph for the capacity of the memoryless binary symmetric channel.

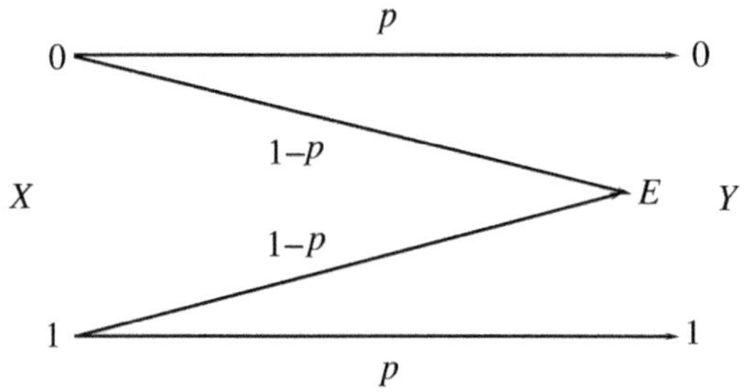


**Figure 4.6** Binary erasure channel.

The average mutual information for this channel is given by

$$I(X;Y) = \sum_{i=0}^{1}\sum_{j=0}^{2} p_{ij} \log \frac{p_{ij}}{p_i q_j}, \tag{4.83}$$

and the probabilities $p_{ij}$ are the following, for $p_0 = r$ and $p_1 = v$, with $r + v = 1$, $p_{00} = rp$, $p_{01} = r(1-p)$, $p_{10} = 0$, $p_{11} = (1-r)(1-p)$, $p_{02} = 0$, $p_{12} = (1-r)p$.

Substituting the probability values in Equation 4.83, one obtains

$$\begin{aligned} I(X;Y) &= [rp] \log \left(\frac{rp}{r^2 p}\right) \\ &+ [(1-p)r] \log \left(\frac{(1-p)r}{(1-p)r}\right), \end{aligned}$$

$$+ \ [(1-r)(1-p)] \log \left( \frac{(1-r)(1-p)}{(1-p)^2} \right)$$
$$+ \ [(1-r)p] \log \left( \frac{(1-r)p}{(1-r)^2 p} \right),$$

Simplifying the terms in the expression, gives

$$I(X;Y) = p\,[r \log r - (1-r) \log (1-r)] = p\,H(r), \qquad (4.84)$$

in which $H(r)$ is the entropy function.

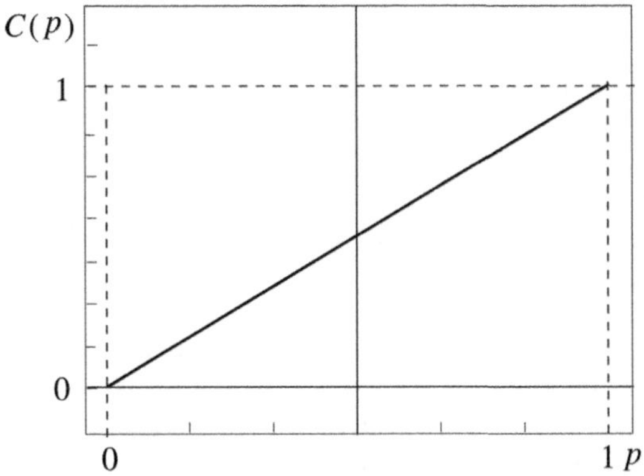


**Figure 4.7** Graph of the capacity for the binary erasure channel.

Because $p$ is determined, $I(X;Y)$ is maximized by the choice of a value for $r$ that produces the highest $H(r)$, that is, $r = 1/2$, for which $H(r) = 1$. Therefore, the capacity of the binary erasure channel is simply $p$. Figure 4.7 shows the graph for the capacity as a linear function of the probability, $C(p) = p$.

# 5

# Error-correcting Codes

*"It is a very sad thing that nowadays there is so little useless information."*
Oscar Wilde

## 5.1 Introduction

The reliable transmission of data over communication networks implies the use of certain codes to protect the messages from noise and interference. An error-correcting code is an algorithm to express a sequence of numbers such that any errors which are introduced can be detected and corrected, based on the remaining numbers. The study of error-correcting codes and the associated mathematics is known as coding theory (Lin and Costello, 1983).

Error-correcting codes add redundancy to the data before transmission or storage. Thus, the receiver, or reading equipment, can recover the original data even if some bits are corrupted by noise. There are different types of error-correcting codes, including block codes, convolutional codes, and turbo codes, that have different properties and applications (Hsiao, 1984).

The basic principle is to encode the data into a longer sequence of bits, called a codeword, that has a certain algebraic structure to allow the detection and correction of errors. For instance, a simple error-correcting code is the parity check code, which adds an extra bit to the data that is the binary sum of all the other bits. If the received bit sequence has an odd number of 1s, then there is an error and the last bit is changed.

The use of error-correcting codes in digital communication involves diverse questions. First, it involves the design of codes that are efficient, with high transmission rate and low error probability. Those codes should be also have low latency and small complexity for encoding and decoding. The codes must also be adequate to the channel characteristics, including the noise level, the bandwidth limitation and the interference.

It is important to consider that some codes perform better in bursty noise environments, while others are more suitable for fading channels.

DOI: 10.1201/9788743813613-5

Another question is to evaluate the advantages of error-correcting codes against the costs of adding redundancy and signal processing complexity. For instance, the addition of bits to the data stream may increase the bandwidth requirement.

The use of error-correcting codes in digital communication offers opportunities and benefits. One possibility is to enhance the performance and reliability of communication systems, including cellular networks, Internet, or satellite communications. Error-correcting codes can decrease the number of retransmissions, improve the quality of service, or increase the coverage area of the system.

New applications and technologies that require high data rates and low error rates, such as multimedia streaming, cloud computing, or quantum communication can be made available, because error-correcting codes can permit the compression and protection of data from interference, noise and eavesdropping.

It is also possible to explore the theoretical limits of information transmission and compression, because error-correcting codes can verify information-theoretic limits and theorems, and develop new concepts and methods in cryptography, to guarantee the data secrecy and inviolability (Konheim, 1981).

The communication systems are always changing, regarding the circuit implementation, according to the new transmission demands and the technological evolution. For example, the old systems evolved from the electromechanical relay to thermionic tubes and, later on, to transistors and integrated circuits. Notwithstanding, the basic components of a communication system remain the same.

In general, a communication system can be represented by the block diagram shown in Figure 5.1.

- **Source:** The source produces the information to be transmitted. Example of sources are: the microphone, the computer keyboard, a telemetry sensor, the cell phone. The source output is mathematically modelled by a stochastic process.
- **Transmitter:** Converts the source output to waveforms that are adequate for transmission over a communication channel. The transmitter function can be subdivided into the following parts.

    1. **Source coder:** Usually an analog to digital converter, the source coder can include additional functions, including removing redundancy.

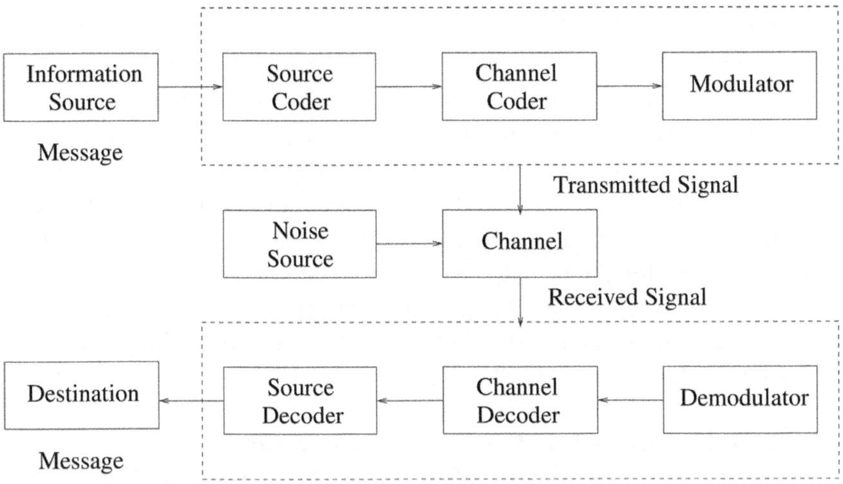


**Figure 5.1** Generic communication system.

2. **Channel coder:** This block adds controlled redundancy to the signal at the source coder output, to remove the noise effects.
3. **Modulator:** The original signal is, usually, not suitable for transmission over a channel. The modulator translates the signal frequency to be adequately transmitted through the channel.

- **Channel:** It is the physical means through which the information passes to reach the receiver. The channel can be a twisted pair, a microwave link, a cellular communication system, or an optical cable. The channel is subject to interference and noise, which disturbs the transmitted signal and must be controlled.
- **Receiver:** The receiver processes the incoming signal to recover the original waveform. It comprises the following parts.

1. **Demodulator:** Based on the received waveform, the demodulator estimates the original signal and delivers its digital version to the channel decoder. This digital signal can include errors.
2. **Channel decoder:** This device applies coding techniques to the digital signal to correct possible errors and provides an estimate of the original sequence at the output of the source coder.
3. **Source decoder:** This block takes the channel decoder output and replaces the redundancy that has been removed at the source coder, to reconstitute the transmitted message to be delivered to the recipient.

- **Destination:** Final receiver of the transmitted information. The recipient may be a human being that receives a phone call, or a computer.

Every communication system suffers some kind of interference, a deterministic effect on the transmitted signal, or noise, a random effect that disturbs the signal. Therefore, the received signal produces messages that could contains errors. The objective of every communications engineer it to design systems that present acceptable error rates for the user. An error rate of $10^{-4}$ is usual for a telephone call, but it is unacceptable for a bank transfer.

The usefulness of error correcting codes was established by Claude E. Shannon, in a paper published in 1949, known as the Shannon coding theorem for a noisy channel, which can be stated as (Omura, 1979):

> **Theorem**. For any memoryless channel, whose input is a discrete alphabet, there are codes with information rates $R$ (nats/symbol), with words of length $n$ digits, for which the probability of error, considering maximum likelihood decoding, is limited by $P_e < e^{1-nE(R)}$, in which, $E(R) > 0$, $0 \leq R < C$, is a decreasing convex function specified by the channel transition probabilities and $C$ is the channel capacity (Omura, 1979).

The coding theorem proves the existence of codes that have the property of reducing the decoding error, but it does not offer any indication of how to develop those codes. On the other hand, note that $P_e$ decreases exponentially as $n$ increases. The system complexity also escalates.

The main objectives of the coding theory are:

- Discover long and efficient codes.
- Find practical and efficient coding and decoding methods.

Recent technological developments in the areas of digital processors, computers, microelectronics, and massive hardware integration make it possible the use of complex coding and decoding circuits. Thus, it is possible to enjoy the full advantages of coding.

### 5.1.1 Error Types

Due to the presence of noise in the channel, errors can occur during the transmission of data. Those errors could be sporadic and independent, being called random errors, or they could occur in sequences of several errors at a time, called bursts, implying that the channel has some sort of memory.

## 5.2 Linear and Nonlinear Codes

Error-correcting codes can be defined in many ways, according to the mathematical operations that generate them, or the nature of the algebraic structure that defined them. Linear and nonlinear codes are the basic definitions.

### 5.2.1 Linear Codes

A linear code is an error-correcting code for which any linear combination of codewords is also a codeword. Linear codes have their redundant digits computed as linear combinations of the information digits. The operation is performed on a finite field.

A linear error correcting code is the set of all linear combinations of $k$ independent vectors in a vector space $C$ of $n$-tuples over a field $F$. Therefore, a linear error-correcting code is a vector subspace and it can be given by a basis called the generator matrix of the code. Linear codes, the primary subject of this chapter, are usually referred to using the notation $(n, k)$ (Nenno, 1987).

In other words, a linear code of length $n$ over the the finite field $F$ is a subspace of $F^n$. Thus the words of linear code the code space $F^n$ are vectors, and it is possible to refer to codewords as codevectors.

If $C$ is a linear code that, as a vector space over the field $F$, has dimension $k$, then ones says that $C$ is an $(n, k)$ linear code over $F$, or simply an $(n, k)$ code. There is no conflict with the definition of the dimension of $C$ as a code, since $|C| = |F|^k$.

**Example**: The repetition code of length $n$ over the field $F$ is an $(n, 1, n)$ linear code. This code has a large distance $d = n$, but few codewords.

In particular the rate of an $(n, k)$ linear code is $R = k/n$. If $C$ has minimum distance $d$, then $C$ is an $(n, k, d)$ linear code over $F$. The number $n - k$ is called the redundancy of $C$.

**Example**: The binary parity check code of length $n$ over $F$ is an $(n, n-1, 2)$ linear code of redundancy 1 and rate $R = (n-1)/n$.

### 5.2.2 Nonlinear Codes

Nonlinear codes use nonlinear circuits or operations, including AND, OR and NOR gates, in the binary case, to combine the information digits to produce the code digits. A nonlinear error-correcting code is a collection of $M$ codewords (or $n$-tuples) with components over some alphabet $F$. We refer to the code as an $(n, M, d)$ code in which $d$ is a positive integer such that any two codewords differ in at least $d$ places and $d$ is the largest such number with this property.

**Example**: Table 5.1 shows a nonlinear binary $(5, 4, 2)$ code over the finite field $F = \{0, 1\}$ (Nenno, 1987).

**Table 5.1** A nonlinear code over the finite field $F = \{0, 1\}$.

| | |
|---|---|
| $c_1$ | 10101 |
| $c_2$ | 10010 |
| $c_3$ | 01110 |
| $c_4$ | 11111 |

Consider what might happen when some of the messages in the set $\{00, 01, 10, 11\}$ are transmitted over a digital communications channel. Suppose the messages are encoded according to Table 5.2.

**Table 5.2** A set of messages that use a nonlinear code to be transmitted over a communications channel.

| | |
|---|---|
| $m_1 = 00$ | $c_1 = 10101$ |
| $m_2 = 01$ | $c_2 = 10010$ |
| $m_3 = 10$ | $c_3 = 01110$ |
| $m_4 = 11$ | $c_4 = 11111$ |

Define $d(x, y)$, in which $x$ and $y$ are each $n$-tuples over some alphabet, as the number of positions in which the two $n$-tuples $x$ and $y$ differ. One can say that the Hamming distance between two codewords, or $n$-tuples, is given by $d(x, y)$. The Hamming weight of a codeword $x$ is the number of nonzero components of $x$ and is denoted by $w(x) = d(x, 0)$.

The minimum weight of the code $C$ is the minimum nonzero weight among all codewords of $C$, and the Hamming distance is translation invariant. In particular, for linear codes, the minimum weight equals the minimum distance,

$$d(x, y) = d(x - y, y - y) = d(x - y, 0). \tag{5.1}$$

A consequence of the this property is that minimum distance for linear codes is much easier to calculate than for nonlinear, or arbitrary codes. It is only necessary to survey $|C|$ codewords for weight rather than roughly $|C|^2$ pairs for distance.

The minimum Hamming distance between pairs of distinct codewords in a code is called the Hamming distance of the code. A code whose minimum Hamming distance is $d$ can correct $t = \lceil \frac{1}{2}(d-1) \rceil$ errors, in which $\lceil \cdot \rceil$ denotes the greatest integer function. Hence, if a code is $t$-error-correcting, then $d \geq 2t + 1$.

This can be proved by the following reasoning. The Hamming distance is given as $d$. Suppose that codeword $c$ is sent and that it is corrupted into $c'$. If $c'$ is to be decoded to $c$, it must be the case that $d(c, c') < \frac{d}{2}$. Thus, the number of correctable errors is $t < \frac{d}{2}$.

If the Hamming distance $d$ is an even number this implies $t < \frac{d}{2} - 1$. Whereas, if $d$ is odd, one has $t < \frac{d-1}{2}$. Hence, the number of errors that can be corrected is finally given by $t = \lceil \frac{1}{2}(d-1) \rceil$.

Sometimes it is possible to correct certain error patterns with $t$ errors even when $d < 2t + 1$, although there is no guarantee of this because it depends upon which codeword is transmitted and on the particular pattern of $t$ errors that occurs in the codeword (Nenno, 1987).

### 5.2.3 Block and Convolutional Codes

Two different types of codes are produced, according with the way the redundancy digits are attached to the information digits. Error-correcting codes for which the redundancy in a block of digits check the occurrence of errors, for that particular block alone, are called block codes.

On the other hand, codes for which the redundancy in a given block check the occurrence of errors in more than one block are called convolutional codes. The convolutional codes are a special case of the tree codes, and are useful in many practical situations (Lin and Costello, 1983).

The choice of a certain type of code depends on several factors, including the data format, the coding delay, and the system complexity that is necessary to attain a given error rate (Markman, 1987) (da Rocha Jr. & R. Palazzo Jr., 1987).

## 5.3 Block Codes

Block codes are characterized by their coding procedure, which involves the segmentation of the message into block of $k$ digits, to which $n - k$ redundant digits are appended. The $n - k$ additional digits are determined from the $k$ message digits by algebraic procedures, and are used to simple detection, or detection and correction of errors that occur in the transmission process.

Block codes can be linear or nonlinear, according to certain mathematical properties. For the linear codes, the redundant digits are computed as linear combinations of the information digits.

The theory that supports the development of linear error-correcting codes, based on Linear Algebra and Finite Field Theory, is well understood and the block codes are well studied. The idea behind the Galois Field was developed by ÉEvariste Galois (1811-1832), a French mathematician and political activist, who determined the necessary and sufficient conditions for a polynomial to be solvable by radicals. This problem was open for more than three centuries.

For practical reasons, considering that the digital circuits and computers use the binary numerical system, only binary linear block codes are considered.

Therefore, an $(n, k, d)$ code is defined as a set of binary $2^k$ $n$-tuples, called codewords, which differ in, at least, $d$ positions and define a vectorial subspace that encompass all $n$-tuples. The following example has the objective of clarifying the previous concepts.

**Example:** Consider the (7, 3, 4) code whose equations to compute the redundant digits are the following (da Rocha Jr., 2001):

$$\begin{aligned} c_1 &= m_1 \oplus m_2, & c_2 &= m_2 \oplus m_3, \\ c_3 &= m_1 \oplus m_3, & c_4 &= m_1 \oplus m_2 \oplus m_3. \end{aligned}$$

Each block, that has thee information digits, is encoded into a codeword with seven digits, which produce the following set of codewords,

$$\overset{\text{Messages}}{\begin{bmatrix} 0 & 0 & 0 \\ 0 & 0 & 1 \\ 0 & 1 & 0 \\ 0 & 1 & 1 \\ 1 & 0 & 0 \\ 1 & 0 & 1 \\ 1 & 1 & 0 \\ 1 & 1 & 1 \\ m_1 & m_2 & m_3 \end{bmatrix}} \mapsto \overset{\text{Codewords}}{\begin{bmatrix} 0 & 0 & 0 & 0 & 0 & 0 & 0 \\ 0 & 0 & 1 & 0 & 1 & 1 & 1 \\ 0 & 1 & 0 & 1 & 1 & 0 & 1 \\ 0 & 1 & 1 & 1 & 0 & 1 & 0 \\ 1 & 0 & 0 & 1 & 0 & 1 & 1 \\ 1 & 0 & 1 & 1 & 1 & 0 & 0 \\ 1 & 1 & 0 & 0 & 1 & 1 & 0 \\ 1 & 1 & 1 & 0 & 0 & 0 & 1 \\ m_1 & m_2 & m_3 & c_1 & c_2 & c_3 & c_4 \end{bmatrix}}$$

### 5.3.1 Matrix Representation

The codewords can be represented by vectors in an algebraic space, with $n$ components. The components of those vectors are, usually, elements of a finite field with $q$ elements, represented by the symbol GF$(q)$, also called Galois Field. It is also usual to use the binary Galois field, with elements 0 and 1, represented as GF$(2)$.

The linear code is a vector subspace, therefore every codeword can be represented by a linear combination of vectors from the subspace base, that is, vectors that are linearly independent. The base vectors can be written as lines of the generating matrix of the code (Lin and Costello, 1983).

Given the generating matrix of a certain linear code, with $k$ lines and $n$ columns, it is possible to form another matrix $H$, with $n - k$ lines and $n$ columns, such that the space of lines from $G$ is orthogonal to $H$. This means that, if $c_i$ is a vector from the space of lines from $G$, then

$$c_i H^T = 0.$$

Matrix $H$ is called the parity check matrix for the error correcting code, and can be represented as

$$H = [h : I_{n-k}],$$

in which $h$ is and $(n-k)\times k$ matrix and $I_{n-k}$ é is unit matrix $(n-k)\times(n-k)$.

It is possible to be demonstrate that matrix $G$ can be written as $G = [I_k|g]$, in which $g$ is a $k \times (n-k)$ matrix and $I_k$ is the unit matrix $k \times k$ (Lin and Costello, 1983).

The matrices $g$ and $h$ are related by the formula $g^T = h$. Because the lines of $H$ are linearly independent, they generate a linear code $(n, n-k, d')$, that is called the dual code of the code $(n, k, d)$ produce by $G$. Code $(n, n-k, d')$ can be considered the dual space of the code $(n, k, d)$ generated by $G$.

**Example:** The generating matrix for the code of the previous example is the following

$$G = \begin{bmatrix} 1 & 0 & 0 & 1 & 0 & 1 & 1 \\ 0 & 1 & 0 & 1 & 1 & 0 & 1 \\ 0 & 0 & 1 & 0 & 1 & 1 & 1 \\ m_1 & m_2 & m_3 & c_1 & c_2 & c_3 & c_4 \end{bmatrix}.$$

Therefore,

$$g = \begin{bmatrix} 1 & 0 & 1 & 1 \\ 1 & 1 & 0 & 1 \\ 0 & 1 & 1 & 1 \end{bmatrix},$$

$$h = g^T = \begin{bmatrix} 1 & 1 & 0 \\ 0 & 1 & 1 \\ 1 & 0 & 1 \\ 1 & 1 & 1 \end{bmatrix}.$$

The parity-check matrix $H$ is thus

$$\begin{bmatrix} 1 & 1 & 0 & 1 & 0 & 0 & 0 \\ 0 & 1 & 1 & 0 & 1 & 0 & 0 \\ 1 & 0 & 1 & 0 & 0 & 1 & 0 \\ 1 & 1 & 1 & 0 & 0 & 0 & 1 \\ m_1 & m_2 & m_3 & c_1 & c_2 & c_3 & c_4 \end{bmatrix}.$$

Using the matrix representation it is possible to verify that the function of a coder is to obtain the product $mG$ of a line matrix $m$, with $k$ elements, which represent the information digits, by the generating matrix $G$. The result of that operation is a linear combination of the lines of $G$, that is, a codeword.

The following example was presented by Jack Keil Wolf (1935-2011), an American researcher in information theory and coding theory, during one of his lectures at the University of California, San Diego (Wolf, 2008).

**Example:** In general, a block code with $k$ information digits and block length $n$ is called an $(n, k)$ code. Thus, this example is called a Hamming $(7, 4)$ code. Consider the sequence $\{m_1 m_2 m_3 m_4\}$ of message digits that form the codeword $\{m_1 m_2 m_3 m_4 c_1 c_2 c_3\}$, based on the following parity check equations:

$$\begin{aligned} m_1 \oplus m_2 \oplus m_3 \oplus c_1 &= 0 \\ m_1 \oplus m_3 \oplus m_4 \oplus c_2 &= 0 \\ m_1 \oplus m_2 \oplus m_4 \oplus c_3 &= 0 \end{aligned}$$

The equations are represented by the intersecting circles in Figure 5.2. Note that there is an even number of 1's in each circle.

The parity check matrix for the that code is given by,

$$\begin{bmatrix} 1 & 1 & 1 & 0 & 1 & 0 & 0 \\ 1 & 0 & 1 & 1 & 0 & 1 & 0 \\ 1 & 1 & 0 & 1 & 0 & 0 & 1. \end{bmatrix}$$

Suppose the message $\{m_1 m_2 m_3 m_4\} = \{0110\}$ is transmitted. The resultant codeword is then $\{0110011\}$, as illustrated in Figure 5.3.

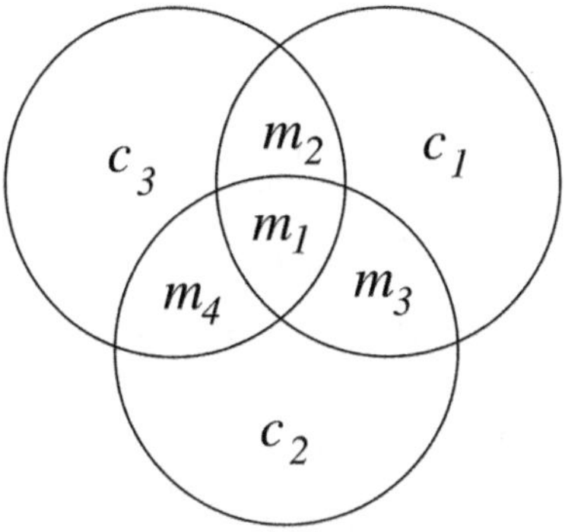


**Figure 5.2** Hamming code explained using a Venn diagram.

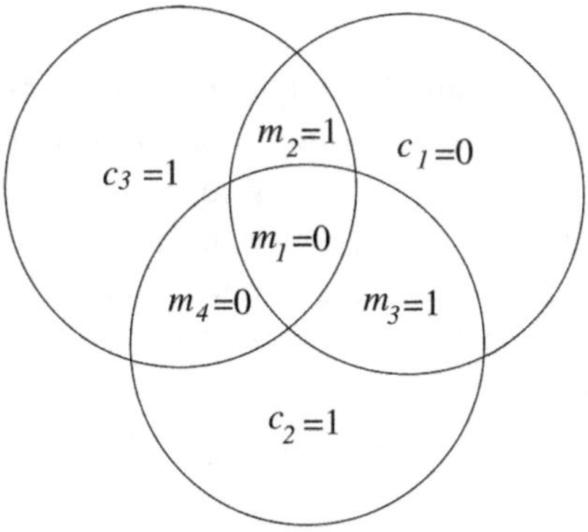


**Figure 5.3** Transmitted codeword using a Venn diagram.

Suppose the transmitted block is received with one error in a message bit, for instance $\{01\underline{0}0011\}$, as depicted in Figure 5.4.

By counting the number of 1's in each circle one finds that there is an error in bottom circle, there is an error in right circle, and there is no error in left circle. Therefore the error is in the third digit.

### 5.3.2 Simple Codes

Some codes that present simple structures, which are suitable to explain the encoding mechanism of more complex ones, are discussed in the following.

#### 5.3.2.1 Repetition Codes

A simple repetition code is characterized by the following parameters: $k = 1$, $c \geq 1$ e $n = k + c = 1 + c$. Because $k = 1$, this code has only two

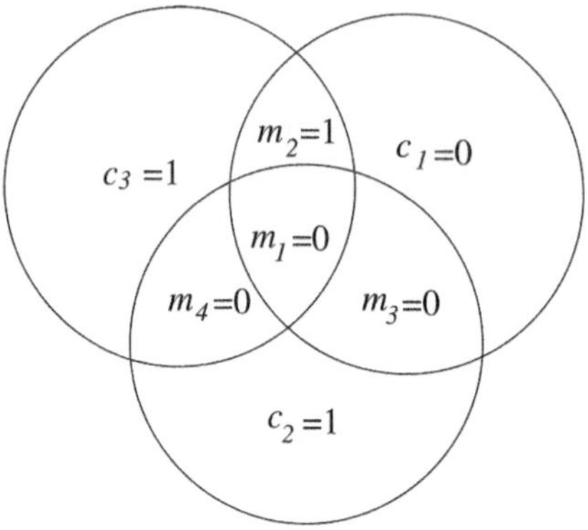


**Figure 5.4** Received codeword with one error in a message bit.

codewords, the sequence of 0's and the sequence of 1's. The parity-check bits are all the same, and are a repetition of the information digit.

A simple decoding rule in this case is to assume that the transmitted digit is the one that occurs more frequently in the received codeword. This is feasible when $n$ is odd. If $n$ is even, and there is a tie in the counting of 0's and 1's, is it only possible to detect the occurrence of errors.

The minimum distance for this type of error-correcting code is $d = n$, and the efficiency is $R = 1/n$. It is clear that any pattern with $t \leq \lfloor n/2 \rfloor$ errors can be fixed.

#### 5.3.2.2 Single Parity Digit Check Codes

The single parity digit check code has a single redundant digit per codeword. This redundant digit is computed in order to make the number of 1's in the codeword even.

In other words, one counts the number of 1's in the codeword and sets the parity digit to 1, if the result is odd. On the contrary, the parity digit is set to 0. The code parameters are $k \geq 1,\ c = 1$ and $n = k + c = k + 1$. The Hamming distance and the code efficiency of this code are, respectively, $d = 2$ and $R = k/n = k/(k + 1)$.

The decoding rule employed for this code is the following. Count the number of 1's in the received word. If the result is even, the received block is assumed free of errors and the message is delivered o the recipient.

On the contrary, it is assumed that the received block of digits has errors, and the recipient is warned about it. Even though this code only permits to detect the occurrence of errors, it is useful and efficient for systems that operate a return channel, to request a retransmission of the message. Soft decision decoding can also profit from this coding strategy.

### 5.3.3 Hamming Code

Richard Wesley Hamming (1915-1998) was an American mathematician who made important contributions to the areas of computer engineering and telecommunications, including the Hamming window for signal processing, the Hamming numbers, the sphere-packing or Hamming bound, the Hamming graph concepts, and the Hamming distance.

Hamming began working with linear error-correcting codes at the Bell Telephone Laboratories in New Jersey, in 1946, after he spent some time working for the Manhattan Project, the U.S. government research project to produce an atomic bomb, at Los Alamos. At Bell Labs he was frustrated because the programs that he was running could not recover from simple errors generated by noise. He then devised a way to both correct a single error in a block and detect a second error.

Hamming was the first coding theorist whose work attracted widespread interest. He was a colleague of Claude E. Shannon at Bell Telephone Laboratories, and published his seminal paper in 1950, after he filed a patent on the coding procedure (Hamming, 1950).

Hamming and Shannon were concerned with the fundamental problem of communication over noisy channels, but Shannon was interested in the statistical properties of the channel and Hamming had an interest in the combinatorial properties of the codes. In a sense, Shannon preferred the existential perspective of the subject, and Hamming had more interest in the construction approach of error-correcting codes.

The Hamming code can be thought as the first non-trivial codes proposed to correct errors. The Hamming code is linear and can correct one error per word, that is, it has minimum distance $d = 3$. The block length is $n \leq 2^c - 1$, in which $c$ the number of redundant digits.

The condition on $n$ ensures that the code has enough redundancy to check the occurrence of one error per word, because the number of non-empty syndromes, $2^c - 1$, is always greater of equal to the number of positions where an error can be.

**Example:** Consider the construction of a Hamming code $(7, 4, 3)$. The procedure can be generalized to the construction of any Hamming code $(n, k, 3)$.

The number of parity-check digits for the code $(7, 4, 3)$ is $c = 7 - 4 = 3$. Consider the non-null binary numbers that can be written with $c = 3$ digits, as in the following

$$\begin{matrix} 0 & 0 & 1 & c_1 \\ 0 & 1 & 0 & c_2 \\ 0 & 1 & 1 & m_1 \\ 1 & 0 & 0 & c_3 \\ 1 & 0 & 1 & m_2 \\ 1 & 1 & 0 & m_3 \\ 1 & 1 & 1 & m_4 \end{matrix}$$

Hamming associated the numbers in the way $2^i$, $i = 0, 1, 2, ...$, with the parity-check positions. The other positions were associated with the information digits, as indicated in the code listing.

Taking a look at the column in a descending manner, the parity-check equations are written as module-2 additions of the information digits, in which 1 appears in the particular column considered. That is,

$$c_1 = m_1 \oplus m_2 \oplus m_4$$

$$c_2 = m_1 \oplus m_3 \oplus m_4$$

$$c_3 = m_2 \oplus m_3 \oplus m_4$$

Upon receiving a word, the decoder computes the parity-check digits and add them modulo-2 to the corresponding digits of the received word to obtain the syndrome.

If, for instance, one error hits digit $m_1$ the syndrome digits at positions $c_1$ and $c_2$ will fail, while the parity-check digit at position $c_3$ never fails, because it does not verify $m_1$. This condition is represented as

$$(c_3, c_2, c_1) = (0, 1, 1).$$

This binary number corresponds to the position of $m_1$ in the preceding code list. Thus, the error has been located and can be corrected. This procedure can be applied to any value of $n$.

The Hamming codes are special ones, because no other class of non trivial codes can be so easily decoded. The Hamming codes are also perfect, according to the following definition.

An error-correcting code $(n, k, d)$ over GF$(q)$, which can correct $t$ errors, is perfect if and only if

$$\sum_{i=0}^{t}(q-1)^i C_n^i = q^{n-k}, \tag{5.2}$$

in which $q$ represents the number of levels.

Excluding the just discussed Hamming codes and the Golay binary $(23, 12, 7)$ and ternary $(11, 6, 5)$ codes, there are no other perfect non-trivial error-correcting codes. (Pless, 1982).

## 5.4 Cyclic Codes

Among the block codes, the cyclic codes are the most important regarding engineering applications (Clark and Cain, 1981). Cyclic codes are used in computer network communication protocols, compact disks, magnetic storage, space transmission and other applications. The code structure is based on discrete Mathematics, which allows the simplification of the coders and decoders.

The more formal treatment of these code requires polynomial rings, modulo $x^n - 1$, with coefficients that belong in the GF$(q)$, in which $n$ is the block length (Berlekamp, 1968a). Nonetheless, a simple way to define the codes is the following.

A code is cyclic when a cyclic permutation, applied to any of its codewords, results in a word of the same code. That is, if

$$\mathbf{c} = \left(c_0, c_1, c_2, ....., c_{n-1}\right) \tag{5.3}$$

is a word that belongs to the code, then

$$\mathbf{c}^i = \left(c_{n-i}, c_{n-i+1}, ..., c_0, c_1, ..., c_{n-i-1}\right) \tag{5.4}$$

is also a word of the code, considering that its indices are reduced modulo-$n$.

As the code $C$ is invariant under this single right cyclic shift, by iteration it is invariant under any number of right cyclic shifts. As a single left cyclic shift is the same as $n - 1$ right cyclic shifts, $C$ is also invariant under a single left cyclic shift and hence all left cyclic shifts. Therefore the linear code $C$ is cyclic when it is invariant under all cyclic shifts.

Some examples of cyclic codes are given in the following. The **0**-code is cyclic and also $F^n$. The repetition codes are cyclic, and the binary parity check code is also cyclic. This goes over to the zero sum codes over any Galois field. The shift invariance criterion does not depend upon the code being linear, and it is possible to define nonlinear cyclic codes.

An $n$-tuple, as $\mathbf{c}$ in the previous expression, can be represented by a polynomial that has maximum degree $n-1$, in the following way

$$c(x) = c_0 + c_1 x + c_2 x^2 + ... + c_{n-1} x^{n-1}. \tag{5.5}$$

Using finite fields properties, it can be proved that all the words of a cyclic code $(n, k, d)$ are multiples of a well-defined polynomial $g(x)$, of degree $n - k$. On the other hand, every polynomial of degree less than or equal to $n-1$, that is divisible by $g(x)$, is a codeword. The polynomial $g(x)$ is called the generator polynomial and is a factor of $x^n - 1$.

#### 5.4.0.1 Matrix Representation

As previously mentioned, the words of a cyclic code are multiples of the generating polynomial $g(x)$. Therefore, the polynomials $g(x)$, $xg(x)$, $x^2g(x)$,...,$x^{k-1}g(x)$ are codewords. It is possible to observe that these words are linearly independent, and can be used to form the generating matrix of a cyclic code, that has a generating polynomial $g(x)$, as shown in matrix form

$$G = \begin{bmatrix} x^{k-1}g(x) \\ . \\ . \\ . \\ x^2g(x) \\ xg(x) \\ g(x) \end{bmatrix}$$

For coding purposes, the cyclic shift property makes it possible to have a sequential implementation of matrix $G$, as discussed in the following section.

#### 5.4.0.2 Coder with $n-k$ Shift-register Stages

The procedure that uses a coder with $n-k$ shift-register stages is based on the property that every word of a cyclic code is a multiple of generator polynomial $g(x)$ of the code.

Therefore, the $k$ information digits can be represented by a polynomial $I(x)$, whose degree is smaller than or equal to $k-1$. If this polynomial is multiplied by $x^{n-k}$ one obtains $I(x)x^{n-k}$, which is a polynomial with degree smaller or equal to $n-1$ that does not contain terms of degree smaller than $n-k$.

Therefore, $I(x)x^{n-k}$ can be written in terms of $g(x)$ as

$$I(x)x^{n-k} = Q(x)g(x) + R(x), \quad (5.6)$$

in which $Q(x)$ and $R(x)$ are, respectively, the quotient and the remaining of the division.

The polynomial $R(x)$ has degree smaller than $g(x)$, that is $R(x)$ has a degree smaller of equal to $n - k - 1$. If $R(x)$ is subtracted from $I(x)x^{n-k}$, the result is a multiple of $g(x)$, that is, it is a codeword.

Therefore, $R(x)$ represents the parity-check digits and has no superimposed non-null terms with $I(x)x^{n-k}$, according to the previous considerations. The operations can be done by the circuit of Figure 5.5 (da Rocha Jr., 2001):

The coder displayed in Figure 5.5 has $n - k$ shift-registers and pre-multiplies the information polynomial by $x^{n-k}$. The circuit switches $g_1, g_2, ..., g_{c-1}$ are closed when the the corresponding component of $g(x)$ equals 1. On the contrary, they are left open.

At the beginning, the contents of the register is zero. Switch $s_1$ is closed and $s_2$ stays in position $a$. The information digits, that represent the incoming message, are sent at the same time of the output and the division circuit.

After the transmission of $k$ information digits, the remaining, which corresponds to the parity-check digits, is stored in the register. Then, switch $s_1$ is open and switch $s_2$ is moved to position $b$. During the next $n - k$ time slots the parity-check digits are transmitted. The procedure is repeated with the subsequent information blocks.

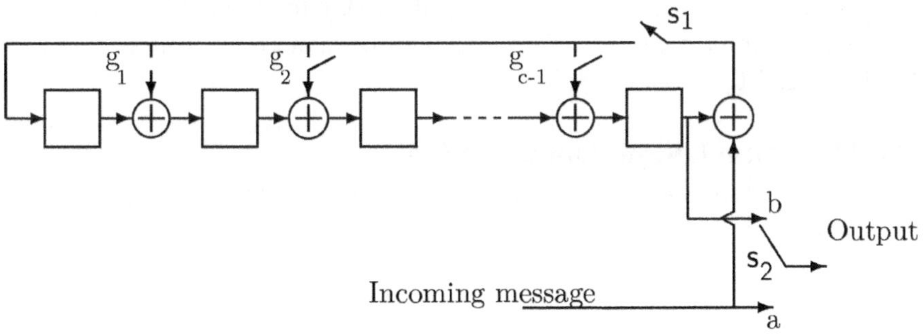


**Figure 5.5** Coder with $n - k$ shift-register stages.

There is another coding procedure for cyclic codes, that is based on the polynomial $h(x) = (x^n - 1)/g(x)$, which employs $k$ shift-register stages, and can be found in the following references (Lin and Costello, 1983) (Clark and Cain, 1981).

#### 5.4.0.3 Cyclic Hamming Code

This section presents a few code classes that use the cyclic structure of the codewords, that is, the circular shifts of each codeword gives another word that belongs to the code.

The Hamming codes also have a cyclic representation. In fact, for every $m$, there is a cyclic, binary Hamming code of redundancy $m$. Then, primitive polynomial of degree $m$ in $F^2[x]$ generates a cyclic Hamming code of redundancy $m$. The polynomial $g(x) \in F^2[x]$ generates a cyclic, binary Hamming code if and only if it is primitive.

The Hamming cyclic codes have a primitive generating polynomial $p(x)$, of degree $m$, and the following parameters

$$n = 2^m - 1, \; k = 2^m - m - 1, \; d = 3.$$

These codes can be decoded by a Meggitt decoder, developed by John E. Meggitt, in 1961, which computes the error syndromes of all correctable error patterns from a small number of error syndromes, therefore, avoiding the need for a syndrome table. In the case of a single-error-correcting code, the Meggitt decoder is simple and appropriate. All the syndromes can be determined from any one error syndrome. Error trap decoders are also used (John E. Meggitt, 1961).

Because the Hamming codes are perfect, they frequently show up in the literature in several applications regarding, for instance, collision resolution in multiple access channels, when reducing the delay for a user to access the channel is more important than maximize the information transmission rate (da Rocha Jr. & J.L. Massey, 1993).

#### 5.4.0.4 Maximum Length Linear Codes

The maximum length linear codes are cyclic and dual of the Hamming codes. The code has the following parameters

$$n = 2^m - 1, \; k = m, \; d = 2^{m-1}, \text{ in which } m \geq 2.$$

The generating polynomial of a linear code of maximum length has the format

$$g(x) = (x^n - 1)/p(x), \tag{5.7}$$

in which $p(x)$ a primitive polynomial of degree $m$.

The dictionary associated to such codes has one null word and $n$ non-null codewords that result from $n$ cyclic shifts of a non-null word. Therefore, all non-null words have the same Hamming weight. These codes are called equidistant, simplex, or sequence-$m$ codes.

Sequence-$m$ codes are made completely orthogonal in only one step and, as a consequence, are decodable by majority logic (Massey, 1963a). The non-null words of those codes are employed to measure the distance in radar and in the global positioning system (GPS).

### 5.4.1 Bose-Chaudhuri-Hocquenghem Code

The Bose-Chaudhuri-Hocquenghem (BCD) codes were invented, in 1959, by French mathematician Alexis Hocquenghem (1908-1990), and independently rediscovered, in 1960, by Raj Chandra Bose (1901-1987), an Indian American mathematician and statistician, and Dwijendra Kumar Ray-Chaudhuri (1933-), a professor emeritus at Ohio State University. Note that the acronym should be written (BRH).

The BCH codes are cyclic and represent one of the most important classes of block code with algebraic decoding algorithms. For any positive integers $m,\ t$ there is a BCH code with the following parameters

$$n = q^m - 1,\ n - k = c \leq mt,\ d \geq 2t + 1.$$

The BCH codes can be seem as a generalization of the Hamming codes, with the ability to correct multiples errors in a word. A conventional way of defining these codes is by the specification of the roots of a generator polynomial.

A primitive BCH code over GF($q$), which can correct $t$ errors, with block length $n = q^m - 1$, has the following generator polynomial roots $\alpha^{m_0}$, $\alpha^{m_0+1}$, ..., $\alpha^{m_0+2t-1}$, for any integer $m_0$, in which $\alpha$ is a primitive element of $GF(q^m)$.

Therefore, the BCH code generator polynomial $g(x)$ can be written as the minimum multiple (MCM) of the minimum polynomials $m_i(x)$, in the following manner

$$g(x) = MMC\{m_0(x), m_1(x), ..., m_{2t-1}(x)\}, \tag{5.8}$$

in which $m_i(x)$ is a minimum polynomial $\alpha^{m_0+i}$, $0 \leq i \leq 2t - 1$.

The non-primitive BCH codes are those in which $\alpha$ is not a primitive element of $GF(q^m)$ and, as a consequence, the block length is given by the order of $\alpha$. Thus, BCH code for which $m_0 = 1$ are called strict sense BCH codes.

An alternative definition for the BCH code can be given as a function of the finite field Fourier transform of the generator polynomial $g(x)$. The roots $\alpha^{m_0}$, $0 \leq i \leq 2t-1$ of $g(x)$ correspond to null components, for the spectrum $G(z)$, at the positions $m_0 + i,\ 0 \leq i \leq 2t-1$.

A primitive BCH code, over GF($q$), that can correct $t$ errors, with block length $n = q^m - 1$, is the set of all the words whose spectrum is zero for $2t$ consecutive positions $m_0 + i,\ 0 \leq i \leq 2t-1$.

The $2t$ consecutive roots of $g(x)$ or, equivalently, the $2t$ spectral components for $G(z)$ guarantee a minimum distance $\delta = 2t + 1$, called designed distance of the code.

The BCH quota theorem states that if any non-null vector **v** has a spectrum **V** with $d-1$ null consecutive components, $V_j = 0,\ j = m_0, m_0+1, .., m_0+ d-2$, then **v** has, at least, $d$ non-null components.

To prove the theorem, suppose that, by hypothesis, **v** has $a,\ a < d$, non-null components at the positions $i_1, i_2, ..., i_a$ and that the Fourier transform of **v** is identically null at the positions $m_0, m_0+1, ..., m_0+d-2$.

Define the following locator polynomial $L(z)$

$$L(z) = \prod_{k=1}^{a}(1 - z\alpha^{ik}) = L_a z^a + L_{a-1} z^{a-1} + ... + L_1 + L_0. \tag{5.9}$$

In this way, the spectral vector $L$ is such that its inverse Fourier transform $l$ has null components for every $i$ such that $c_i \neq 0$, that is, $l_i = 0$ when $c_i \neq 0$. Hence, for the original code domain, one has $l_i c_i = 0$ and, therefore its Fourier transform is also null, this is

$$\sum_{k=0}^{n-1} L_k V_{j-k} = 0 \tag{5.10}$$

Nonetheless, $L(z)$ degree is not superior to $d-1$ and $L_0 = 1$, therefore Summation 5.10 can be written as

$$V_j = \sum_{k=1}^{d-1} L_k V_{j-k} \tag{5.11}$$

The Expression 5.11 shows how to generate the $V_j$'s from a block of known $d-1$ $V_j$'s. But, from the hypothesis, there is a block of null $d-1$ $V_j$'s, at the positions $m_0, m_0+1, ..., m_0+d-2$. If such block is used as an initial condition, then all the $V_j$'s will be null and the vector $v$ will be completely null. Thus, any non-null vector has, necessarily, at least $d$ non-null components.

### 5.4.2 Reed–Solomon Code

The Reed–Solomon codes are block-based error correcting codes with a wide range of applications in digital communications and storage. Reed–Solomon codes are used to correct errors in several electronic equipment, such as magnetic tape, compact disk, digital video disk; storage devices, which include hard disks; digital communication systems, such as digital television and digital radio; consumer technology, including bar-codes, QR codes, Mini-Disks; transmission technologies, such as DSL and WiMAX; and broadcast systems such as satellite communications, DVB and ATSC.

The Reed–Solomon codes were introduced, in 1960, by Irving Stoy Reed (1923-2012), an American mathematician and engineer, and Gustave Solomon (1930-1996), an American mathematician and electrical engineer who was one of the founders, along with Reed, of the algebraic theory of error detection and correction.

A Reed–Solomon code is a set of length-$n$ vectors, the codewords, in which the elements of the vector, the symbols, consist of $m$ binary digits. A Reed–Solomon code operates on a block of data that is manipulated as a set of finite-field elements. The Reed–Solomon codes are able to detect and correct multiple symbol errors.

The only restriction is that $n$ must be chosen no larger than $2^m$. Of the $n$ symbols in each code word, $k$ of them carry information and the other $(n-k)$ are redundant symbols. At the transmitter side, an encoder is used to compute the $(n-k)$ redundant symbols from the $k$ information symbols.

The $n$ symbols of a codeword are then transmitted, or stored. When the $n$ symbols are received, or read, some of them have errors. Note that, since a symbol is a binary $m$-vector, one says that a symbol is in error if one or more of the $m$ binary digits are incorrect.

By adding $t = n - k$ check symbols to the data, a Reed–Solomon code can detect, but not correct, any combination of up to $t$ erroneous symbols, or locate and correct up to $\lfloor t/2 \rfloor$ erroneous symbols at unknown locations.

Consider that, of the total $n$ symbols, $t$ are received in error. Which implies that the other $n - t$ are received correctly. Reed–Solomon codes have the property that if $t \leq (n - k)/2$, then the correct information can be computed from this defective codeword.

Furthermore, if $s$ of the received symbols are erased, probably considered imperfect, and another $t$ symbols are received in error, the correct information can be computed from the defective code word provided that $s + 2t \leq n - k$ (Wolf, 2021).

The multi-level BCH code, for which $m = m_0 = 1$, defined by the parameters

$$n = q - 1,\ n - k = 2t \text{ e } d = 2t + 1,$$

are called Reed–Solomon code. The generating polynomial of these codes has the following format

$$g(x) = (x - \alpha)(x - \alpha^2)(x - \alpha^3)...(x - \alpha^{2t}), \qquad (5.12)$$

in which $\alpha$ is an element of order $n$ from $GF(q)$.

Reed–Solomon code with $q = 2^r$ have many practical applications, with multi-level digits represented by binary $r$-tuples. Because $d = n-k+1$, these codes are also maximum distance separable codes (MDS) (MacWilliams and Sloane, 1977).

Some efficient codes to correct random and burst errors are, in fact, Reed–Solomon codes in $GF(2)^n$, that are used to correct $t$ incorrect binary $r$-tuples, for a code that contains $rn$ binary digits per block. For concatenated encoding it is usual to employ a Reed–Solomon as the external code (Clark and Cain, 1981).

### 5.4.3 Golay Code

Golay codes, which are perfect error-correcting codes that generalize the Hamming code were discovered, in 1949, by Marcel Jules Edouard Golay (1902-1989), a Swiss mathematician, physicist, and information theorist. The Golay code was used in the Voyager probes, and its discovery led to advances in the theory of finite groups.

There are four versions of the Golay code, the binary Golay code, the extended binary Golay code, the ternary Golay and the extended ternary Golay code. They are known to have interesting properties. For example, binary and ternary Golay codes are perfect codes, while their extended versions are self-dual codes.

The Golay code have the following parameters

$$n = 23,\ k = 12 \text{ e } d = 7,$$

with binary alphabet, and

$$n = 11,\ k = 6 \text{ e } d = 5,$$

with ternary alphabet.

The Golay codes, along with the Hamming codes and the repetition code with odd length, are the only perfect error-correcting codes that exist (van Lint, 1982).

The Golay code $(23, 12, 7)$ can be seen as a primitive BCH code that are generated in the following way.

Consider $\alpha$ a primitive element over $GF(2^{11})$ and observe that $2^{11} - 1 = 89 \times 23$, therefore $\beta = \alpha^{89}$ is a non-primitive element of order 23. The code is specified by the roots $\beta,\ \beta^2,\ \beta^3$ and $\beta^4$ of $g(x)$. The roots of the minimum polynomial of $\beta$ are:

$$\beta, \beta^2, \beta^4, \beta^8, \beta^{16}, \beta^9, \beta^{18}, \beta^{13}, \beta 3, \beta^6, \beta^{12}$$

in which one used the fact that $\beta^{23} = 1$. Factoring $x^{23} + 1$ gives

$$x^{23}+1 = (x-1)(x^{11}+x^{10}+x^6+x^5+x^4+x^2+1)(x^{11}+x^9+x^7+x^6+x^5+x+1).$$

Depending on the choice of the primitive polynomial, to generate $GF(2^{11})$, one of the factors of order 11, in the previous set, will be the generating polynomial $g(x)$.

Observe that, by the BCH quota this code has a designed distance $\delta = 5$, while the exact value of the minimum distance is 7. The extended Golay $(24, 12, 8)$ is obtained from the code (23, 12, 7) adding to each word one digit that makes the number of 1's even.

### 5.4.4 Reed–Muller Code

The BCH codes are usually introduced as a generalization of Hamming codes. The generalization of the dual of Hamming codes, the Hadamard codes, results in another family of algebraic codes called Reed–Muller codes, which are among the oldest, simplest and perhaps most ubiquitous family of codes. They are used in many areas of coding theory in both electrical engineering and computer science (Abbe et al., 2020).

Reed–Muller codes were first introduced by David Eugene Muller (1924-2008), an American mathematician and computer scientist, who was a professor of mathematics and computer science at the University of Illinois, in 1954. Shortly afterwards, Irving Stoy Reed (1923-2012) provided the first efficient decoding algorithm for these codes

Reed–Muller codes generalize the Reed–Solomon codes and the Walsh–Hadamard code, they are linear block codes that are locally testable, locally decodable, and list decodable. These codes are used in wireless communications applications, including deep-space communication. The proposed standard for the fifth generation of cellular communications (5G) relies on the closely related polar codes for error correction in the control channel (Wikipedia, 2023).

Those codes are binary and are equivalent to cyclic codes with an appended parity digit. A formal definition of Reed–Muller codes requires the introduction of the Hadamard same length vector product as the vector whose components are the product of the factors' components.

For example, the Hadamard product **xyz** of vectors $\mathbf{x} = (x_1, x_2, ..., x_n)$, $\mathbf{y} = (y_1, y_2, ..., y_n)$ and $\mathbf{z} = (z_1, z_2, ..., z_n)$ is given by

$$\mathbf{xyz} = (x_1 y_1 z_1, x_2 y_2 z_2, ...., x_n y_n z_n). \tag{5.13}$$

Consider $c_0$ a vector with $2^m$ components equal to 1, and $c_1, c_2, ..., c_m$ the lines of a matrix whose $2^m$ columns are all the binary $m$-tuples. The Reed–Muller code of order $r$ has a generating matrix whose lines are the vectors $c_0, c_1, ...., c_m$ and their pairwise Hadamard products, their three by three products and the $r$ by $r$ products. For any integer value of $m$, the Reed–Muller code of order $r$ has the following parameters

$$n = 2^m, \; k = \sum_{i=0}^{r} C_m^i, \; d = 2^{m-r}.$$

The Reed–Muller constitute a large class of codes, but with an error-correction power that is inferior to the BCH codes of similar code rate. Two important aspects of the code are the decoding facility using majority logic, and the property that they are constructed from Euclidean geometry.

### 5.4.5 Quadratic Residue Code

The history and development of quadratic residues (QR) and non-residues leads to the research on number theory led by Johann Carl Friedrich Gauss (1777-1855), a German mathematician, astronomer, geodesist, and physicist who contributed to many fields in mathematics and science.

Gauss's *Disquisitiones Arithmeticae*, published in 1801, developed the fundamental ideas of the subject, focusing on quadratic residues and non-residues. Gauss referred to the theorem related to these concepts as the *Theorema Aureum*[2]. The study of quadratic residues has been important to mold modern number theory.

A quadratic residue code is a type of cyclic code, which can be defined in terms of their idempotent generators. These codes present many good properties which are analogous in many respects to those of quadratic residue codes over a field. A quadratic residue is defined in the following.

An integer $r$ is a quadratic residue of a prime number $p$, if and only if there is an integer $s$ such that $s^2 \equiv r$, modulo $p$.

It is possible to demonstrate that if $n = 8m \pm 1$ is a prime number then 2 is a quadratic residue of $n$. In this case, $x^n + 1$ can be factored as $(x + 1)G_r(x)G_{\overline{r}}(x)$, as follows

$$G_r(x) = \prod_{r \in Q} (x + \alpha^r), \tag{5.14}$$

$$G_{\overline{r}}(x) = \prod_{\overline{r} \in \overline{Q}} (x + \alpha^{\overline{r}}), \tag{5.15}$$

in which $\alpha$ is an element of order $n$ in an extension of the field $GF(2)$, $Q$ is the set of quadratic residues modulo $n$ and $\overline{Q}$ is the set of non-quadratic residues modulo $n$, and $r$ is a primitive $p$th root of unity in some finite extension field GP$(r)$.

The cyclic codes with generating polynomial $G_r(x)$ $(1+x)G_r(x)$ $G_{\overline{r}}(x)$ and $(x+1)G_{\overline{r}}(x)$ are called quadratic residue codes. An efficient manner to decode those codes is by the use of permutations.

Decoders that employ permutations are usually more complex than BCH decoders. On the other hand, the minimum distance of some quadratic residue codes is larger than the minimum distance associated to BCH codes of comparable length.

An algebraic approach for decoding the quadratic residue codes, was proposed, in 1990, by Irving Stoy Reed, Xiaowei Yin and Trieu-Kien Truong. The idea of the algorithm was to find the error locator polynomial by a systematic use of the Newton identities, developed by Isaac Newton (1642–1726), an English mathematician, physicist, astronomer, alchemist, theologian, writer and natural philosopher.

The Newton identities were actually first introduced by Albert Girard (1595–1632), a French-born mathematician, who was the first to use the abbreviations sin, cos and tan for the trigonometric functions in a treatise (Wikipedia, 2024) .

The identities relate two types of symmetric polynomials, namely between power sums and elementary symmetric polynomials, which are associated with the code syndromes. The developed technique extended the algebraic decoding algorithm developed, in 1987, by Michele Elia, from the Politecnico di Torino, Italy (Elia, 1987) (Reed et al., 1990) (Reed et al., 1992).

### 5.4.6 Alternant Codes

Alternant codes, which were introduced by Hermann Josef Helgert, in 1974, is a class of codes defined by the parity check matrix of a linear code of minimum distance at least $t + 1$ (Helgert, 1974). Helgert is a professor of the Electrical & Computer Engineering Department, The George Washington University. The parity check matrix of the code is obtained by restricting some of its elements to sub-fields of GF$(q^m)$.

They form a large and important class of codes and include, as particular cases, all Bose-Chaudhuri-Hocquenghem (BCH), the classical Goppa codes, the Chien-Choy generalized BCH codes, the generalized Srivastava codes and the general Reed–Solomon codes (MacWilliams and Sloane, 1977).

Regarding the decoding procedure, the important concepts are the error-location and the error evaluation polynomials, and the so-called key equation, a congruence that they satisfy. Any method to solve the key equation produces a decoding algorithm.

The most effective decoding method is due to Elwyn Ralph Berlekamp (1940-2019), who was a professor of mathematics and computer science at the University of California, Berkeley. It is usually called the Berlekamp-Massey decoder. Berlekamp gave a computationally efficient iterative algorithm to solve the key equation for the two polynomials (Berlekamp, 1968b).

James Lee Massey (1934-2013), who was an American information theorist and cryptographer, professor of digital technology at ETH Zurich, showed that the algorithm gives a general solution to the problem of synthesizing the shortest linear feedback shift register that generates the syndrome sequence (Massey, 1969b).

Another decoding method, that is considerably easier to understand, considering that it is a variation of the Euclidean algorithm for the greatest common divisor (GCD), was devised by Y. Sugiyama (Y. Sugiyama and Namekawa, 1975).

A simple modification of the parity-check matrix of the BCH codes produces the alternant codes. A BCH code of length $n$, and designed distance $\delta$ over $GF(q)$, has a parity-check matrix $H = [h_{ij}]$, in which $h_{ij} = \alpha^{ij}$, $1 \leq i \leq \delta - 1, 0 \leq j \leq n - 1$, and $\alpha \in GF(q^m)$ is an $n$-th primitive root of the unit.

Alternant code are obtained by making the parameters $h_{ij} = x_j^{i-1} y_j$, in which $x = (x_1, x_2, ..., x_n)$ is a vector with distinct components that belong to $GF(q^m)$ and $y = (y_1, y_2, .., y_n)$ is a vector of non-null components, which also belong to $GF(q^m)$.

## 5.5 Convolutional Codes

The convolutional codes offer a different error-correcting approach, regarding the block codes. A convolutional encoder converts a whole data sequence, regardless of its length, into a single codeword. Recall that the block encoders segment a data sequence into fixed-length blocks. A convolutional code is an error-correcting code that produces parity-check symbols by convolving a boolean polynomial function with a data stream polynomial.

These blocks of $k$ digits are mapped into codewords of length $n$. This implies a completely different approach regarding the design of convolutional codes. While the block codes are developed based on algebraic and combinatorial techniques, the design of convolutional codes rely on heuristic construction techniques.

One of the important capacities of convolutional codes is maximum likelihood soft decision decoding. This differ from block codes, which use hard decision decoding. Convolutional codes $(k, n, M)$ are characterized by the base code rate $k/n$, and by the depth, or memory, of the encoder $M$, in which $k$ is the input data rate and $n$ is the encoded data rate. The memory $M$ is also called the constraint length, because the output is a function of the current input as well as the previous $M - 1$ inputs.

Convolutional codes are used to achieve reliable data transmission in several applications, including digital video, digital radio, mobile communications and satellite communications. These codes are usually concatenated, for internal error protection, with a hard-decision code, such as Reed–Solomon. An interleaver is frequently used to scramble the digits before transmission.

The convolutional codes were initially studied by Peter Elias (1923-2001), a pioneer in the field of information theory, who was a member of the Massachusetts Institute of Technology (MIT) faculty. In an address to the American National Academy of Engineering, Robert Gallager stated that Elias' 1954 technical report for the MIT, "Error-Free Coding" provided a major step in this evolution by developing the concepts of product codes and iterative decoding (Elias, 1954).

In the document Elias used these concepts to invent the first algorithm for achieving error freedom at a strictly positive transmission rate. Elias' paper "Coding for Noisy Channels" was perhaps the most influential early information theory paper after Shannon's original work (Elias, 1955).

Elias created the name convolutional codes, in 1955, and his basic motivation was to show that it was in principle possible, by using a convolutional code with infinite constraint length, to transmit information at a rate equal to channel capacity with probability one that no decoded symbol will be in error (Willems, 2009).

In summary, he showed that a redundancy can be introduced in a data sequence using a linear shift register, and demonstrated that the resulting codes are good when chosen at random. This interesting result has a connection with Shannon's work, that proved the existence of codes, randomly selected, that might, in the mean, attain high levels of confiability for transmission at data rates that are below the channel capacity (Shannon, 1948b).

In 1961, Wozencraft and Reiffen described the first practical decoding algorithm for convolutional codes. That was the first one of a class of sequential algorithms that provide fast sub-optimal decoding of the convolutional codes (Wozencraft and Reiffen, 1961). John McReynolds Wozencraft (1925-2009), a pioneer of coding theory, was an electrical engineer and information theorist, professor emeritus at the Massachusetts Institute of Technology (MIT). Barney Reiffen (1927-2012) was a professor at the MIT, where he worked on reliable communications at Lincoln Laboratory until his retirement in 1988.

In 1963, Roberto Mario Fano (1917-2016), an Italian-American computer scientist and professor of electrical engineering and computer science at the Massachusetts Institute of Technology (Fano, 1963), and, in 1969, Frederick Jelinek (1932-2010), a Czech-American researcher in information theory, automatic speech recognition (Jelinek, 1969), described modifications on the sequential algorithms that improved the performance of the Wozencraft-Reiffen, which remains sub-optimal to these days.

In 1967, Andrea Giacomo Viterbi, (1935-), an Italian Jewish-American electrical engineer and businessman who co-founded Qualcomm Inc. and invented the Viterbi algorithm, discovered a third approach to the decoding of convolutional codes, which he showed to be asymptotically optimal (Viterbi, 1967).

Later on, Jim K. Omura (1940-), a member of the American National Academy of Engineering for contributions in spread-spectrum communications and data encryption, demonstrated that the Viterbi algorithm was a solution to find the minimum wight path in an weighted oriented graph (Omura, 1969).

In 1973, George David Forney Jr. (1940-), an American electrical engineer who made contributions in coding theory and information theory, showed that the Viterbi algorithm is similar to a maximum likelihood algorithm for the decoding of convolutional codes (Forney Jr., 1973).

### 5.5.1 Linear Convolutional Coders

A typical linear convolutional encoder, with code rate $R = 1/2$ is depicted in Figure 5.6. It consists of three connected delay elements, that form the shift register, and two modulo-2 adders. The code rate is computed using the fact that there are two output bits for each input bit (da Rocha Jr., 2001).

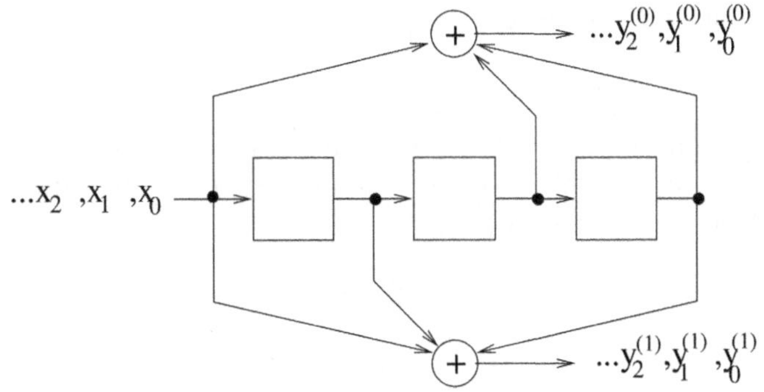


**Figure 5.6** Linear convolutional encoder of rate $R = 1/2$.

In general, an encoder with $k$ inputs and $n$ outputs has rate $R = k/n$. For example, the encoder of Figure 5.7 has rate $R = 2/3$.

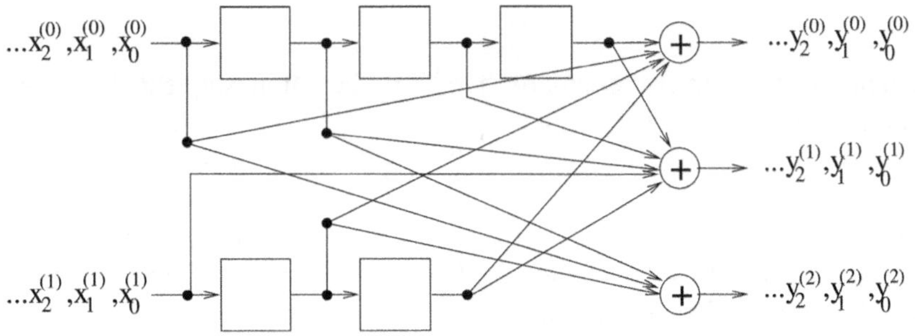


**Figure 5.7** Linear convolutional encoder of rate $R = 2/3$.

In Figure 5.6, the data binary sequence $\boldsymbol{x} = (x_0, x_1, x_2, \ldots)$ is applied at the input of a shift-register. From the input bits and the stored values in the register a pair of coded data sequences is produced

$$\boldsymbol{y}^{(0)} = (y_0^{(0)}, y_1^{(0)}, y_2^{(0)}, \ldots)$$

and

$$\boldsymbol{y}^{(1)} = (y_0^{(1)}, y_1^{(1)}, y_2^{(1)}, \ldots).$$

The output sequences can be multiplexed to create a unique output sequence

$$\boldsymbol{y} = (y_0^{(0)} y_0^{(1)}, y_1^{(0)} y_1^{(1)}, y_2^{(0)} y_2^{(1)}, \ldots),$$

in which $\boldsymbol{y}$ is the convolutional codeword.

Each element of the output sequence is a linear combination of the elements from the input sequences.

$$\boldsymbol{x}^{(0)}, \boldsymbol{x}^{(1)}, \boldsymbol{x}^{(2)}, \ldots, \boldsymbol{x}^{(k-1)}.$$

For instance, the output sequence of Figure 5.6 is computed from a single input sequence $\boldsymbol{x}$. Is is usually assumed that the contents of the shift-register is null at the beginning. Therefore,

$$\begin{aligned} y_0^{(1)} &= x_0^{(0)} + 0 + 0 \\ y_1^{(1)} &= x_1^{(0)} + x_0^{(0)} + 0 \\ y_2^{(1)} &= x_2^{(0)} + x_1^{(0)} + 0 \\ y_3^{(1)} &= x_3^{(0)} + x_2^{(0)} + x_0^{(0)} \\ y_4^{(1)} &= x_4^{(0)} + x_3^{(0)} + x_1^{(0)} \\ &\vdots \end{aligned} \tag{5.16}$$

In general, an arbitrary element of the $y_j^{(1)}$ of the output sequence $y^{(1)}$ can be computed as

$$y_i^{(1)} = x_i^{(0)} + x_{i-1}^{(0)} + x_{i-3}^{(0)}. \tag{5.17}$$

**Example:** The sequential coder of rate $R = 1/2$ of Figure 5.6 is used to encode the information sequence $\boldsymbol{x} = (10110)$. The output coded sequences are the following (da Rocha Jr., 2001):

$$\boldsymbol{y}^{(0)} = (10001010),$$

$$\boldsymbol{y}^{(1)} = (11111110).$$

The codeword corresponding to the input $\boldsymbol{x} = (10110)$ is then

$$\boldsymbol{y} = (11, 01, 01, 01, 11, 01, 11, 00).$$

After the whole input sequence $\boldsymbol{x}$ has been stored in the coder, a sequence of zeros is introduced to guarantee that, at the end of the process, the register content is null. This is a necessary condition to carry out the decoding of that class of codes.

It is possible to observe from Equation 5.17 that the encoders shown in Figures 5.6 and 5.7 are linear. If $\boldsymbol{y}_1$ and $\boldsymbol{y}_2$ are codewords that correspond to inputs $\boldsymbol{x}_1$ and $\boldsymbol{x}_2$, respectively, then $(\boldsymbol{y}_1 + \boldsymbol{y}_2)$ is the codeword that corresponds to the input $(\boldsymbol{x}_1 + \boldsymbol{x}_2)$.

The linear structure of those codes allows them to be studied using linear systems techniques. A response to the impulse $\boldsymbol{g}_j^{(i)}$ is obtained from the $i$-th coder output by the application of an input of 1 followed by a sequence of zeros at the $j$-th input.

Sequences of zeros are applied to all inputs. The data sequence $\boldsymbol{x}^{(j)} = \delta(j) = (1000\ldots)$ can be used as a Kronecker delta, named after Leopold Kronecker (1823-1891), a German mathematician who worked on number theory, algebra and logic, which is the discrete equivalent of the Dirac delta for continuous systems, named after Paul Adrien Maurice Dirac (1902-1984), an English mathematical and theoretical physicist who is considered to be one of the founders of quantum mechanics and quantum electrodynamics.

The impulse responses for the encoder of Figure 5.6 are:

$$\begin{aligned} \boldsymbol{g}^{(0)} &= (1011), \\ \boldsymbol{g}^{(1)} &= (1101). \end{aligned} \tag{5.18}$$

The coder of Figure 5.7 has the following impulse responses:

$$\begin{aligned} \boldsymbol{g}_0^{(0)} &= (1001) \qquad & \boldsymbol{g}_1^{(0)} &= (0110) \\ \boldsymbol{g}_0^{(1)} &= (0111) \qquad & \boldsymbol{g}_1^{(1)} &= (1010) \\ \boldsymbol{g}_0^{(2)} &= (1100) \qquad & \boldsymbol{g}_1^{(2)} &= (0100). \end{aligned} \tag{5.19}$$

The impulse responses are often referred to as generating sequences, because their relationship with the generated codewords is similar to that between the generating polynomials and the codewords of the cyclic code.

Considering that there are three memory elements in the encoder of Figure 5.6, each input bit can affect a maximum of four bits, which is the maximum length of the generating sequence of Equation 5.18.

In general, an input data sequence $\boldsymbol{x}^{(i)}$ to a given convolutional encoder is place in a shift-register with $m_i$ memory elements. The number of memory elements determines the extension of direct interference of a single bit on the input data sequence.

The constraint length $k$ of a convolutional encoder is the maximum number of bits in an output sequence that can be affected by any input bit. Because the parity bits are the only bits sent over the channel, a larger constraint length generally implies a greater resilience to bit errors. It is defined as,

$$k \triangleq 1 + \max_i m_i. \tag{5.20}$$

It takes considerably longer to decode codes of long constraint length, therefore one cannot increase the constraint length arbitrarily and expect fast decoding. In fact, the decoding complexity is exponential in the constraint length.

The total memory $M$ of a convolutional code is defined as the total number of memory elements in the coder. Therefore,

$$M = \sum_{i=0}^{k-1} m_i. \tag{5.21}$$

The total memory of a convolutional code has a strong impact on the complexity of the Viterbi decoder. Also, the greater the number of parity bits, the higher the resilience to bit errors, but the trade-off is that a proportionally higher amount of communication bandwidth is required to coding overhead.

### 5.5.2 Representation of Convolutional Codes

A convolutional code can be represented by a state diagram or by a trellis diagram, among other representation forms. The state diagram, or state machine, corresponds to regarding the encoder as a set of states with well-defined transitions between them. The state diagram is useful in figuring out how to decode a set of parity bits to reconstruct the original message bits.

An important point to consider is that the state diagram for a convolutional code is identical for all codes with a given constraint length $k$ and the number of states is always $2^{k-1}$.

#### 5.5.2.1 State Diagram

As mentioned, the convolutional encoder can be considered a finite state machine. The contents of its memory elements determine the mapping between the next set of input and output bits.

Consider the encoder of Figure 5.6, which contains three binary memory elements that can assume any of eight possible states. These states are designed $\{S_0, S_1, \ldots, S_7\}$ and are associated with the contents of the respective memory elements, as follows.

$$\begin{array}{ll} S_0 \leftrightarrow (000), & S_4 \leftrightarrow (001) \\ S_1 \leftrightarrow (100), & S_5 \leftrightarrow (101) \\ S_2 \leftrightarrow (010), & S_6 \leftrightarrow (011) \\ S_3 \leftrightarrow (110), & S_7 \leftrightarrow (111) \end{array}$$

The encoder can only move between the states in a limited manner, as atypical state machine. Given the current state $S_i S_j S_k$, the next state could be $0 S_j S_k$, that corresponds to an input zero, or $1 S_j S_k$ which corresponds to an input one. The state diagram of Figure 5.8 presents this restriction.

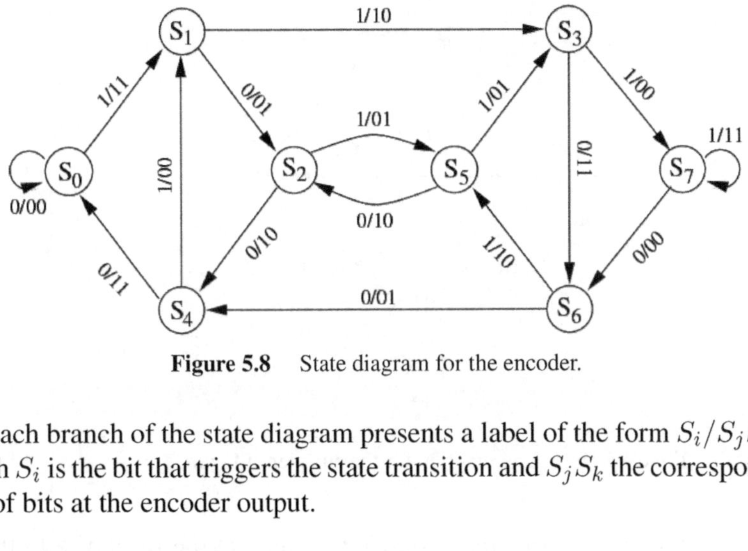


**Figure 5.8** State diagram for the encoder.

Each branch of the state diagram presents a label of the form $S_i/S_j S_k$, in which $S_i$ is the bit that triggers the state transition and $S_j S_k$ the corresponding pair of bits at the encoder output.

#### 5.5.2.2 Trellis Diagram

A trellis diagram is ans extension of the sate diagram that shows explicitly the passage of time, representing each instant of time with a separate state diagram. For example, consider the convolutional encoder shown in Figure 5.9.

The coder has rate $R = 1/3$ and two memory cells, thus the state diagram has four states, as can be observed in Figure 5.10.

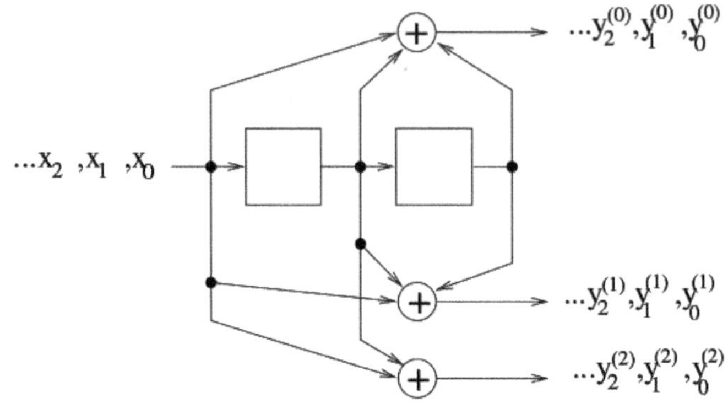


**Figure 5.9** Linear convolutional encoder with rate $R = 1/3$.

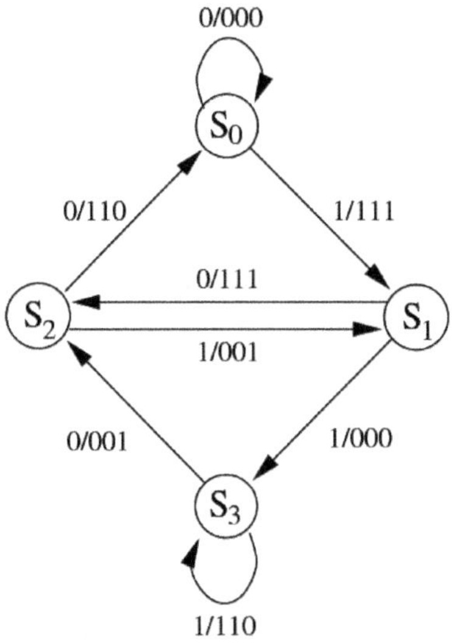


**Figure 5.10** State diagram for the encoder of Figure 5.9

Figure 5.11 shows the diagram extended in time, in the form of a trellis diagram. The trellis branches are labeled with the output bits that correspond to the associated state transitions.

Each convolutional codeword corresponds to a single path, which begins and ends at state $S_0$, by means of the associated trellis diagram. The trellis structure permits certain counting exercises that bring some useful results.

Consider a generic convolutional encoder $(n, k)$ with total memory $M$ and maximum memory order $m$. The trellis associated diagram has $2^M$ nodes

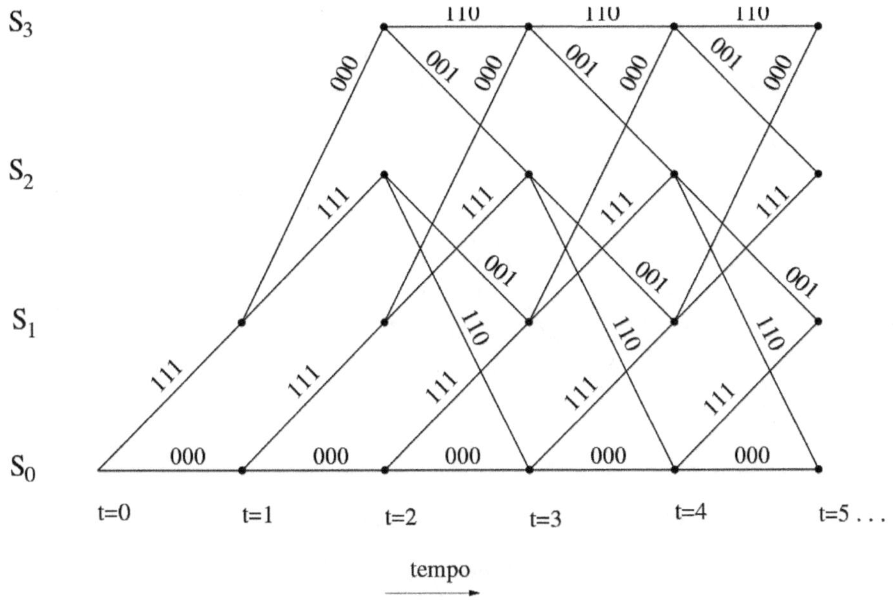


**Figure 5.11** Trellis diagram for the encoder of Figure 5.9

in each state. There are $2^k$ branches that leave each node, a branch for each possible combination of input bits. After instant $t = m$, there are $2^k$ branches arriving at each node.

Assume that, after the sequence has entered the decoder, it is necessary to have $m$ state transitions for the coder to return to state $S_0$. Given an input sequence with $k \cdot L$ bits, in which $L$ is any integer number, the trellis diagram must have $L + m$ stages, the first and the last stages begin and end, respectively, at state $S_0$.

This way, there are $2^{kL}$ distinct paths in a general trellis, each one corresponding to a convolutional codeword of length $n(L+m)$. For example, the input sequence of length three $\boldsymbol{x} = (011)$ is presented in Figure 5.12, that corresponds to the associated path, with five branches, for the convolutional codeword with $3(3+2) = 15$ bits, $\boldsymbol{y} = (000, 111, 000, 001, 110)$.

The complexity of the Viterbi algorithm is linear in the codeword length. The complexity is linear in the number of states at each time. In general the number of states is $2^M$, in which $M$ is the number of delay elements in the encoder. Therefore, Viterbi decoding is practical for $M$ not much higher than say 10, that is, the number of states is not much more than $2^{10} = 1024$ (Willems, 2009).

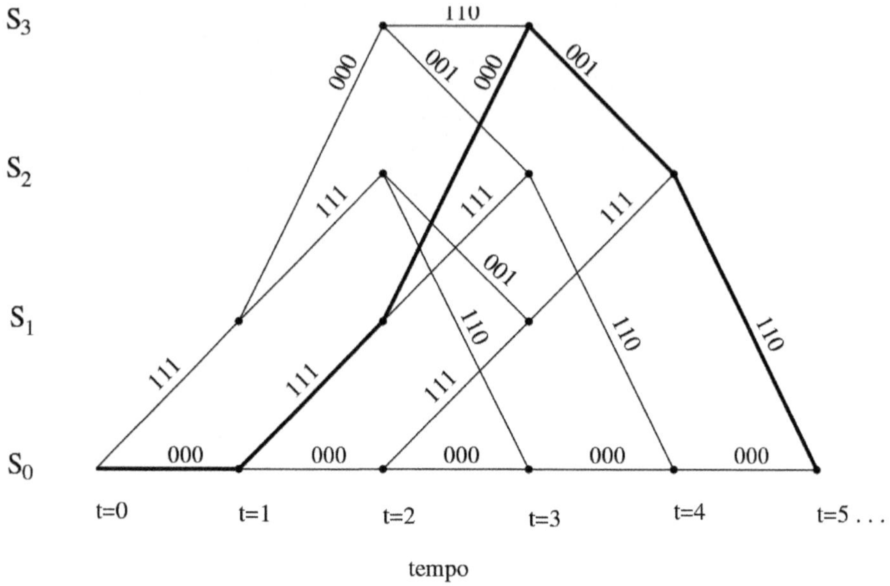


**Figure 5.12** Trellis diagram for input of length 3 for the encoder of Figure 5.9

# 6

# Decoding Algorithms

*"Glamour is a beautiful illusion – the word 'glamour' originally meant a literal magic spell – that promises to transcend ordinary life and make the ideal real. It depends on a special combination of mystery and grace. Too much information breaks the spell."*
Virginia Postrel

## 6.1 Introduction

The simple detection capacity of a code, or the detection and correction of errors is directly linked to the previously mentioned minimum distance of the code. The important concepts of Hamming weight of a vector and the Hamming distance between two vectors are formally stated in the following.

The Hamming distance is a metric on the space of all $n$-tuples over $\mathrm{F}(q)$ which means that $d$ satisfies the following properties for any $x, y, z \in \mathrm{F}(q^n)$:

1. $d(x, x) = 0$,
2. $d(x, y) = d(y, x)$,
3. $d(x, y) \leq d(x, z) + d(z, y)$.

The third condition is called the triangle inequality.

### 6.1.1 Minimum Distance

The Hamming weight of a vector is the number of null positions in it, and the Hamming distance between two vectors, with same number of components, is the number of differing positions. The Hamming distance is a metric to evaluate the proximity of the information vectors.

**Example.** Consider vectors $v_1 = (1, 2, 0, 0, 3)$ and $v_2 = (1, 1, 0, 2, 3)$, in $\mathrm{F}(4)$. The Hamming weights of $v_1$ and $v_2$ are, respectively, 2 and 4 and the Hamming distance between $v_1$ and $v_2$ is 2.

DOI: 10.1201/9788743813613-6

It is important to consider that the minimum distance of a certain code is the smallest Hamming distance between any of its codewords.

Denote by $q$, $q = p^m$, the cardinality of the code alphabet, in which $p$ is a prime number and $m$ is a positive integer. Because the code is linear, the addition module-$p$ of any two words of the code is another codeword. It is possible to conclude that find the minimum Hamming distance of a linear code is equivalent to determine the word with minimum Hamming weight, apart from the all-zero word.

This is a simplification, computer-wise, because in case the code has $M$ words it is only necessary to compute the Hamming weight of $M - 1$ codewords. For special situations, in which the linear code has an additional mathematical structure, the computation of the code minimum distance, or its inferior or superior quotas, can be more simplified.

For a code of minimum distance $d$, the smallest number of changes to convert a codeword into another is, at least, $d$. Therefore, the occurrence of, at least, $d$ transmission errors can be detected, because the result is an $n$-tuple that does not belong to the code.

Regarding the correction of errors, it is important to observe that, after the their detection, it is necessary to decide which codeword was effectively transmitted. If one supposes that the codewords were equiprobable, it is reasonable to choose the one that is closest to the received $n$-tuple, in terms of Hamming distance. This choice is the correct one when the error pattern, containing $t$ errors per word, satisfies the relation $2t + 1 \leq d$.

### 6.1.2 Error Syndrome and Decoding

Suppose that a word from a linear code, with generating matrix $G$ and parity-check matrix $H$, is transmitted through a noisy channel. At the receiver, an $n$-tuple $r$ is received, which could be different from the transmitted word $v$ due to the noise introduced during the transmission process.

The decoder task is to recover $v$ from knowledge of $r$. The first step in the decoding process if to verify if $r$ is a valid codeword. This can be represented by the following equation

$$rH^T = s,$$

in which $s$ is a vector with $n - k$ components, called syndrome, as previously defined.

If $s = 0$, which means that $n - k$ components are equal to zero, it is supposed that no errors had occurred, that is, one presumes that $r = v$. However, if $s \neq 0$, $r$ does not correspond to the space of lines from $G$ and the decoder uses this error syndrome to provide the detection, or detection and correction, of the actual word. The received $r$ $n$-tuple can be written as

$$r = v + e,$$

in which $e$ is an $n$-tuple representing the error configuration.

The decoding process involves a decision regarding which codeword has been transmitted. A systematic way to implement the decision process consists of distributing the $2^n$ $n$-tuples into $2^{n-k}$ disjoint sets, in such a way that each one contains only one codeword.

This way, the decoding is correctly performed if the received $n$-tuple $r$ is in the subset associated to the transmitted word. The $2^k$ $n$-tuples of the code are written in a line and, below the all-zero $n$-tuple one places an $n$-tuple $e_1$ that does not appear in the first line. The second line is formed by the addition, module-2, of $e_1$ to the first line elements, as shown in the following.

$$\begin{array}{ccccc} 0 & v_1 & v_2 & \cdots\cdots\cdots & v_{2^k-1} \\ e_1 & e_1 \oplus v_1 & e_1 \oplus v_2 & \cdots\cdots\cdots & e_1 \oplus v_{2^k-1} \end{array}$$

The subsequent lines are formed in an analogous way, each new line begins with a previously unused element. This results in the following table, which is a standard array,

$$\begin{array}{lllll} 0 & v_1 & v_2 & \cdots\cdots & v_{2^k-1} \\ e_1 & e_1 \oplus v_1 & e_1 \oplus v_2 & \cdots\cdots & e_1 \oplus v_{2^k-1} \\ e_2 & e_2 \oplus v_2 & e_2 \oplus v_2 & \cdots\cdots & e_2 \oplus v_{2^k-1} \\ \vdots & \vdots & \vdots & \cdots\cdots & \vdots \\ e_{2^k-1} & e_{2^k-1} \oplus v_1 & e_{2^k-1} \oplus v_2 & \cdots\cdots & e_{2^k-1} \oplus v_{2^k-1} \end{array}$$

The obtained lines are called coset classes and the leftmost element in each coset class is called the leader. The previous matrix array is called the standard arrangement and the described procedure is the code decomposition into coset classes.

To use the standard array it is necessary to find the class and, therefore the associated leader, to which the received $n$-tuple belongs. This is, in general, difficult to implement. Therefore, the standard array concept is useful as a way to understand the structure of the linear codes, but it is not a practical decoding algorithm. Potentially more practical decoding methods for linear codes are presented in the following.

#### 6.1.2.1 Maximum Likelihood Decoding

If the word of a code $(n, k, d)$ are independently selected and all have the same probability of being sent over a communication channel, an optimum decoding manner is the following. When receiving the $r$ $n$-tuple, the decoder compares it with all possible codewords. In the binary case, that means comparing $r$ with the $2^k$ distinct $n$-tuples that form the code.

The codeword that is nearest to $r$, in terms of Hamming distance, is selected. This is, the selected codeword is the one that differs from $r$ at the smallest number of positions. This is, therefore, the supposed transmitted word.

Unfortunately, the time required to decode a received $n$-tuple can become too long, even for moderate values of $k$. Note that the decoder must compare $r$ with $2^k$ words, during a time interval that corresponds to the duration of $n$ channel digits. This makes the decoding process unfeasible for practical cases.

#### 6.1.2.2 Decoding by Systematic Search

A general procedure for decoding linear block codes consists of associating each non-null syndrome with an error-correctable configuration. One of properties of the standard array is that all $n$-tuples, belonging to the same coset class, has the same syndrome.

Furthermore, the coset classes leaders should be chosen as the most probable error configurations, in the respective coset classes. Based on the mentioned properties, it is possible to apply the following decoding procedure.

1. Compute the syndrome for the received $n$-tuple.
2. Use systematic search to find the correctable error pattern, that is, the coset leader associated to the syndrome of the received $n$-tuple.
3. Subtract from the received $n$-tuple the error configuration found in the previous step, to correct it.

To implement this procedure, it is necessary to successively generate all correctable error configurations and feed them to a combinational circuit, which presents the respective syndromes at the output.

Using a multiple-input logic gate it is possible to detect when the locally generated syndrome coincides with the syndrome of the $n$-tuple received. If this code $(n, k, d)$ corrects $t$ errors per block, the number of distinct error-correcting configurations that are correctable, which is necessary to generate in the systematic search process, is given by

$$N = C_n^1 + C_n^2 + ... + C_n^t = \sum_{i=1}^{t} C_n^i \leq 2^{n-k} - 1.$$

It is possible to observe, from the previous expression, that the number of distinct configurations grows rapidly with $n$ and $t$. Because of this, the decoding technique has limited application.

#### 6.1.2.3 Probabilistic Decoding

In the last few years, several decoding algorithms of probabilistic essence have appeared in the specialized literature. Hartmann and Rudolph introduced an algorithm for decoding that is optimum, in the sense that it minimizes the probability of error per digit, when the codewords are equiprobable and transmitted in the presence of additive noise, on a channel without memory (Hartmann and Rudolph, 1976).

This algorithm is exhaustive, as every word of the dual code is used in the decoding process. This characteristic makes it practical for use with high-efficiency codes, contrary to what happens with conventional techniques.

Wolf introduced an algorithm that consists of a rule for walking in a trellis-like structure, which depends on the matrix $H$ of the code. The received $n$-tuple is used to determine the most likely path, that is, the transmitted codeword. These procedures are known as soft decision techniques (Wolf, 1978).

## 6.2 Decoding Cyclic Codes

Linear block code decoding procedures are also applicable to cyclic codes. However, the algebraic properties resulting from the cyclic structure allow for some important simplifications in the decoder implementation, both in the calculation of the syndrome, as in the correction of errors (da Rocha Jr, 2014).

The syndrome computation consists of dividing the word received from the channel by the generating polynomial $g(x)$. The rest of this division is the desired syndrome $s(x)$. If $s(x)$ is zero, the received word is accepted as belonging to the code. Otherwise, if $s(x) \neq 0$, errors are considered to have occurred.

This way, it is possible to perceive the simplicity of a circuit to detect errors when cyclic codes are used. The question of locating errors in a received word, in order to correct them, is generally more difficult to be resolved in a practical way. The most important decoding techniques are those based on the Berlekamp-Massey algorithm (Massey, 1969a) and in Euclid's algorithm (MacWilliams and Sloane, 1977).

Some of the most important decoding procedures for cyclic codes are presented in the following. Recall that a cyclic code is a block code, in which the circular shifts of each codeword gives another word that is a member of the code.

### 6.2.1 Meggitt Decoder

Meggitt's algorithm consists of employing a circuit to identify syndromes that correspond to error patterns containing an error in the highest order position of the received word, this is, an error in position $x^{n-1}$ (Lin and Costello, 1983).

This way, when this digit is delivered to the recipient, it will be changed or not, depending on the decision of the circuit that identifies errors in this position. By making the received word move cyclically, digit by digit, in a shift register, all the digits of this word will necessarily occupy position $x^{n-1}$, after a certain number of shifts, and it will be therefore examined by the error identification circuit.

The convenience of using the Meggitt algorithm is a function of the complexity of the error identifying circuit at position $x^{n-1}$ of the received word. One way to implement such a circuit, in a relatively simple manner, is by the use of programmable memories of the programmable read-only memory (PROM) type.

### 6.2.2 Error Trap Decoder

Another algorithm, known as error trapping, consists of cyclically shifting, bit by bit, the syndrome of the received word, always observing its Hamming weight. When the Hamming weight of the syndrome becomes less than or equal to $t$, the number of correctable errors, the corresponding segment of length $n-k$ of the error vector, where the errors are contained, coincides with this syndrome. Once the pattern of errors has been identified, the correction is immediate (Lin and Costello, 1983).

If, on the other hand, after $n$ displacements, the weight of the syndrome is not smaller than $t$, the decoder declares the occurrence of a pattern of errors that spreads over a number of positions, cyclically consecutive, that exceeds than $n - k$. This procedure is more appropriate for use with low-efficiency codes, considering that for its efficient application the condition

$$n/k > t$$

must be satisfied.

### 6.2.3 Decoding with Information Set

In a linear code $(n, k, d)$, any set of $k$ positions of a word, which can be specified independently, constitute a information set (Clark and Cain, 1981). As a consequence, the symbols in an information set define a codeword.

If there are no errors in the positions of the information set, then it is possible to reconstruct the transmitted word. The information set decoding algorithm consists of the following steps:

1. Build diverse information sets for the code used.
2. Form several estimates of the transmitted word, decoding the received word using each of the information sets constructed previously.
3. Compare the estimates obtained in step 2 with the received word and decide on the word that is closest to the received word.

### 6.2.4 Threshold Decoding

Threshold decoding is also known as majority logic decoding. The vast majority of this method's applications are focused on cyclic codes (Rudolph, 1969a). The concept of majority decoding of linear block codes using orthogonal parity checks, or can be orthogonalized in steps, was first proposed by Irving Stoy Reed, in 1954 (Reed, 1954). This idea was further developed by James Lee Massey and M. E. Mitchell, in the 1960's. In a technical report, Massey described two procedures for decoding linear systematic codes, majority decoding and a posteriori probability decoding (Massey, 1963b) (et al., 1963).

Subsequently, L. D. Rudolph proposed a one-step majority decoding scheme based on parity checks that are, in general, not orthogonal. In 1968, E. J. Weldon presented some improved majority decoding algorithms for block codes associated with finite geometries (Rudolph, 1964) (Jr., 1968) (Rudolph, 1969b).

Before describing this method, it is necessary to conceptualize what parity checksums or parity sums are. As described previously, the syndrome is represented by a vector of $n - k$ coordinates,

$$S = (s_0, s_1, ....., s_{n-k-1}),$$

in which, for a given code $(n, k, d)$ with parity check matrix $H$ and an error vector $(e_0, e_1, ..., e_{n-1})$, one has (Massey, 1963a).

$$S = eH^T,$$

in which each syndrome component $s_j$, $0 \leq j \leq n-k-1$ is given by

$$s_j = \sum_{i=0}^{n-1} e_i h_{ij}. \tag{6.1}$$

The linear combination of the syndrome digits

$$A = \sum_{i=0}^{n-k-1} a_i s_i,$$

in which $a_i$ is 0 or 1, can, with the help of Equation 6.1, be written as

$$A = \sum_{i=0}^{n-1} b_i e_i, \tag{6.2}$$

in which $b_i$ is 1 or 0.

An error in position $e_i$ is said to be verified by $A$ if the corresponding coefficient $b_i$ in Equation 6.2) is 1. Equation 6.2 is called parity-check sum.

Given a set of $J$ parity checksums $A_1, A_2, ..., A_J$, such that a position $e_l$ of the error vector is checked by all of them and all other positions $e_i$, $i \neq l$, of the vector appear, at most, in a single parity checksum, then this set is said to be orthogonal in position $e_l$.

Assuming the occurrence of $t \leq \lfloor J/2 \rfloor$ errors in the received word, the decoding procedure is based on the following reasoning,

1. $e_l = 1$. This means that the remaining $t-1$ errors will reach, at most, $t-1 \leq \lfloor J/2 \rfloor - 1$ parity sums, leaving, therefore, at least, $J - \lfloor J/2 \rfloor + 1 = \lceil J/2 \rceil + 1$ sums equal to a 1.
2. $e_l = 0$. In this case, the $t$ errors will reach, at most, $\lfloor J/2 \rfloor$ parity sums, that is, half the parity sum, for the worst case.

The decoding rule consists of making $e_l = 1$, that is, declaring the presence of an error in this position when the majority of parity sums are equal to 1. Otherwise, make $e_l = 0$, that is, if there is an equal number of parity sums parity equal to 1 or 0, or if the majority is 0.

When the code used is cyclic, after a given position of the received word is decoded, a cyclic shift is applied to it and use is made of same set of $J$ parity checksums to decode position $e_{l-1}$, and so on with the other positions, until the entire word is decoded.

Codes for which $J = d - 1$ are said to be completely orthogonalizable. It is not always possible to directly obtain $J$ orthogonal parity sums at a given position in a codeword. For several classes of codes this is obtained in $L$ steps, in which at each step orthogonal parity sums are used in a sum of positions (Lin and Costello, 1983).

**Example.** Consider a cyclic code of maximum length $(7, 3, 4)$, is produced by a polynomial $g(x) = x^4 + x^2 + x + 1$. The following three parity-check sums, that are orthogonal at position $e_6$, are obtained (da Rocha Jr., 2001):

$$\begin{aligned} A_1 &= e_6 + e_5 + e_3 \\ A_2 &= e_6 + e_4 + e_0 \\ A_3 &= e_6 + e_2 + e_1. \end{aligned}$$

This code, as can be seen, is completely orthogonalizable in a single step and, by threshold decoding, can correct one error per word.

**Example.** Consider the Hamming cyclic code $(7, 4, 3)$, generated by the polynomial $g(x) = x^3 + x + 1$. This code is decodable using majority logic, as described in the following, using matrix $H$.

$$H = \begin{bmatrix} 1 & 1 & 1 & 0 & 1 & 0 & 0 \\ 0 & 1 & 1 & 1 & 0 & 1 & 0 \\ 1 & 1 & 0 & 1 & 0 & 0 & 1 \end{bmatrix}.$$

From the $H$ matrix for the code $(7, 4, 3)$ the following parity sums are obtained

$$\begin{aligned} A_1 &= s_2 &&= e_6 + e_5 + e_4 + e_2 \\ A_2 &= s_2 + s_1 &&= e_6 + e_3 + e_2 + e_1 \\ A_3 &= s_0 &&= e_6 + e_5 + e_3 + e_0. \end{aligned}$$

The sums $A_1$ and $A_2$ were used to estimate the sum $e_6 + e_2$, while $A_1$ and $A_3$ are used to estimate $e_6 + e_5$. This constitutes the first decoding step. From it one obtains,

$$A_4 = e_6 + e_2$$

$$A_5 = e_6 + e_5,$$

that are orthogonal in $e_6$, they constitute the second steep and complete the orthogonalization process of the code.

## 6.3 Algebraic Decoding

As a rule, for a given code $(n, k, d)$, the decoding process is always more complex than the encoding process. From a practical point of view, therefore, the best code is chosen within a given budget. This may result in the use of sub-optimal codes, but whose decoding is no so complex.

For some classes of algebraic codes, computationally efficient algorithms have been developed to decode them. The problem of decoding algebraic codes consists of solving a system of non-linear equations, whose solution, in general, is not at all obvious.

### 6.3.1 Algebraic Decoding in the Frequency Domain

This procedure can be applied to any cyclic code, but it is more efficient for BCH codes. The received vector $\mathbf{r}$, is supposed to result from the sum $\mathbf{v} + \mathbf{e}$, over $GF(q)$, of a codeword $\mathbf{v}$ and an error vector $\mathbf{e}$, that is, $\mathbf{r} = \mathbf{v} + \mathbf{e}$ (Blahut, 1983). The necessary steps for decoding are shown in the following (da Rocha Jr, 2014).

1. Fourier transform of the received vector – Calculate the Fourier transform $R$ of the received vector $\mathbf{r}$, which can be expressed as a function of the corresponding transforms $\mathbf{v}$ and $\mathbf{e}$, as $R = V + E$.
2. Syndrome computation – The code syndrome is computed as follows,

$$S(z) = \sum_{j=0}^{2t-1} S_j z^j$$

$$S_j = R_{j+m_0} = \sum_{i=0}^{n-1} r_i \alpha^{i(j+m_0)}, j = 0, 1, ..., 2t-1.$$

3. Computation of the error-locator polynomial – This step is also known as the key equation solution. The error locator polynomial, $L(z)$, is of the form

$$L(z) = \sum_{k=0}^{\nu-1} L_z z^k = \prod_{k=1}^{\nu} (1 - z\alpha^{i_k}),$$

in which $i_1, i_2, ..., i_\nu, \nu \leq t$, correspond to the error localization. The Euclidean algorithm is applied, with $a(z) = z^{2t}$ and $b(z) = S(z)$. The algorithm stops when the degree of $r_i(z)$ is smaller than $t$. Then, one takes $L(z) = g_i(z)$.

4. Computation of the Fourier transform of the error vector – The error vector $\mathbf{e}$ has a Fourier transform $E$, whose polynomial representation is the following,
$$E(z) = \sum_{j=0}^{n-1} E_j z^j.$$
Because the code has $2t$ consecutive roots, it follows that the coefficients $E_j, j = m_0, m_0 + 1, ..., m_0 + 2t - 1$ are known. The other coefficients are calculated using the following recurrence formula,
$$\sum_{k=0}^{n-1} L_k E_{j-k} = 0.$$

5. Error correction – The error vector is obtained by the inverse transform of the vector $E$, obtained in the fourth step. Hence, the transmitted word estimate is given by,
$$v = r - e.$$

**Example.** Consider the BCH code $(7, 4, 3)$, whose roots of the generating polynomial are $\alpha, \alpha^2$ and $\alpha^4$, in which $\alpha$ is a primitive element of $GF(2^3)$ (da Rocha Jr., 2001). Suppose the received word is
$$r(x) = x^6 + x^3,$$
that is,
$$r = (1, 0, 0, 1, 0, 0, 0).$$

Its Fourier transform is
$$R = (\alpha^2, \alpha^4, \alpha^2, \alpha, \alpha, \alpha^4, 0),$$
in which
$$R_j = \sum_{i=0}^{6} r_i \alpha^{ij} = \alpha^{6j} + \alpha^{3j}.$$

Computing the code syndrome, one obtains $S_j = R_{j+1}, j = 0, 1$. Thus,
$$S_0 = R_1 = \alpha^4$$
$$S_1 = R_2 = \alpha,$$

Therefore,
$$S(z) = \alpha z + \alpha^4.$$

Computation of $L(z)$ using the Euclidean algorithm

| $i$ | $g_i(z)$ | $r_i(z)$ | $q_i(z)$ |
|---|---|---|---|
| $-1$ | $0$ | $z^2$ | $-$ |
| $0$ | $1$ | $\alpha z + \alpha^4$ | $-$ |
| $1$ | $\alpha^6 z + \alpha^2$ | $\alpha^6$ | $\alpha^6 z + \alpha^2$ |

therefore, $L(z) = \alpha^6 z + \alpha^2$.

Computing the error vector transform, one obtains

$$\sum_{k=0}^{\nu-1} L_k.E_{j-k} = 0$$

$$L_0.E_j + L_1.E_{j-1} = 0$$

It is known that $E_j = S_{j-1},\ j = 1, 2$. Therefore, $E_1 = \alpha^4$ and $E_2 = \alpha$. Substituting these values into the previous expression, one obtains

$$E_j = \alpha^4 E_{j-1}.$$

Using this recurring expression it is possible to compute the remaining components, which result in

$$E = (\alpha^3, \alpha^6, \alpha^2, \alpha^5, \alpha, \alpha^4, 1),$$

whose inverse transform is given by

$$e = (0, 0, 1, 0, 0, 0, 0).$$

Therefore, $e(x) = x^4$, is the corrected word, which is given by

$$v(x) = r(x) - e(x),$$
$$v(x) = x^6 + x^4 + x.$$

## 6.4 Soft Decision Decoding

Decoding with soft decision is an approach to the decoding problem which aims to avoid degradation in the performance of a communication system that uses two-level hard quantization of symbols, before decoding. The soft-decoder takes a stream of bits, or a block of bits, and decodes them by considering a whole range of possible values. It considers the reliability of each received pulse to improve the estimation of the input data.

In a paper published, in 1974, B. G. Dorsch described a decoder for linear binary block $(n, k)$ codes using soft decisions quantized to $J$ levels. The decoder can be applied to any linear block code does not depend upon any particular feature of the code, such as being a concatenated code or having a sparse parity-check matrix (Dorsch, 1974).

In the Dorsch decoder, hard decisions are derived from the soft decisions using standard bit by bit detection, choosing the binary state closest to the received coordinate.

The power of the Dorsch decoder arises from the relatively unknown property that most codes, on average, can correct almost $n-k$ erasures, which is considerably more than the guaranteed number of correctable erasures of $d - 1$, or the guaranteed number of correctable hard decision errors of $\frac{d-1}{2}$, in which $d$ is, as previously defined, the minimum Hamming distance of the code (Tomlinson et al., 2017).

The soft decision decoding algorithm for cyclic codes, for instance, especially the maximum likelihood (ML) decoding algorithm, can obtain significant performance that is superior to that of algebraic decoding, but the complexity is higher.

Due to the difficulties of practical implementation, most detectors consist of an analog demodulator, operating on individual signal elements, followed by a digital decoder operating on blocks of digits, produced using hard decisions by the demodulator.

This situation can be improved by retaining part of the information about the reliability of the received symbols, which would otherwise be dismissed at the demodulator, using it to assist in the decoding process. The resulting systems are, in general, less complex to implement than those employing coherent detection with correlation, or matched filters.

The use of soft decision can provide an additional gain of about 2.0 dB with respect to the two-level hard decision, operating in the presence of additive Gaussian noise. A maximum likelihood decoder, employing soft decision, selects the code word whose Euclidean distance to the received signal is as small as possible.

Strictly speaking, the analog voltage read at the demodulator output should be the value to be processed by the system. Due to practical problems, these voltages are quantized and made available for further processing, in the form of a group of numbers, which represent the various quantization levels.

Quantization details and the choice of the optimal metric for the symbols will not be discussed. A sub-optimal metric, that is used in engineering, because it represents a good compromise for different values of the signal to noise ratio, consists of using integer numbers. For example, when quantizing the demodulator output into eight levels, the metric used consists of the integers from zero to seven.

Some decoding algorithms are presented in the following, which employ soft-decision. The aforementioned algorithms are well known in the technical literature in which they are also compared with each other, in terms of performance (Clark and Cain, 1981). The choice of one of these algorithms is dictated by particularities of the application, for example, limitation on the processing capacity in the decoder.

### 6.4.1 Massey Algorithm

The Massey algorithm is a generalization of majority logic decoding, which makes use of the *a posteriori* probability of orthogonal parity digits. Only the first version of the algorithm, known as Type I, is presented (Massey, 1963a).

In what follows, one assumes that the noise sequence is additive and independent from digit to digit, and suppose that $\{A_i\}$ is a set of $J$ orthogonal parity check equations in position $e_m$. This algorithm aims to allocate to $e_m$ the value $V$ that maximizes the conditional probability $P(e_m = V|\{A_i\})$.

Applying Bayes' rule, making use of the conditions of orthogonality and independence from digit to digit, and taking logarithms, one obtains the rule: choose for $e_m$ the value $V$ that maximizes the expression

$$\log P(e_m = V) + \sum_{i=1}^{J} \log P(A_i|e_m = V).$$

To apply the rule, in the binary case, some definitions are necessary. The probability of error for the digit $e_m$ is represented by $p_0 = 1 - q_0$, that is, $P(e_m = 1) = p_0$. Denote by $p_i = 1 - q_i$ the probability of an odd number of 1's in the digits verified by $A_i$, at the $i$-th orthogonal parity-check equation in $e_m$, at the exception of $e_m$. Therefore one obtains,

$$P(A_i = 0|e_m = 1) = P(A_i = 1|e_m = 0) = p_i$$

$$P(A_i = 0|e_m = 0) = P(A_i = 1|e_m = 1) = q_i.$$

Because $e_m$ can take only two values, 0 or 1, the decoding rule becomes: choose $e_m = 1$, if and only if,

$$\log(p_0) + \sum_{i=1}^{J} \log P(A_i|e_m = 1) > \log(q_0) + \sum_{i=1}^{J} \log P(A_i|e_m = 0). \quad (6.3)$$

After some simplification, Inequation 6.3 can be written as,

$$\sum_{i=1}^{J} (2A_i - 1) \log(q_i/p_i) > \log(q_0/p_0)$$

or

$$\sum_{i=1}^{J} A_i \log(q_i/p_i) > (1/2) \sum_{i=1}^{J} \log(q_i/p_i).$$

In practical applications the quantities $w_i = \log(q_i/p_i)$ are normalized and approximated by whole numbers, which entails a small degradation in the performance of the algorithm.

### 6.4.2 Hartmann and Rudolph Algorithm

Carlos R. P. Hartmann and Luther D. Rudolph, from the Syracuse University, developed an algorithm for decoding linear codes, which is optimal in the sense that it minimizes the probability of error per symbol, in a situation in which the words are equiprobable and the channel is discrete and memoryless (Hartmann and Rudolph, 1976).

Hartmann and Rudolph presented a decoding rule which minimizes the probability of symbol error over a time-discrete memoryless channel, for any linear error-correcting code, when the codewords are equiprobable. The complexity of this rule varies inversely with code rate, that makes the technique interesting for high rate codes.

This algorithm is an exhaustive procedure, considering that all words in the dual code are used in the decoding process. From a practical point of view, this feature makes it attractive for use with high-rate and relatively long codes which, in general, is uncommon for conventional techniques. The Hartmann and Rudolph algorithm is statistical in nature and is applicable to both block and convolutional codes.

The decoding rule for binary block codes is as follows: Choose $\tilde{c}_m = 0$ if

$$\sum_{j=1}^{2^{n-k}} \prod_{s=0}^{n-1} \rho_s^{(c'_{js} \oplus \delta_{ms})} > 0,$$

otherwise do $\tilde{c}_m = 1$. In expression, $n$ represents the length of the block, $k$ represents the number of information digits, $\tilde{c}_m$ is the estimated value of the transmitted symbol $c_m$ and $c'_{js}$ is an element of the dual code,

$$\delta_{ms} = \begin{cases} 0, & m \neq s \\ 1, & m = s \end{cases}$$

$$\rho = \frac{1-\phi_s}{1+\phi_s}, \quad \Phi = \frac{P(r_s|1)}{P(r_s|0)},$$

$P(r_s|c_m)$ is the conditional probability of receiving symbol $r_s$ when $c_m$ is transmitted.

**Example:** Consider the Hamming cyclic code (7,4,3), whose dual code is given in the following,

$$\begin{matrix} 0 & 0 & 0 & 0 & 0 & 0 & 0 \\ 1 & 1 & 1 & 0 & 1 & 0 & 0 \\ 0 & 1 & 1 & 1 & 0 & 1 & 0 \\ 1 & 0 & 0 & 1 & 1 & 1 & 0 \\ 0 & 1 & 0 & 0 & 1 & 1 & 1 \\ 1 & 1 & 0 & 1 & 0 & 0 & 1 \\ 0 & 0 & 1 & 1 & 1 & 0 & 1 \\ 1 & 0 & 1 & 0 & 0 & 1 & 1 \end{matrix}$$

If eight quantization levels are used, the decoding rule is the following: choose $\tilde{c}_0 = 0$ if

$$\begin{aligned} \rho_0 &+ \rho_1\rho_2\rho_4 + \rho_0\rho_1\rho_2\rho_3\rho_5 + \rho_3\rho_4\rho_5 + \rho_0\rho_1\rho_4\rho_5\rho_6 \\ &+ \rho_1\rho_3\rho_6 + \rho_0\rho_2\rho_3\rho_4\rho_6 + \rho_2\rho_5\rho_6 > 0, \end{aligned} \tag{6.4}$$

otherwise, choose $\tilde{c}_0 = 1$.

### 6.4.3 Weldon Algorithm

The algorithm developed by E. J. Weldon Jr., Emeritus Professor in the Department of Electrical Engineering at the University of Hawaii, is sub-optimal, but has the advantage of implementation simplicity. Some error patterns, correctable by a maximum likelihood decoder, are not correctable using the Weldon algorithm.

For this algorithm, several estimates are formed for each transmitted symbol, weighted according to their respective reliability, and applied to a decision function, in order to determine the value of the transmitted symbols. In the following, a particular version of the Weldon algorithm is described that allows the visualization of the involved steps (Jr., 1971).

1. The decoder receives a word of $n$ positions, occupied with soft decisions by the demodulator, whose output was quantized in $Q = 2^m$ regions. To each level is allocated a weighting function $\sigma_i, 0 \leq i \leq 2^m - 1$, in which, sub-optimally, the $\sigma_i$'s will be represented by the integers from 0 to $2^m - 1$.
2. Each $\sigma_i$ is then represented by a binary $m$-tuple, and $m$ binary sequences of length $n$ are constructed as follows. The $r$-th binary sequence of length $n$, $0 \leq r \leq m - 1$, is composed of the most significant bits $2^r$ of the $n$ $\sigma_i$'s.
3. Each of the binary sequences is decoded using a hard-decision decoder.
4. The $m$ decoded binary sequences are combined, position by position, using the decision function $f_d(i, j)$ for the $j$-th symbol of the decoded $i$-th $n$-tuple.

$$f_d(i,j) = \sum_{i=0}^{m-1} (1 - 2B_{ij}) w_i \begin{cases} > & 0, \quad c_j = 0 \\ < & 0, \quad c_j = 1 \end{cases}$$

in which $B_{ij}$ represents the $j$-th symbol in the $i$-th decoded sequence, $c_j$ represents the estimated symbol and $w_i$ is a weighting factor that is proportional to the reliability of the estimate, whose computation is described in the following.

$$\begin{aligned} w_i = &\ V_i R_i \quad , 0 \leq i \leq m - 1 \\ V_i = &\ 2^i \qquad , R_i = \text{máx}(0, d - 2n_i), \end{aligned}$$

in which $d$ is the Hamming distance of the code and $n_i$ is the number of positions changed by the $i$-th decoder. Using this algorithm it is possible to correct soft error patterns with soft weights of up to $(Q - 1)d/2$. The symbol $Q$ represents the number of quantization levels.

**Example:** Consider the Hamming code (7,4,3) used with a demodulator with $Q = 2^3$ quantization levels. Suppose that the all-zero word was transmitted and that the sequence $(0, 2, 0, 6, 0, 0, 0)$ was received. The soft weight of the error is 2+6=8, which is correctable because $8 < (Q - 1)d/2 = 21/2$. The three sequences to be decoded with hard decision are:

$$S_0 = (0, 0, 0, 0, 0, 0, 0)$$

$$S_1 = (0, 1, 0, 1, 0, 0, 0)$$
$$S_2 = (0, 0, 0, 1, 0, 0, 0)$$

The decoder will decode $S_0$ as an all-zero sequence, performing $n_0 = 0$ corrections, $S_1$ as a sequence of weight 3 with $n_1 = 1$ correction and $S_2$ as an all-zero sequence with $n_2 = 1$ correction. The corresponding $w_i$'s are:

$$w_0 = 1(3 - 0) = 3$$
$$w_1 = 2(3 - 2) = 2$$
$$w_2 = 4(3 - 2) = 4$$

When these values $w_i$ are applied to the decision function expression, $w_0$ and $w_2$ are always multiplied by 1 while $w_1$ is sometimes multiplied by -1. In a worst case scenario, one has: min$f_d(i, j) = 3 - 2 + 4 = 5 > 0$ and, therefore, the all-zero sequence is recovered correctly. The reader can check out the following situation.

The sequence $(0, 0, 0, 0, 0, 0, 0)$ is transmitted over the channel and the sequence $(1, 2, 0, 4, 4, 0, 0)$ is received. The smooth weight of the error vector is $1+2+4+4 = 11$, which is at least 12 away from the nearest Hamming word of weight 3. This means that the correction of this error is feasible using a maximum likelihood decoder, however, such correction is not possible when using the Weldon algorithm.

### 6.4.4 Chase Algorithm

David Chase introduced his algorithm, in 1972. It is a type of decoding algorithm that utilizes channel measurement information, in addition to the conventional use of the algebraic properties of the code. The maximum number of errors that can, with high probability, be corrected is equal to $1-d$, the minimum Hamming distance of the code (Chase, 1972).

The Chase algorithm makes use of decoders with hard decision, generating a set of estimates of the transmitted word, in an approximate version of a maximum likelihood decoder. Chase's original article contains three variations of the algorithm, the steps of which are:

1. The received sequence is transformed into the vector $Y$, by hard decisions in each of its symbols.
2. Various error patterns $T$ are generated and added to $Y$ for the generation of $S$ test sequences. Each generated test sequence is decoded by an hard decision decoder.

3. The soft distance between the received sequence and each of the decoded words is calculated. One decides for the code word that presents the smallest distance.

The three variations of the Chase algorithm differ in terms of the number of error patterns which are generated for the formation of test sequences and are described in the following.

1. The list of error patterns $T$ contains the all-zero $n$tuple and all weight patterns $\lfloor d/2 \rfloor$.
2. The error patterns $T$ are formed like this: The $\lfloor d/2 \rfloor$ positions of lowest reliability are filled with the possible $2^{\lfloor d/2 \rfloor}$ combinations of 1's and 0's, and the other positions are filled with 0's.
3. This version is almost identical to the previous one, except that the number of error patterns is $\lfloor (d/2)+1 \rfloor$, instead of $2^{\lfloor d/2 \rfloor}$. The vectors $T$ contain 1's in the $i$-th positions with the lowest reliability and 0's in the other positions, in which:

$$i = \begin{cases} 0, 2, 4, ..., d-1 & , \quad \text{for } d \text{ odd} \\ 0, 1, 3, ..., d-1 & , \quad \text{for } d \text{ even.} \end{cases}$$

**Example:** Consider the Hamming code (7,4,3) used with a demodulator with $Q = 2^3$ quantization levels. Suppose that the all-zero word was transmitted and that the sequence $r = (1, 2, 0, 4, 4, 0, 0)$ was received. Using the $b$ version of the Chase algorithm, the following test sequences are produced:

$$S_1 = (0, 0, 0, 1, 1, 0, 0)$$
$$S_2 = (0, 0, 0, 1, 0, 0, 0).$$

The hard-decision decoder for this code will decode $S_2$ as the all-zero sequence, whose soft distance for $r$ is 11. For $S_1$, after decoding, one obtains: $(0, 1, 0, 1, 1, 0, 0)$, which has distance 12 from $r$. It is possible, therefore, to decode correctly, in a situation when Weldon algorithm fails.

The $c$ version of Chase's algorithm makes use of the following test sequences:

$$S_1 = (0, 0, 0, 1, 1, 0, 0)$$
$$S_2 = (0, 0, 0, 0, 0, 0, 0)$$

The decoded sequences are identical to those obtained and the correct decoding is achieved.

### 6.4.5 Decoding Convolutional Codes

Algorithms for decoding convolutional codes can be divided into two classes: sequential algorithms and the Viterbi algorithm. The popularity of sequential algorithms decreased rapidly after the development of the Viterbi algorithm, in 1967, which is a maximum likelihood algorithm, while sequential algorithms are not.

In the next section, the Viterbi algorithm is presented in detail. Sequential algorithms are studied in depth in (Wicker, 1995).

#### 6.4.5.1 The Viterbi Algorithm

Consider the decoding problem presented in Figure 6.1. An information sequence $\boldsymbol{x}$ is encoded into a convolutional codeword $\boldsymbol{y}$, which is transmitted through a noisy channel. The convolutional decoder receives the vector $\boldsymbol{r}$ and generates an estimate $\boldsymbol{y}'$ of the transmitted codeword.

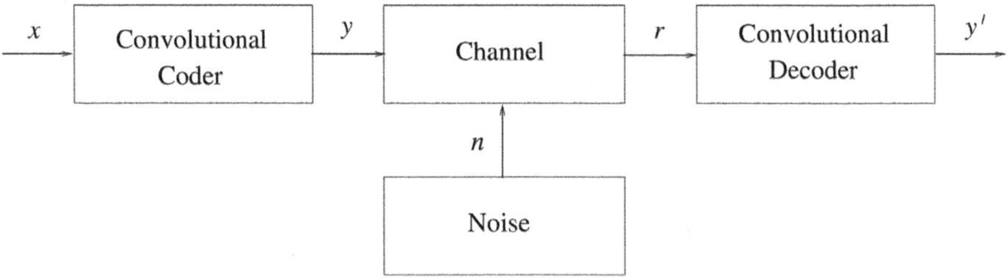


**Figure 6.1** Decoding problem associated with convolutional coding.

The maximum likelihood decoder selects, by definition, the estimate that maximizes the probability $p(\boldsymbol{r}\,|\boldsymbol{y}')$, while a *maximum a posteriori* (MAP) decoder selects the estimate that maximizes the probability $p($ boldmath$y'|\boldsymbol{r})$. If the source distribution is uniform, then the two decoders give identical responses. In general, they can be related by Bayes' rule (Papoulis, 1984),

$$p(\boldsymbol{r}|\boldsymbol{y}) \cdot p(\boldsymbol{y}) = p(\boldsymbol{y}|\boldsymbol{r}) \cdot p(\boldsymbol{r}).$$

A convolutional encoder with rate $k/n$ receives $k$ input bits and generates $n$ output bits with each shift of its registers. Assuming an input sequence $\boldsymbol{x}$ composed of $L$ blocks of $k$-bits, one obtains

$$\boldsymbol{x} = \left(x_0^{(0)}, x_0^{(1)}, \ldots, x_0^{(k-1)}, x_1^{(0)}, x_1^{(1)}, \ldots, x_1^{(k-1)}, x_{L-1}^{(0)}, \ldots, x_{L-1}^{(k-1)}\right). \tag{6.5}$$

The output sequence $\boldsymbol{y}$ consists of $L$ blocks of $n$ bits, one bit for each input block, plus $m$ additional blocks, with $m$ being the number of cells in the longest shift register.

$$\boldsymbol{y} = \left(y_0^{(0)}, y_0^{(1)}, \ldots, y_0^{(n-1)}, y_1^{(0)}, y_1^{(1)}, \ldots, y_1^{(n-1)}, y_{L+m-1}^{(0)}, \ldots, y_{L+m-1}^{(n-1)}\right). \tag{6.6}$$

The noisy version of the transmitted codeword reaches the receiver and the maximum likelihood decoder generates an estimate $\boldsymbol{y}'$ of the transmitted sequence. The sequences $\boldsymbol{r}$ and $\boldsymbol{y}'$ have the following forms

$$\boldsymbol{r} = \left(r_0^{(0)}, r_0^{(1)}, \ldots, r_0^{(n-1)}, r_1^{(0)}, r_1^{(1)}, \ldots, r_1^{(n-1)}, r_{L+m-1}^{(0)}, \ldots, r_{L+m-1}^{(n-1)}\right), \tag{6.7}$$

$$\begin{aligned} \boldsymbol{y}' = \Big(&{y'_0}^{(0)}, {y'_0}^{(1)}, \ldots, {y'_0}^{(n-1)}, {y'_1}^{(0)}, {y'_1}^{(1)}, \ldots, \\ &{y'_1}^{(n-1)}, {y'_{L+m-1}}^{(0)}, \ldots, {y'_{L+m-1}}^{(n-1)}\Big). \end{aligned} \tag{6.8}$$

Assuming that the channel is memoryless, that is, the noise that affects a given bit of the received word $\boldsymbol{r}$ is independent of the noise that affects the other bits, and using the fact that the joint probability of independent events is the product of the probabilities of the individual events, one obtains

$$\begin{aligned} p(\boldsymbol{r}|\boldsymbol{y}') &= \prod_{i=0}^{L+m-1} \left[p(r_i^{(0)}|{y'_i}^{(0)})p(r_i^{(1)}|{y'_i}^{(1)}) \cdots p(r_i^{(n-1)}|{y'_i}^{(n-1)})\right] \\ &= \prod_{i=0}^{L+m-1} \left(\prod_{j=0}^{n-1} p(r_i^{(j)}|{y'_i}^{(j)})\right). \end{aligned} \tag{6.9}$$

Equation 6.9 is sometimes called the likelihood function from $\boldsymbol{y}'$ (Viterbi, 1971). Since the logarithm function is monotonically increasing, the estimate that maximizes $p(\boldsymbol{r}|\ \boldsymbol{y}')$ also maximizes $\log p(\boldsymbol{r}|\boldsymbol{y}')$. Applying the logarithm to each side of Equation 6.9 one has the likelihood logarithmic function.

$$\log p(\boldsymbol{r}|\boldsymbol{y}') = \sum_{i=0}^{L+m-1} \left(\sum_{j=0}^{n-1} \log p(r_i^{(j)}|{y'_i}^{(j)})\right). \tag{6.10}$$

In hardware implementations of the Viterbi decoder, the elements of the sum of Equation 6.10 are usually converted into a more easily manipulated form called bit metric ($M(r_i^{(j)}|y_i'^{j})$), given by

$$M(r_i^{(j)}|y_i'^{(j)}) = a\left[\log p(r_i^{(j)}|y_i'^{(j)}) + b\right]. \tag{6.11}$$

The coefficients $a$ and $b$ are chosen so that the bit metrics are small integers that can be quickly processed by digital logic circuits. The path metric for the codeword $\boldsymbol{y}'$ is calculated as follows,

$$M(\boldsymbol{r}|\boldsymbol{y}') = \sum_{i=0}^{L+m-1}\left(\sum_{j=0}^{n-1} M(r_i^{(j)}|y_i'^{(j)})\right). \tag{6.12}$$

If the value of $a$ in Equation 6.11 is real and positive, and the value of $b$ is also real, then the codeword $\boldsymbol{y}'$ which maximizes $p(\boldsymbol{r}|\boldsymbol{y}')$ also maximizes $M(\boldsymbol{r}|\boldsymbol{y}')$. A negative value can also be chosen for $a$, in this case $\boldsymbol{y}'$ is chosen in order to minimize $M(\boldsymbol{r}|\boldsymbol{y}')$.

Sometimes it useful to measure the contribution to the path metric made by a simple block of $\boldsymbol{r}$ and $\boldsymbol{y}$. A block corresponds to a branch on the trellis. The $k$-th branch metric, $M(\boldsymbol{r}_k|\boldsymbol{y}_k')$, for a codeword $\boldsymbol{y}'$ is defined as the sum of the bit metrics of the $k$-th block of $\boldsymbol{r}$, given $\boldsymbol{y}'$.

$$M(\boldsymbol{r}_k|\boldsymbol{y}_k') = \sum_{j=0}^{n-1} M(r_k^{(j)}|y_k'^{(j)}). \tag{6.13}$$

The $k$-th partial path metric, $M^k(\boldsymbol{r}|\boldsymbol{y}')$, for a given path is obtained by the sum of the branch metrics for the $k$-th first branches through which the path passes,

$$M^k(\boldsymbol{r}|\boldsymbol{y}') = \sum_{i=0}^{k-1} M(\boldsymbol{r}_i|\boldsymbol{y}_i') = \sum_{i=0}^{k-1}\left(\sum_{j=0}^{n-1} M(r_i^{(j)}|y_i'^{(j)})\right). \tag{6.14}$$

Trellis diagrams can be used to calculate path metrics in the Viterbi Algorithm. It is worth mentioning that the branches of the presented trellis were labeled with the output bits corresponding to a particular input in the decoder and its current state. It is assumed that $\boldsymbol{r}$ is the received sequence, written at the bottom of the trellis, a block at each instant of time, with each block corresponding to a stage of the trellis.

For example, in the case of the code whose trellis, shown in Figure 5.11, the beginning of the trellis should present the aspect depicted in Figure 6.2.

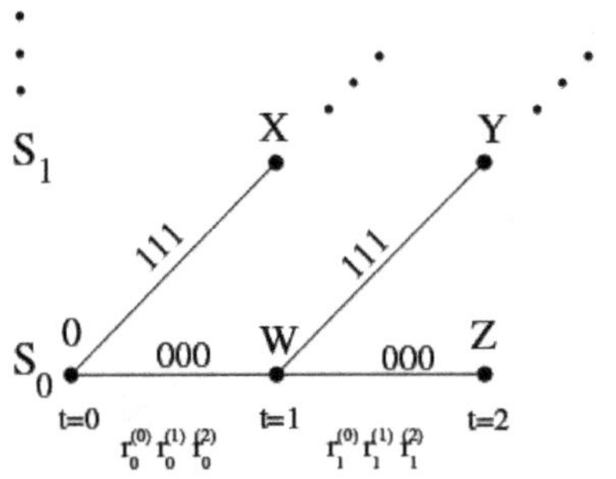


**Figure 6.2** Computing the branch metrics at the beginning of the decoding process.

In the Viterbi Algorithm, each node on the trellis is designated by a number. This number is the partial metric of the path that starts in the state $S_0$, at the time instant $t = 0$, and ends at that node.

For example, in Figure 6.2, the label $Y$ corresponds to the path with two branches that ends in the state $S_1$ at the time instant $t = 2$. As the output bits corresponding to this path consist of three zeros followed by three ones, one has

$$\begin{aligned} Y =& M^2(\boldsymbol{r}|\boldsymbol{y}' = (000, 111)) \\ =& W + M(\boldsymbol{r}_1|\boldsymbol{y}_1' = (111)) \\ =& \left(M(r_0^{(0)}|0) + M(r_0^{(1)}|0) + M(r_0^{(2)}|0)\right) + \\ &+ \left(M(r_1^{(0)}|1) + M(r_1^{(1)}|1) + M(r_1^{(2)}|1)\right). \end{aligned} \tag{6.15}$$

The assignment of numbers to the trellis nodes is done until a point in the routine is reached in which more than one path enters the same node. In this case, the route that has the best partial metric is chosen among all the paths that arrive at that node. The best metrics can be the largest or the smallest, depending on the value of $a$ and $b$ in Equation 6.11).

The path with the best metric is the survivor, while the others are non-survivors. Observing Figure 6.3 and assuming that the path metrics have been chosen so that the path with the lowest metric presents the codeword of maximum-likelihood, the label $Z$ can be determined as follows

$$\begin{aligned} Z = \min \Big\{ & \left[X + M(r_t^{(0)}|0) + M(r_t^{(1)}|0) + M(r_t^{(2)}|1)\right], \\ & \left[Y + M(r_t^{(0)}|1) + M(r_t^{(1)}|1) + M(r_t^{(2)}|1)\right] \Big\}. \end{aligned} \tag{6.16}$$

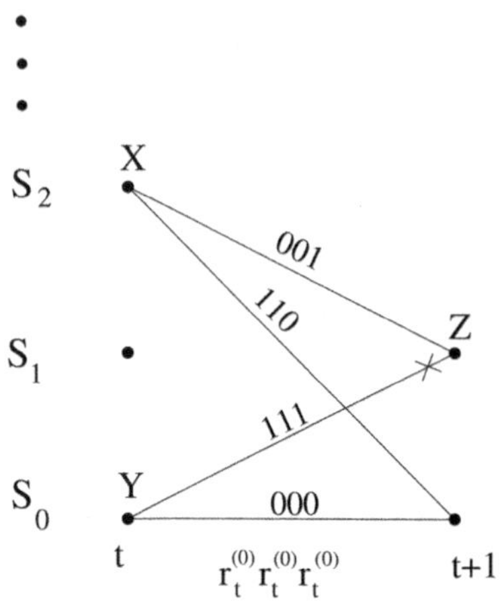


**Figure 6.3** Computing the branch metrics for a state at which two paths arrive.

The algorithm stops when all nodes of the trellis have been labeled and the survivors determined. Going the opposite way from the last node of the trellis a, state $S_0$ at the time instant $L + m$, one obtains a single path, because only one path can survive as input in a given node. This path is the route of maximum likelihood. A summary of the Viterbi Algorithm is presented in the following.

### Viterbi Algorithm

Assuming that $S_{j,t}$ is the state $S_j$ at the time instant $t$, then to each node of the trellis a metric $V(S_{j,t})$ can be associated. These metrics can be computed as follows.

1. Do $V(S_{0,0}) = 0$ and $t = 0$;
2. At each time instant $t$, compute the partial metrics for all paths entering each node;
3. Make $V(S_{k,t})$ equal to the best partial metric entering the corresponding state $S_k$ at time instant $t$;
4. If $t < L + m$, increment $t$ and return to Step 2.

After the metrics at all nodes have been computed, the unique path obtained from state $S_0$, at the time instant $t = L + m$, following the opposite path towards state $S_{0,0}$ is the maximum likelihood path.

The path selected by the Viterbi algorithm is the path of maximum likelihood. If the maximum likelihood path (ML) $\boldsymbol{y}$ is not selected by the decoder, then, at some time instant $t$, the partial path of ML does not survive when compared to some other partial path $z$.

If the complement of $y$ is added to $z$, then the resulting path presents a better metric than the $y$ path. This contradicts the assumption that $y$ is the ML path.

#### 6.4.5.2 Hard Decision Decoding

In hard-decision decoding, each signal is analyzed and a hard decision is made about the signal transmitted represent a 0 or a 1. This decision forms the input to the Viterbi decoder. Assuming that the channel is memoryless, it can be modeled as shown in Figure 6.4. The branches are labeled with likelihood functions. This channel is commonly called a memoryless binary channel.

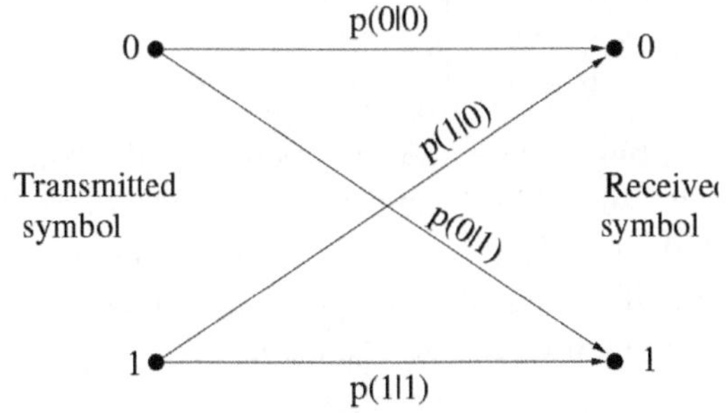


**Figure 6.4** Memoryless binary channel.

If for the binary channel the probability of bit error is independent of the transmitted bit, the channel is called a symmetric binary channel (BSC), that can be seen in Figure 6.5.

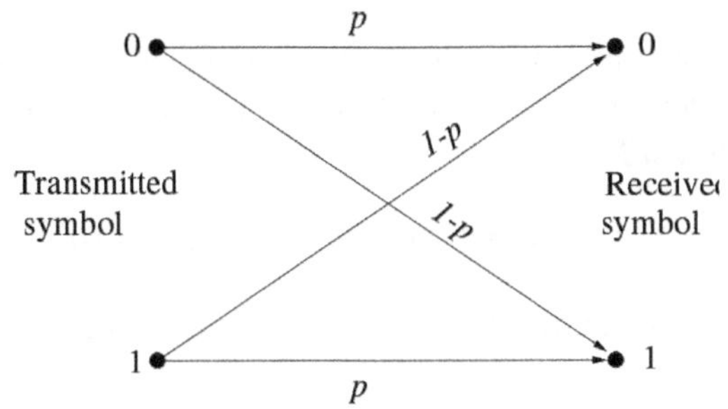


**Figure 6.5** Binary symmetric channel.

## Computing the Metric for a Memoryless Symmetric Binary Channel

The first step in determining the bit metrics for binary channels is the calculation of the likelihood functions. These conditional probabilities are then converted into likelihood logarithm functions, to finally be converted into bit metrics using Equation 6.11.

If $a$ and $b$, in Equation 6.11, are selected to be equal to $[\log_2 p - log_2(1-p)]^{-1}$ and $-\log_2(1-p)$, respectively, the bit metrics are independent of the crossover probability $p$.

$$M(r_i^{(j)}|y_i^{(j)}) = \frac{1}{\log_2 p - \log_2(1-p)}\left[\log_2 p(r_i^{(j)}|y_i^{(j)}) - \log_2(1-p)\right]$$

| $M(r_i^{(j)}\|y_i^{(j)})$ | $r_i^{(j)} = 0$ | $r_i^{(j)} = 1$ |
|---|---|---|
| $y_i^{(j)} = 0$ | 0 | 1 |
| $y_i^{(j)} = 1$ | 1 | 0 |

For the symmetric binary case, the path metric for the codeword $\boldsymbol{y}$, given a received word $\boldsymbol{r}$ is simply the Hamming distance $d(\boldsymbol{y}, \boldsymbol{r})$. The surviving paths are those with the smallest partial metric at each node.

On the other hand, if $a$ is equal to $[\log_2(1-p) - \log_2 p]$ and $b$ is equal to $-\log_2 p$, the following metrics can be obtained.

| $M(r_i^{(j)}\|y_i^{(j)})$ | $r_i^{(j)} = 0$ | $r_i^{(j)} = 0$ |
|---|---|---|
| $y_i^{(j)} = 0$ | 1 | 0 |
| $y_i^{(j)} = 1$ | 0 | 1 |

With this set of metrics, the surviving paths are those with the largest partial metric at each node.

**Example** Viterbi decoding with hard-decision for the symmetric binary channel. The encoder in Figure 5.9 encodes the sequence $\boldsymbol{x} = (110101)$ generating the codeword

$$\boldsymbol{y} = (111, 000, 001, 001, 111, 001, 111, 110),$$

which is transmitted via a noisy binary symmetric channel.

The received word

$$\boldsymbol{r} = (1\bar{0}1, \bar{1}00, 001, 0\bar{1}1, 111, \bar{1}01, 111, 110)$$

leaves the receiver's detection circuit and is sent to the Viterbi decoder. Erroneously decoded bits are identified with a slash. The metrics used are those from the second set of metrics calculated previously. The surviving paths are those that have the highest partial metric.

The decoding operation of the received word can be seen in Figure 6.6. Each node of the trellis is labeled with the value calculated with the Viterbi algorithm. The maximum likelihood path, denoted by a thicker line, is obtained from the state $S_{0,8}$ going in the direction of state $S_{0,0}$ through the surviving paths. The decoded word is equal to the codeword that was transmitted, the Viterbi decoder corrected four errors in the received word.

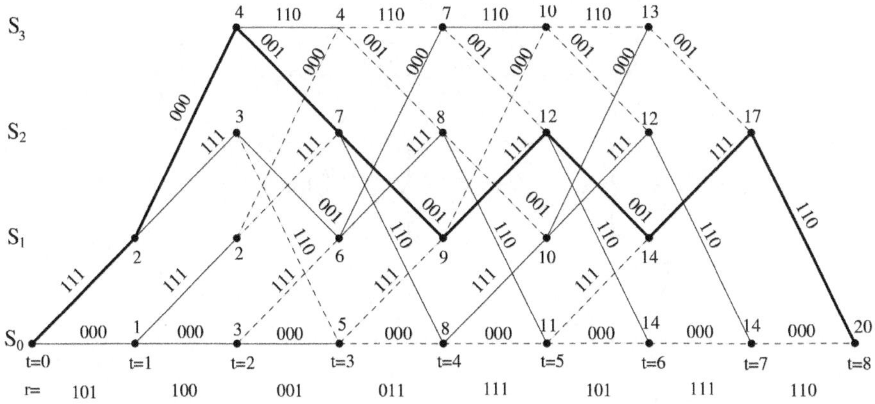


**Figure 6.6** Viterbi decoding with hard decision.

### 6.4.5.3 Soft Decision Decoding

In soft decision decoding, the decoder is more flexible, as it uses multi-bit quantization, that is, instead of assigning a 1 or a 0 to each noisy binary signal received, four or more decoding regions are established, varying from the decision region by a 1-strong($\underline{1}$) until a 0-strong($\underline{0}$).

Intermediate values are given to signals with less clear decision levels. On channels with additive white Gaussian noise, soft decision decoding increases the decoding gain by 2 dB to 3 dB in relation to hard decision.

Consider the case of a Binary Phase Shift Keying (BPSK) system operating on an additive white Gaussian noise (AWGN) channel. In which $E_b$ is the bit energy and $N_0$ W/Hz is the noise power spectral density. If the transmitted bits $\{y_i^{(j)}\}$ take on the values $\pm 1$, then the received signals can be represented by random Gaussian variables with average value $y_i^{(j)}\sqrt{E_b}$ and variance $N_0/2$. Thus the likelihood function is

$$p(r_i^{(j)}|y_i^{(j)}) = \frac{1}{\sqrt{\pi N_0}} e^{-(r_i^{(j)} - y_i^{(j)}\sqrt{E_b})^2/N_0}. \tag{6.17}$$

The log-likelihood function can be simplified if it is noted in the formula that $(y_i^{(j)})^2 = 1$, regardless of the value of $y_i^{(j)}$. All terms that are function of $\boldsymbol{y}$ are grouped into a pair of constants $C_1$ and $C_2$ (Viterbi, 1971).

$$\begin{aligned}
\log p(\boldsymbol{r}|\boldsymbol{y}) &= \sum_{i=0}^{L-1} \left( \sum_{j=0}^{n-1} \log p(r_i^{(j)}|y_i^{(j)}) \right) \\
&= \sum_{i=0}^{L-1} \left\{ \sum_{j=0}^{n-1} \left[ -\frac{(r_i^{(j)} - y_i^{(j)}\sqrt{E_b})^2}{N_0} - \log \sqrt{\pi N_0} \right] \right\} \\
&= \frac{-1}{N_0} \sum_{i=0}^{L-1} \left\{ \sum_{j=0}^{n-1} (r_i^{(j)}\sqrt{E_b})^2 \right\} - \frac{Ln}{2} \log \pi N_0 \\
&= \frac{-1}{N_0} \sum_{i=0}^{L-1} \left\{ \sum_{j=0}^{n-1} [r_i^{(j)^2} - 2r_i^{(j)} y_i^{(j)} \sqrt{E_b} + y_i^{(j)^2} E_b] \right\} \\
&\quad - \frac{Ln}{2} \log \pi N_0 \\
&= C_1 \sum_{i=0}^{L-1} \left\{ \sum_{j=0}^{n-1} r_i^{(j)} y_i^{(j)} \right\} + C_2 \\
&= C_1(\boldsymbol{r} \cdot \boldsymbol{y}) + C_2
\end{aligned} \tag{6.18}$$

The path metrics can then be obtained by the inner product between the received word and the codewords. The bit metrics are

$$M\left(r_i^{(j)}|y_i^{(j)}\right) = r_i^{(j)} y_i^{(j)}. \tag{6.19}$$

The minimization of the path metric of Equation 6.18 is equivalent to finding the codeword $\boldsymbol{y}$ that is closest to $\boldsymbol{r}$ in terms of the Euclidean distance.

The previous analysis assumes that the receiver is capable of processing real numbers with infinite precision. In practice, however, digital circuits quantize signals at some point, somehow sacrificing the effectiveness of the Viterbi algorithm.

Figure 6.7 shows a discrete symmetric channel (DSC) to which the receiver associates one of four values for each received signal. The underlined 0 or 1 represents the the reception of a strong signal, while a regular 0 or 1 represents the the reception of a weak signal (da Rocha Jr., 2001).

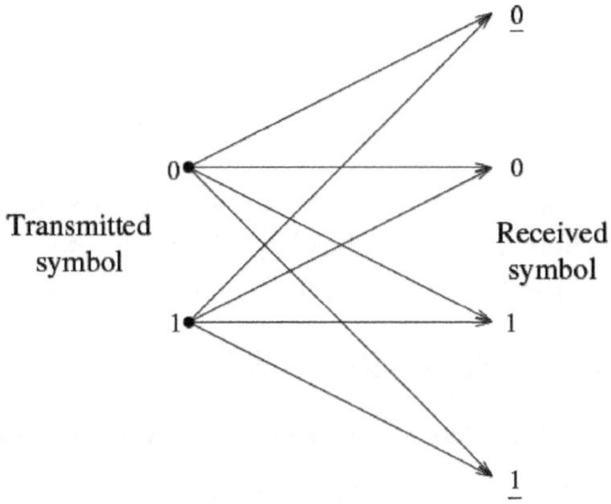


**Figure 6.7** Discrete symmetric channel.

Bit decisions in a hard-decision receiver are made with a hard limiter. In receivers with soft decision, this element is replaced by a multi-bit analog-to-digital converter (ADC). For example, the model in Figure 6.7 implies the use of a 2-bit ADC in the decision circuit.

**Example:** A Viterbi decoder with soft decision is presented. Consider the following values for the conditional probabilities in Figure 6.7.

| $p(r_i^{(j)}\|y_i^{(j)})$ | $r_i^{(j)} = \underline{0}$ | $r_i^{(j)} = 0$ | $r_i^{(j)} = 1$ | $r_i^{(j)} = \underline{1}$ |
|---|---|---|---|---|
| $y_i^{(j)} = 0$ | 0.50 | 0.32 | 0.13 | 0.05 |
| $y_i^{(j)} = 1$ | 0.05 | 0.13 | 0.32 | 0.50 |

From these probabilities the following logarithmic likelihood functions can be obtained.

| $\log_2 p(r_i^{(j)}\|y_i^{(j)})$ | $r_i^{(j)} = \underline{0}$ | $r_i^{(j)} = 0$ | $r_i^{(j)} = 1$ | $r_i^{(j)} = \underline{1}$ |
|---|---|---|---|---|
| $y_i^{(j)} = 0$ | $-1.00$ | $-1.64$ | $-2.94$ | $-4.32$ |
| $y_i^{(j)} = 1$ | $-4.32$ | $-2.94$ | $-1.64$ | $-1.00$ |

Using the expression $M(r_i^{(j)}|y_i^{(j)}) = 1.5[\log_2 p(r_i^{(j)}|y_i^{(j)}) - \log_2(0.05)]$ some bit metrics are obtained that can be easily implemented using digital circuits.

| $M(r_i^{(j)} \mid y_i^{(j)})$ | $r_i^{(j)} = \underline{0}$ | $r_i^{(j)} = 0$ | $r_i^{(j)} = 1$ | $r_i^{(j)} = \underline{1}$ |
|---|---|---|---|---|
| $y_i^{(j)} = 0$ | 5 | 4 | 2 | 0 |
| $y_i^{(j)} = 1$ | 0 | 2 | 4 | 5 |

Assume that the codeword

$$\boldsymbol{y} = (111, 000, 001, 001, 111, 001, 111, 110)$$

has been transmitted and corrupted by a burst of errors at the end of the codeword. However, there is the availability of two-bit soft decision in the decoder. Then, one has the following input for the Viterbi decoder,

$$\boldsymbol{r} = (\underline{1}\overline{0}1, \underline{\overline{1}00}, 0\underline{01}, \underline{0}\overline{1}1, \underline{11}\overline{0}, \overline{110}, 1\underline{11}, 1\underline{1}0)$$

The decoding of the received word can be observed in Figure 6.8.

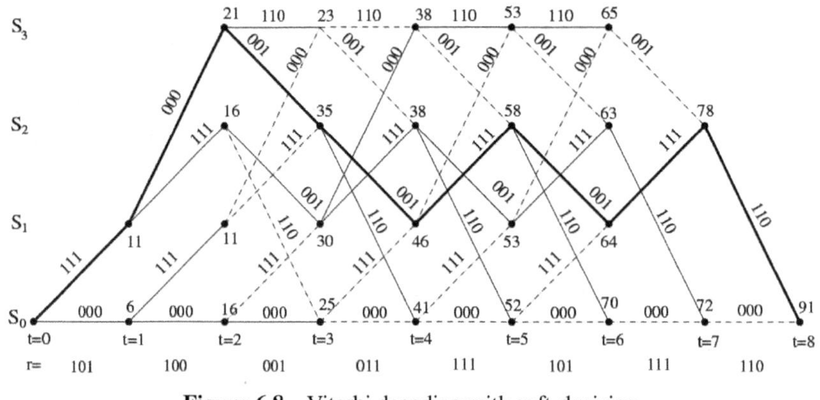


**Figure 6.8** Viterbi decoding with soft-decision.

To make the gain resulting from the use of convolutional codes more evident, simulations were carried out using the encoder in Figure 5.6. The system uses the orthogonal BPSK modulation scheme operating on a channel with additive white Gaussian noise.

The performance of the code can be seen in Figure 6.9, measured in terms of the error probability as a function of the ratio between the bit energy $E_b$ and noise power spectral density $N_0$, for the case of hard-decoding and for the case of decoding using soft decision.

Using soft-decision causes a gain of approximately 2 dB compared to the hard-decoding. Also shown in Figure 6.9 is the probability of error for a

BPSK system without coding, whose performance much worse than that of the coded system. It is of the order of 5 dB when the system error probability is $10^{-3}$).

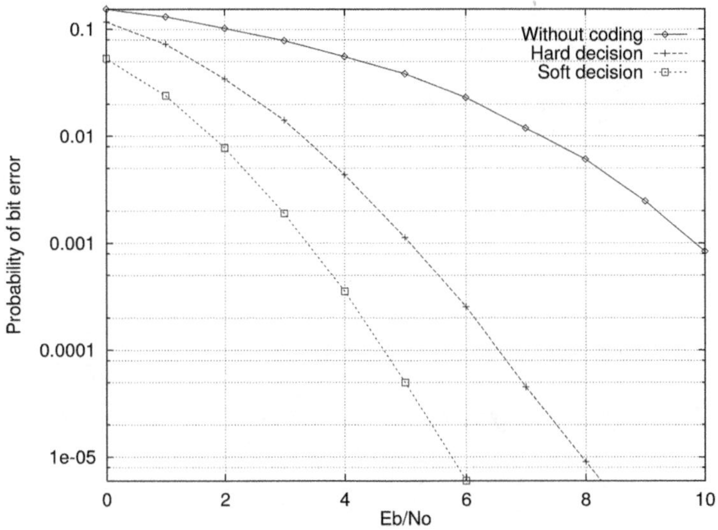


**Figure 6.9** Error probability of a BPSK system for three different cases: without encoding, encoded with hard-decoding and encoded with soft decoding.

# 7

# Spread Spectrum Coding

*"For having lived long, I have experienced many instances of being obliged, by better information or fuller consideration, to change opinions, even on important subjects, which I once thought right but found to be otherwise."*
Benjamin Franklin

The first developments using concepts related with current spread spectrum techniques occurred in the 1940's, involving applications to military problems (Scholtz, 1982). From the beginning until the present date, there has been a process of evolution due mainly to improvements in electronic components.

Spread spectrum techniques became very popular in the communications community, since technical articles on this subject began to appear in the specialized literature, after almost decades of secrecy due to military interests.

## 7.1 Spread Spectrum

The main characteristic of spread spectrum systems is concerned with its bandwidth, which is far greater than that of baseband signals, or modulated signals produced by conventional techniques. The manner by which the spectrum is spread is done with the help of a code, independent of the transmitted data. The receiver needs an identical copy of the code, synchronized in time, in order to recover the data.

The process of spreading introduces a large amount of redundancy in the transmitted signal. This allows the receiver to suppress a considerable portion of the interference introduced by the channel in the transmitted signal. This feature constitutes one of the major advantages of the process. However, it is possible to name other advantages of spread spectrum systems (Pickholtz, R.L., Schilling D.L., Milstein L.B., 1982; Scholtz, 1982) as follows.

DOI: 10.1201/9788743813613-7

- Low intercept probability (jamming) of the signal, due to the random-like nature of the spreading code;
- Allows the addressing of a select group of users in the same channel, this is, Code Division Multiple Access (CDMA);
- Use of the signal to measure propagation delay, which is important for radar systems to determine the position and direction of targets;
- It is possible to hide the signal in background noise, so as to make it difficult to detect by those for which the spreading code is unknown.
- Useful as a means of achieving diversity in channels with multipath.

One of the current strategies in use to spread the spectrum is the technique of Direct Sequence (DS) modulation, in which a fast Pseudo-Noise (PN) causes amplitude switching in the data signal. Figure 7.1 illustrates this technique.

Another used technique is called Frequency Hopping (FH), in which the signal is subjected to switching in frequency, according to a pre-determined pseudo-random sequence. This technique is illustrated in Figure 7.2.

It is also possible to produce a spread spectrum by means of transmission of signal bursts at random time instants. The technique is known as Time Hopping (TH) and is illustrated in Figure 7.3.

Other systems may be conceived by combining the techniques presented earlier. In this manner, the spread spectrum system is the antithesis of the usual communication system. This follows because, contrasting with the usual assumptions for designing communication systems, spread spectrum systems require a very large bandwidth and a very low power spectral density for the transmitted signal.

However, what happened then was that spread spectrum was recommended sometimes to applications were apparently it was not very effective, as pointed out by Viterbi (Viterbi, 1985).

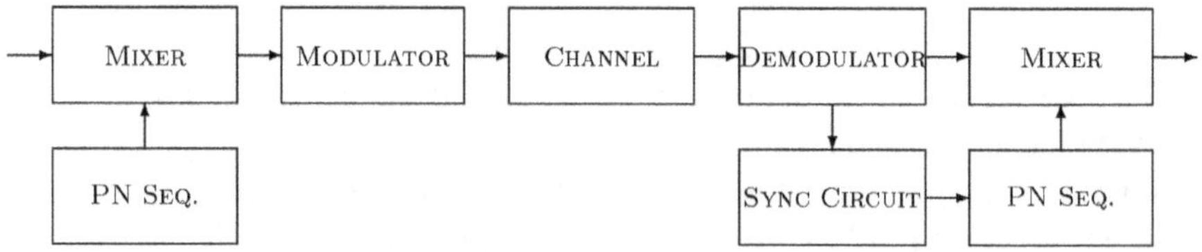


**Figure 7.1** Direct sequence spread spectrum system.

Transmission of the spread signal is done by means of digital modulation of a carrier. The digital modulator is referred to as a mixer in the above figures. Many modulation techniques can be employed, e.g., BPSK and QPSK.

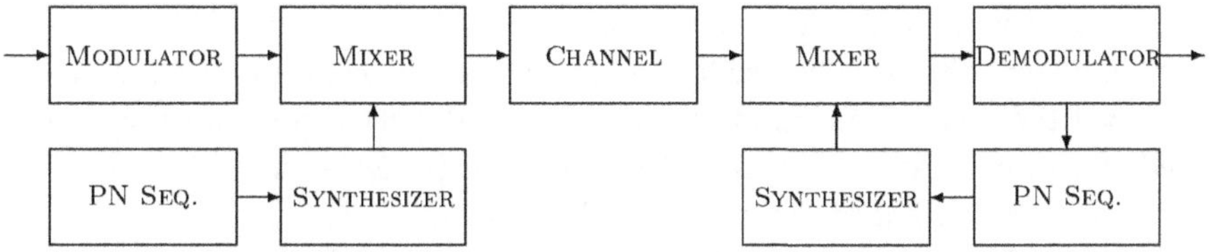


**Figure 7.2** Frequency hop spread spectrum system.

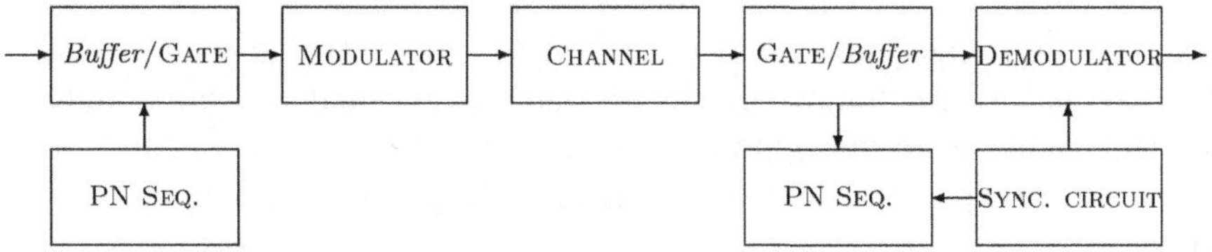


**Figure 7.3** Spread spectrum using random time windows.

### 7.1.1 Generation of Pseudo-Random Sequences

In principle pseudo-random sequences could be stored in a memory and a search algorithm could be used for selecting a particular sequence. However, usually sequential techniques are fast enough and offer lower implementation costs for producing such sequences.

Using Galois field theory, a branch of abstract algebra, it is possible to generate pseudo-random sequences in a sequential manner.

In the sequel only unipolar sequences will be considered, i.e., sequences the elements of which are 0's and 1's. Figure 7.4 shows a general purpose shift-register, a pseudo-random sequence generator.

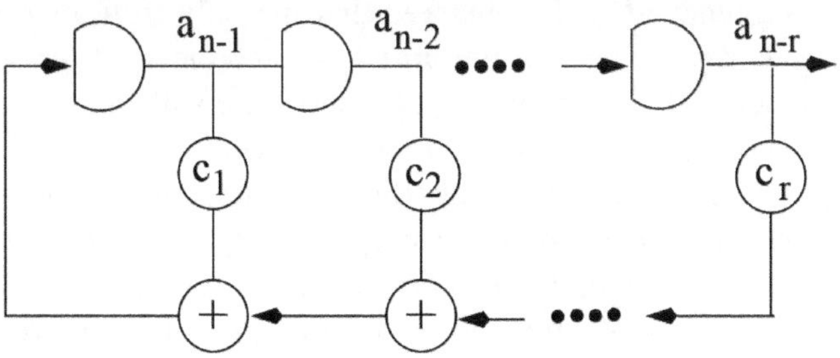


**Figure 7.4** Pseudo-Random Sequence Generator.

The shift-register is started with some set of bits as the initial state. At each clock period the contents $a_j$ of the shift-register are shifted to the right. There are $r$ stages in the shift-register, the outputs of which may be connected to a modulo-2 adder. The modulo-2 adders are part of the shift-register feedback circuit. The feedback connections depend on the value of $c_j$; if $c_j = 1$ there is a connection present, if $c_j = 0$ there is no connection to the feedback circuit. At each clock pulse a bit of the pseudo-random sequence is produced at the output of the generator denoted by $a_{n-r}$.

Note that all processes employed are linear and each bit entering the first stage of the shift-register influences the generation of the next $r$ bits, characterizing the memory property of the shift-register.

For each generator there is a characteristic polynomial the degree of which is equal to the number of shift-register stages, and the polynomial coefficients indicate the connections between stages and the modulo-2 adders. The characteristic polynomial corresponding to the generator in Figure 7.4 is given by

$$f(D) = 1 + c_1 D + c_2 D^2 + \ldots + c_r D^r, \qquad (7.1)$$

in which, for example, $D^2$ is associated with the second shift-register stage and $c_2$ indicates a connection of the second stage with a modulo-2 adder. An example of a generator with 42 stages is given in the simulation presented in Figure 7.8.

Considering an $r$-stage shift-register, there is a maximum of $2^r$ possible binary $r$-tuples. However, because of the linear feedback, the all-zero ($r$ 0 bits) initial state would lead to an all-zero sequence. Therefore, for the sequences of interest there are at most $2^r - 1$ distinct $r$-tuples which can be used as initial state in the shift-register.

Suppose then that a primitive characteristic polynomial is available, i.e., a feedback connection polynomial for which all non-zero $2^r - 1$ $r$-tuples appear in the $r$ stages of the shift-register. In this case a pseudo-random sequence of period $2^r - 1$ is generated. It is remarked that the only truly random data in this sequence is represented by the initial state of the shift-register. The initial state together with the primitive polynomial are sufficient to generate the corresponding complete pseudo-random sequence.

Primitive polynomials and their properties are studied in abstract algebra. A necessary but not sufficient condition for a given polynomial to be primitive is that it must be irreducible in the field containing its coefficients.

An important property of irreducible polynomials is that any irreducible polynomial $p(x)$ of degree $r$, with binary ({0,1}) coefficients divides the polynomial

$$f(x) = x^{2^r - 1} - 1. \qquad (7.2)$$

Let $p(x)$ be a binary irreducible polynomial of degree $r$. The polynomial $p(x)$ is called a primitive polynomial if and only if the least degree polynomial $x^n + 1$ divisible by $p(x)$ has degree $n = 2^r - 1$. In general, it is not an easy matter to tell whether a polynomial is primitive, let alone to find one. Usually one resorts to tables of primitive polynomials in order to select a primitive polynomial of a desired degree.

The following equation gives the number of binary primitive polynomials $N_p(r)$ of a given degree $r$:

$$N_p(r) = \frac{2^r - 1}{r} \prod_{i=1}^{J} \frac{P_i - 1}{P_i}, \tag{7.3}$$

in which $P_i, P_i > 1, i = 1, 2, \ldots, J$ are the natural numbers that divide $2^r - 1$.

## 7.2 Convolutional Coding

A convolutional encoder is a device that inserts redundancy to the binary data, with the objective of correcting transmission errors, before the spread spectrum process. As a consequence of the insertion of redundant digits usually the transmission rate is reduced. The insertion of controlled redundancy is a way to achieve error-correction.

Besides convolutional coding, there is at least one more coding technique for error-correction. That technique is called block coding, in which $k$-bit blocks of data are encoded into $n$-bit long codewords by means of a predefined encoding algorithm, in which $n > k$.

Convolutional codes were first studied by Peter Elias (1923–2001), in 1955. As a result of the effort of many researchers convolutional coding experienced great development, culminating in 1967, when Andrew Viterbi (1935–), an Italian, and later American, electrical engineer and businessman, who co-founded Qualcomm Inc., developed the decoding algorithm for convolutional codes now known as the Viterbi decoding algorithm.

George David Forney (1940–) showed that the Viterbi decoder is a maximum likelihood decoder. In 1993, Claude Berrou (1951–) *et al.* introduced the recursive systematic convolutional codes, called turbo codes, based on convolutional codes (Berrou et al., 1993).

Convolutional codes have been widely used in wireless communications, including WiFi, mobile cellular, and satellite transmission, and are the basis of the widely used turbo coding. Convolutional codes do not have a finite block length, such as the block codes, and may be considered as linear digital filters, either Infinite Impulse Response (IIR) or Finite Impulse Response (FIR).

### 7.2.1 The Structure of Convolutional Codes

The implementation of a convolutional encoder is simple for it employs procedures similar to those adopted in the generation of pseudo-random sequences, in Section 7.1.1. Decoding, however, is a more elaborate issue and will be discussed later.

In the generation of pseudo-random sequences, see Figure 7.4, the output of the furthest right stage is the only output, and there are no external inputs in this circuit. On the other hand, in a convolutional encoder, see Figure 7.5 for example, the encoder has at least one external input and more than one output.

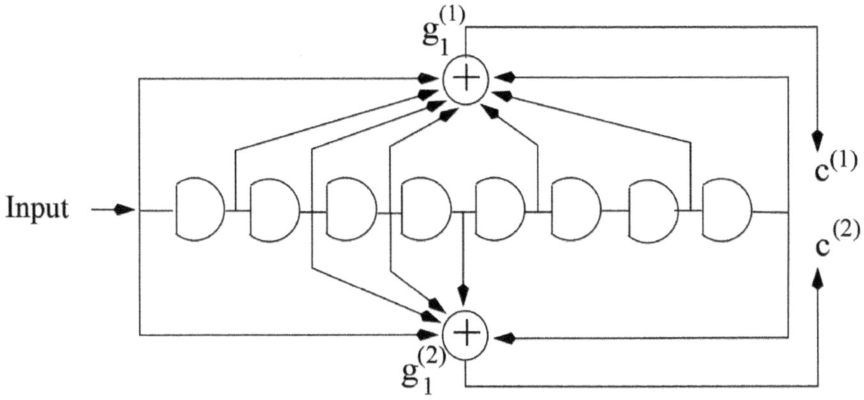


**Figure 7.5** Convolutional encoder diagram.

Since the job of the encoder is to introduce redundancy, it follows that the number of external inputs to the encoder is less than the number of its outputs.

The encoder shift-register stages are assumed to contain zeros initially. If an information bit equal to 1 is present at the encoder input, then at the next clock pulse the shift-register contents are shifted one stage to the right and the information bit enters the first stage of the encoder shift-register. Simultaneously, the encoder outputs are generated with the aid of modulo-2 adders; see Figure 7.5 as an example.

For every $k$ input information bits the encoder outputs $n$ bits (a sub-block) and retains $r$ bits in its memory. The code rate is defined as the ratio between the number of input bits and the number of output bits. Therefore if transmission ends after $N$ sub-blocks, the code rate is $kN/(nN + r)$, which asymptotically approaches $k/n$ for large values of $N$. The code constraint length $K$ is an important parameter defined as the number of encoder shift-register stages plus 1, i.e., $K = r + 1$.

In order to fully characterize the identification of the encoder it is necessary to specify the connections between the shift-register and the modulo-2 adders, i.e., it is necessary to specify each encoder output as a linear function of the input and current state; see Figure 7.5.

The encoder connections are specified by a set of sequences given by

$$g_i^{(j)} = (g_{i,0}^{(j)}, g_{i,1}^{(j)}, \ldots, g_{i,r}^{(j)})$$

in which $i = 1, \ldots, n$ refers to the inputs, and $j = 0, \ldots, r$ refers to the outputs. If $g_{i,m}^{(j)} = 1$, then there is a connection from the output of the $m^{th}$ shift-register stage to a modulo-2 adder, to produce an output bit at output $c^{(j)}$. If $g_{i,m}^{(j)} = 0$ then there is no connection present at the output of the $m^{th}$ shift-register stage. For $m = 0$ there is just a connection from the input of the shift-register.

From the example illustrated in Figure 7.5 it follows that.

$$g_1^{(1)} = (1, 1, 1, 1, 0, 1, 0, 1, 1)$$

$$g_1^{(2)} = (1, 0, 1, 1, 1, 0, 0, 0, 1)$$

thus characterizing outputs $c^{(1)}$ and $c^{(2)}$.

The structure of the convolutional encoder used in the reverse link, in the IS-95 standard, is shown in Figure 7.13.

## 7.3 CDMA and the IS-95 Standard

The technology of spread spectrum appeared initially in connection with military applications and only in the 1980's it began to be considered for commercial applications.

Spread spectrum techniques were used in military applications mainly due to its privacy properties, since the spread signal looks like noise and its detection is dependent on the sequence employed to perform the spreading.

Resistance to interference is another advantage, because even if a signal is transmitted with the same carrier frequency as the spread signal, depending on the signal to noise ratio it may be still possible to recover the original signal by employing the spreading sequence.

In wireless communication, each spread spectrum system has a frequency band to perform its transmissions. Since, in a given frequency band, there are many users trying to send their signals, a technique is required to discriminate users so as to allow transmissions to operate with a prescribed quality. Operation of many users in this manner characterizes what is known as multiple access.

Various multiple access digital systems were proposed and commercially used, as the GSM system in Europe, the TDMA in USA, and PDC in Japan. CDMA was first commercially used in USA and became a standard under the name IS-95, later changed by Qualcomm to CDMA2000.

### 7.3.1 Processing Gain and CDMA Capacity

From an analysis of the code division multiple access system, it is possible to derive an equation for the number of calls per cell as a function of the data rate, final bandwidth, signal to noise ratio, voice activity factor, frequency reuse and sectorization.

An important parameter when determining capacity is the ratio between the power of the received signal, $C = R \cdot E_b$, and the interference, $I = W \cdot N_0$, i.e.,

$$\frac{C}{I} = \frac{RE_b}{WN_0}, \tag{7.4}$$

in which $R$ denotes the data rate in kbit/s, $W$ denotes the bandwidth spread in frequency and $E_B/N_0$ is the ratio between the bit energy and the noise power spectral density.

For a system using CDMA, the interfering power is given by $I = C \cdot (N - 1)$, in which $N$ is the number of users transmitting in the bandwidth $W$, and thus $C/I = 1/(N - 1)$. It is assumed that all signals are transmitted with a controlled power level, which is the case for the Qualcomm systems.

Using the expressions given earlier it follows that the capacity of a CDMA system, in a non-cell environment is given by

$$N = 1 + \frac{W}{R} \frac{1}{E_b/N_0}, \tag{7.5}$$

in which $\frac{W}{R}$ is called the capacity gain of the CDMA scheme, denoted by $G_P$.

The voice activity factor, $V$, reflects the fact that in a full-duplex conversation, the fraction of time actually used by the voice signal is usually less than 0.35. With CDMA it is possible to reduce the transmission rate when there is no signal to transmit and, in this manner, to minimize the interference caused to other users. The consideration of the voice activity factor, thus practically doubles capacity, since the interfering power is given by $NV$. The modified equation for capacity then becomes

$$N = 1 + \frac{W}{R} \frac{1}{E_b/N_0} \frac{1}{V}. \tag{7.6}$$

In a cellular system, as a consequence of interference by adjacent cells, the signal to interference ratio becomes

$$\frac{C}{I} = \frac{1}{N + 6Nk_1 + 12Nk_2 + 18Nk_3 + \cdots} \tag{7.7}$$

in which $N$ is the number of mobile stations per cell and $k_1,\ k_2,\ k_3, \ldots$ represent the contributions of individual cells in the layers around the cell under consideration. By defining

$$F = \frac{1}{1 + 6k_1 + 12k_2 + 18k_3 + \cdots} \tag{7.8}$$

as the efficiency of frequency reuse, Equation 7.7 can be rewritten as

$$\frac{C}{I} = \frac{F}{N}. \tag{7.9}$$

Finally, capacity can still be increased as a function of the sectorization gain, $G$, thus yielding the full capacity equation

$$N = 1 + \frac{W}{R} \frac{1}{E_b/N_0} \frac{1}{V} FG, \tag{7.10}$$

in which $N$ denotes the number of calls per cell (assuming Rayleigh fading), $W$ is the bandwidth spread in frequency (1.25 MHz), $R$ denotes the data rate in kbit/s (assuming 9.6 kbit/s), $E_B/N_0$ is the ratio between bit energy and noise power spectral density (assuming 7.0 dB), $V$ is the voice activity factor (assuming 40 %), $F$ is the efficiency of frequency reuse (assuming 60 %), $G_S$ denotes the sectorization gain (assuming 3 sectors: 2.55).

In order to increase capacity it is a usual practice to reduce both the transmitting power level and the date rate whenever there is no voice activity. The capacity is then proportionally incremented with transmission rate reduction. This proportionality factor is called (as mentioned earlier) the voice activity gain $V$.

As mentioned earlier, another way to increase capacity is to sectorize an area of coverage, thus reducing interference by a factor factor due to the antenna. Other factors like interference from other cells and noise in the channel itself can be incorporated to the equation for channel capacity, in order to investigate by simulation the effect of these factors in the system.

### 7.3.2 Channel Layout for IS-95

In each cell there are two data links, one for direct channels (transmission from the base station to the mobile) and the other for the reverse channels (transmission from the mobile to the base station).

The direct link consists of a pilot channel, a synchronization channel, seven paging channels and at most 64 channels of direct traffic. The reverse link consists of access channels and channels for traffic.

There are then six distinct types of channels in the IS-95 standard. The task of each type of channel will be described in the following sections. In (Rhee, 1998) one finds a quantitative description of these channels with the associated transmission procedures. Figures 7.6 and 7.7 illustrate the structure of these channels.

#### Pilot Channel

The pilot channel is a reference. It uses the mobile station to acquire the clock, and as a phase reference for coherent demodulation. It is continuously transmitted by each base station on every active CDMA frequency. The mobile stations monitor this signal periodically. The structure of this channel is illustrated in Figure 7.6.

#### Synchronization Channel

Communication between the base station and the mobile is synchronous. Synchronization is performed by employing the pilot channel and the synchronization channel. The mobile station uses the synchronization channel only when it is enters the system, at the beginning of its connection to the base station. After that the mobile station will hardly use the synchronization channel again.

After the synchronization channel is acquired, the mobile station adjusts its timing and initiates monitoring the paging channels (described next).

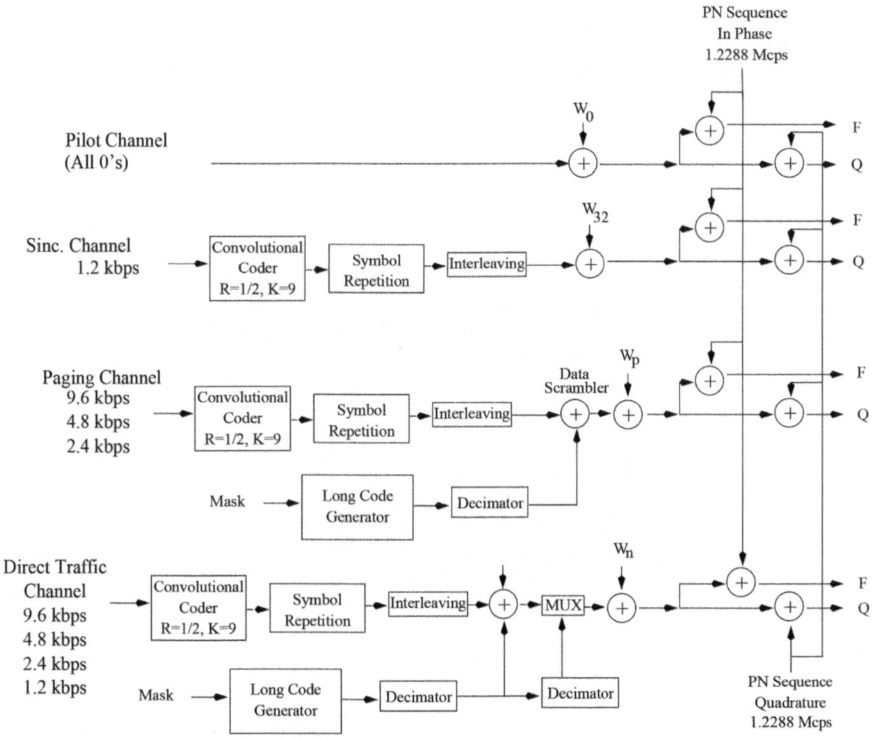


**Figure 7.6** CDMA direct channel block diagram.

Figure 7.7 shows the structure of the data link for reverse channels, which will be discussed later.

## Paging Channel

The base station uses the paging channel to transmit system information and specific information to a given mobile station. Information like, for example, beginning and end of a call and register of a mobile station flow in this channel.

Each mobile station monitors only one paging channel. Figure 7.6 also shows the structure of the paging channel.

## Channels for the direct and for the reverse traffic

Both channels, for direct and for reverse traffic, use control structures consisting of frames of 20 ms. Transmission can be done at rates of 9,600, 4,800,

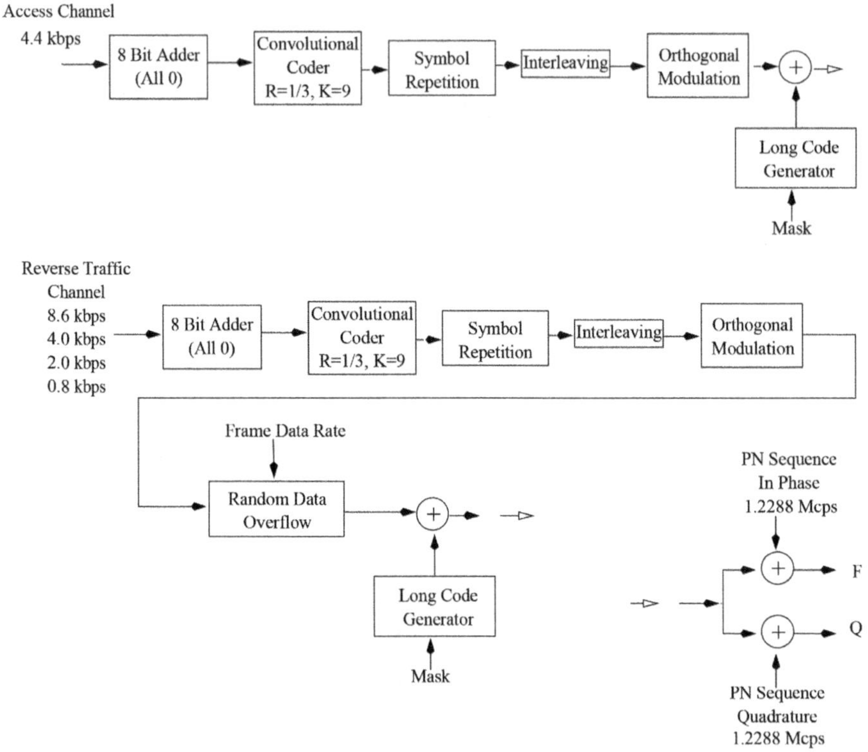


**Figure 7.7** CDMA reverse channel block diagram.

2,400 and 1,200 bits/s. In these channels flow conversations and the following five types of messages.

- Call control messages;
- Handoff control messages;
- Power control messages;
- Security and authentication messages;
- Messages to obtain/provide special information from/to a mobile station.

The structure of channels of direct traffic and channels of reverse traffic are illustrated in Figures 7.6 and 7.7, respectively.

## Access Channel

The access channel provides communication between a mobile station and the base station, when the mobile station is not using a traffic channel. The mobile station randomly chooses an access channel, which is distinguished from other channels through its associated pseudo-random sequence.

This channel is used to send short signaling messages from the mobile station to the base station, as for example messages for originating a call, channel response, state of the mobile station and register.

Each frame in an access channel has 96 bits and 20 ms duration, which corresponds to a transmission rate of $\frac{96 \text{ bits}}{20 \text{ ms}} = 4.8$ kbit/s. Out of the 96 bits only 88 bits are data bits. The remaining 8 bits are all-zeros and are used for synchronization with the convolutional encoder. Figure 7.7 shows the structure of the access channel.

### Transmission on the Access Channel

In the sequel a description is presented of the process of generating digits for transmission on the access channel. According to the structure of the access channel, illustrated in Figure 7.7, there are 88 information bits at the input and 24,576 chips at the output, of which 12,288 phase modulate the carrier and 12,288 modulate the carrier in quadrature. The following sections describe in more detail the main blocks illustrated in Figure 7.7.

## 7.3.3 Orthogonal Modulation

A set of 64 orthogonal sequences is employed, each sequence being 64 bits long, called Walsh sequences, which guarantee orthogonality among the transmitted data. Each sequence has a number called modulation symbol index – MSI.

The Walsh sequences can be recursively generated with Hadamard matrices

$$H_{2n} = \begin{bmatrix} H_n & H_n \\ H_n & \overline{H_n} \end{bmatrix}, \tag{7.11}$$

for $n = 1, 2, 4, 8, 16, 32$ and $H_1 = 0$. Matrix $H_{64}$ is shown in Tables 7.1 and 7.2.

In orthogonal modulation 6 input bits are used to calculate a MSI value. Once calculated, the output has the 64 bits of the Walsh sequence corresponding to the MSI value. This value is determined by the equation

$$MSI = C_0 + 2C_1 + 4C_2 + 8C_3 + 16C_4 + 32C_5. \tag{7.12}$$

## 7.3.4 Direct Sequence Spreading

As shown in Figure 7.7, scattering results from the modulo-2 addition of the output sequence of the modulation block with the sequence at the output of the PN generator, Figure 7.8.

**Table 7.1** The 64 Walsh sequences (First part).

| MSI | Walsh sequences |
|---|---|
| 0 | 0000000000000000000000000000000000000000000000000000000000000000 |
| 1 | 0101010101010101010101010101010101010101010101010101010101010101 |
| 2 | 0011001100110011001100110011001100110011001100110011001100110011 |
| 3 | 0110011001100110011001100110011001100110011001100110011001100110 |
| 4 | 0000111100001111000011110000111100001111000011110000111100001111 |
| 5 | 0101101001011010010110100101101001011010010110100101101001011010 |
| 6 | 0011110000111100001111000011110000111100001111000011110000111100 |
| 7 | 0110100101101001011010010110100101101001011010010110100101101001 |
| 8 | 0000000011111111000000001111111100000000111111110000000011111111 |
| 9 | 0101010110101010010101011010101001010101101010100101010110101010 |
| 10 | 0011001111001100001100111100110000110011110011000011001111001100 |
| 11 | 0110011010011001011001101001100101100110100110010110011010011001 |
| 12 | 0000111111110000000011111111000000001111111100000000111111110000 |
| 13 | 0101101010100101010110101010010101011010101001010101101010100101 |
| 14 | 0011110011000011001111001100001100111100110000110011110011000011 |
| 15 | 0110100110010110011010011001011001101001100101100110100110010110 |
| 16 | 0000000000000000111111111111111100000000000000001111111111111111 |
| 17 | 0101010101010101101010101010101001010101010101011010101010101010 |
| 18 | 0011001100110011110011001100110000110011001100111100110011001100 |
| 19 | 0110011001100110100110011001100101100110011001101001100110011001 |
| 20 | 0000111100001111111100001111000000001111000011111111000011110000 |
| 21 | 0101101001011010101001011010010101011010010110101010010110100101 |
| 22 | 0011110000111100110000111100001100111100001111001100001111000011 |
| 23 | 0110100101101001100101101001011001101001011010011001011010010110 |
| 24 | 0000000011111111111111110000000000000000111111111111111100000000 |
| 25 | 0101010110101010101010100101010101010101101010101010101001010101 |
| 26 | 0011001111001100110011000011001100110011110011001100110000110011 |
| 27 | 0110011010011001100110010110011001100110100110011001100101100110 |
| 28 | 0000111111110000111100000000111100001111111100001111000000001111 |
| 29 | 0101101010100101101001010101101001011010101001011010010101011010 |
| 30 | 0011110011000011110000110011110000111100110000111100001100111100 |
| 31 | 0110100110010110100101100110100101101001100101101001011001101001 |
| 32 | 0000000000000000000000000000000011111111111111111111111111111111 |

The PN sequence has a period of $2^{42} - 1$. The PN sequence generator, denoted by the polynomial $p(x)$, is given by

$$p(x) = 1 + x + x^2 + x^3 + x^5 + x^6 + x^7 + x^{10} + x^{16} + x^{17} + x^{18} + x^{19}$$
$$+x^{21} + x^{22} + x^{25} + x^{26} + x^{27} + x^{31} + x^{33} + x^{35} + x^{42}.$$

At the initial state of the process of generating the PN sequence the register contents are 1000000000000000000000 00000000000000000000. At each clock pulse there is a displacement of the register contents to the right, and those register cells which receive as input the output of a modulo-2 adder receive the sum of the contents of the previous cell and that of cell number 42.

**Table 7.2** The 64 Walsh sequences (Continuation).

| MSI | Walsh sequences |
|---|---|
| 33 | 0101010101010101010101010101010110101010101010101010101010101010 |
| 34 | 0011001100110011001100110011001111001100110011001100110011001100 |
| 35 | 0110011001100110011001100110011010011001100110011001100110011001 |
| 36 | 0000111100001111000011110000111111110000111100001111000011110000 |
| 37 | 0101101001011010010110100101101010100101101001011010010110100101 |
| 38 | 0011110000111100001111000011110011000011110000111100001111000011 |
| 39 | 0110100101101001011010010110100110010110100101101001011010010110 |
| 40 | 0000000011111111000000001111111111111111000000001111111100000000 |
| 41 | 0101010110101010010101011010101010101010010101011010101001010101 |
| 42 | 0011001111001100001100111100110011001100001100111100110000110011 |
| 43 | 0110011010011001011001101001100110011001011001101001100101100110 |
| 44 | 0000111111110000000011111111000011110000000011111111000000001111 |
| 45 | 0101101010100101010110101010010110100101010110101010010101011010 |
| 46 | 0011110011000011001111001100001111000011001111001100001100111100 |
| 47 | 0110100110010110011010011001011010010110011010011001011001101001 |
| 48 | 0000000000000000111111111111111111111111111111110000000000000000 |
| 49 | 0101010101010101101010101010101010101010101010100101010101010101 |
| 50 | 0011001100110011110011001100110011001100110011000011001100110011 |
| 51 | 0110011001100110100110011001100110011001100110010110011001100110 |
| 52 | 0000111100001111111100001111000011110000111100000000111100001111 |
| 53 | 0101101001011010101001011010010110100101101001010101101001011010 |
| 54 | 0011110000111100110000111100001111000011110000110011110000111100 |
| 55 | 0110100101101001100101101001011010010110100101100110100101101001 |
| 56 | 0000000011111111111111110000000011111111000000000000000011111111 |
| 57 | 0101010110101010101010100101010110101010010101010101010110101010 |
| 58 | 0011001111001100110011000011001111001100001100110011001111001100 |
| 59 | 0110011010011001100110010110011010011001011001100110011010011001 |
| 60 | 0000111111110000111100000000111111110000000011110000111111110000 |
| 61 | 0101101010100101101001010101101010100101010110100101101010100101 |
| 62 | 0011110011000011110000110011110011000011001111000011110011000011 |
| 63 | 0110100110010110100101100110100110010110011010010110100110010110 |

At each time instant there are 42 bits in the register. Each one of the bits is fed to one input of a two-input AND gate, and the other input is fed with

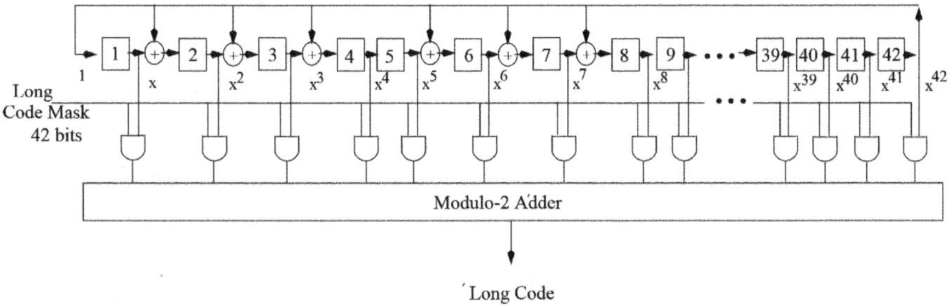


**Figure 7.8** Generator of long code sequence with period $2^{42} - 1$.

bits from another 42 bit long sequence called mask. The mask is formed from data belonging to the particular mobile station. The description of the mask is illustrated in Figure 7.9.

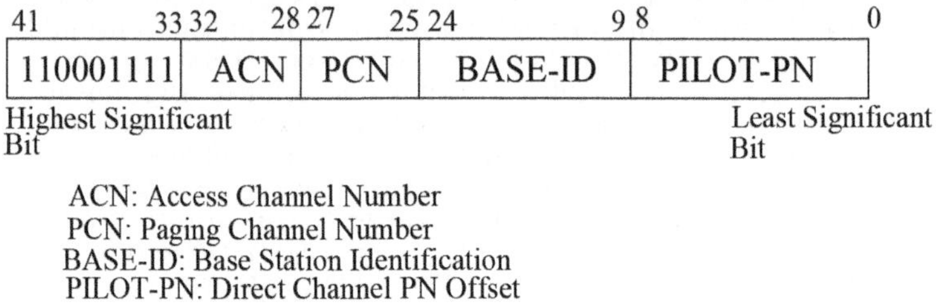


**Figure 7.9** Mask code for the access channel.

The output of each AND gate is connected to a modulo-2 adder the output of which is a bit of the long code.

In the access channel, the long code sequence is four times faster than the orthogonally modulated sequence. Each input bit is added (modulo-2) successively with four bits of the long code, thus resulting in four bits at the output of the direct sequence spreading circuit.

### 7.3.5 Quadrature Scattering

Quadrature scattering, Figure 7.10, is similar to direct sequence scattering. The bits received from the scattering block are divided into two sequences, one for phase scattering (even bits) and the other in quadrature (odd bits).

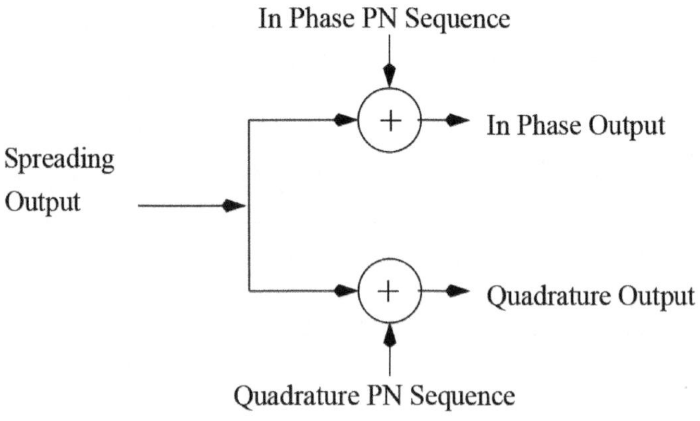


**Figure 7.10** Quadrature scattering.

The phase sequence is added bit-by-bit with the PN phase spreading sequence. The scattering sequence is obtained from the generator shown in Figure 7.11. The associated characteristic polynomial is $P_I(x) = 1 + x^5 + x^7 + x^8 + x^9 + x^{13} + x^{15}$.

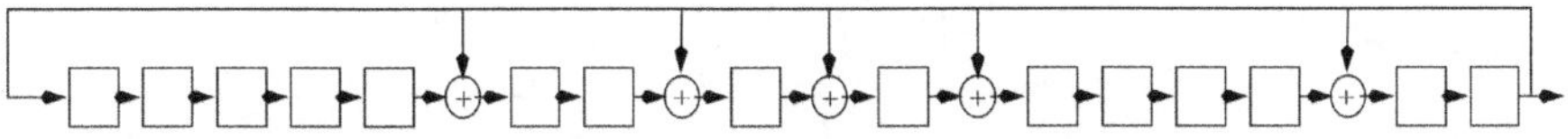

**Figure 7.11** Generator for PN phase spreading sequences.

The quadrature sequence is added bit-by-bit with the quadrature PN spreading sequence. The spreading sequence is obtained from the generator shown in Figure 7.12. The associated characteristic polynomial is $P_Q(x) = 1 + x^3 + x^4 + x^5 + x^6 + x^{10} + x^{11} + x^{12} + x^{15}$.

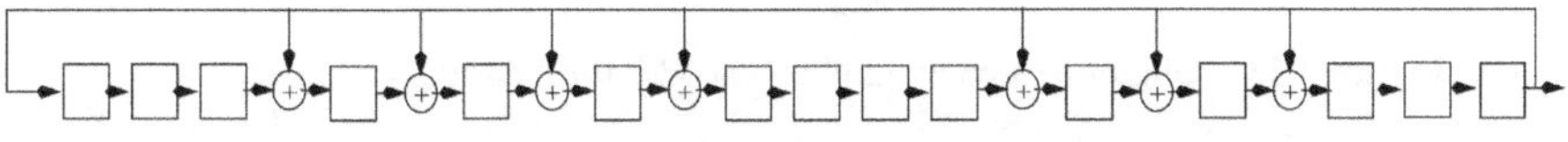

**Figure 7.12** Generator for quadrature PN spreading sequences.

### 7.3.6 Convolutional Encoder

The convolutional encoder has 96 bits input bits at a transmission rate of 4.8 kbit/s, producing at the output 288 bits at 14.4 kbit/s. Its asymptotic coding rate is $R = 1/3$ and the sub-block length is nine. Figure 7.13 shows the encoder structure (Rhee, 1998).

For each bit $b(k)$, $k = 0, 1, \ldots, 95$ at the encoder input, three bits are generated at the output, denoted as $c_k^1, c_k^2, c_k^3$. Initially the shift-registers $D_i, i = 1, 2, \ldots, 8$ are all set to zero.

At each clock pulse the register contents of a cell is moved to its neighbor cell on the right. Register cell $D_1$ is fed with the input bit, according to the order from bit $b_0$ to $b_{95}$.

The outputs are calculated in the following manner.

$$\begin{aligned} c_k^0 &= d_8 + d_6 + d_5 + d_3 + d_2 + d_1 + b_k, \\ c_k^1 &= d_8 + d_7 + d_5 + d_4 + d_1 + b_k, \\ c_k^2 &= d_8 + d_7 + d_6 + d_3 + +b_k, \end{aligned}$$

in which $k = 0, \ldots, 95$ and $d_i$ is the output of register cell $D_i$. This procedure is repeated until $b_{95}$ is encoded. The output is read out in series, from the first to the last bit, as follows.

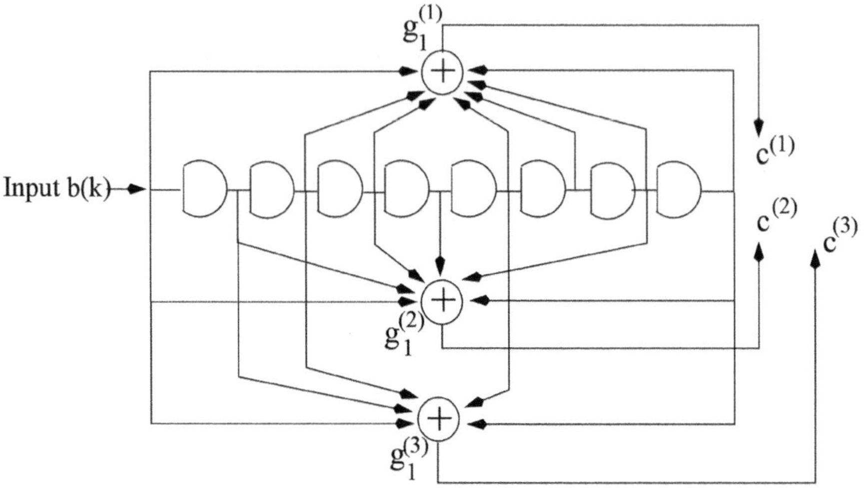


**Figure 7.13** Diagram of convolutional encoder for the access channel.

$$c_0^0, c_0^1, c_0^2, c_1^0, c_1^1, c_1^2, \ldots, c_95^0, c_95^1, c_95^2.$$

## Symbol Repetition Block

At the input to the symbol repetition block there are 288 bits and at the output there are 576 bits. There is no further processing of the input bits, apart from their repetition. The bits are read out in the following order.

$$c_0^0, c_0^0, c_0^1, c_0^1, c_0^2, c_0^2, \ldots$$

## Interleaving Block

The purpose of the interleaving block is to help correct burst errors, during data transmission through a channel with multipath fading. Another reason is to reduce the excess in redundancy, thus improving system efficiency.

The interleaving block receives 576 bits and changes their order. Suppose that the bits are ordered in matrix form 32x18, column by column. The output is then obtained by reading the matrix in a row-by-row manner. Reading is performed alternately, i.e., first line 1 is read out then line 17 is read out, and so on successively in the following order.

1 17 9 25 5 21 13 29 3 19 11 27 7 23 15 31
2 18 10 26 6 22 14 30 4 20 12 28 8 24 16 32

# 8

# Theoretical Cryptography

*"Cryptography is the ultimate form of non-violent direct action."*
Julian Assange

## 8.1 Introduction

Cryptography is the basis for network security. It comes from the Greek word *kryptos*, for tomb, hidden or secret, combined with *graphein*, or writing. A free translation is hidden writing, which defines the proposal of ciphering a message. Cryptology, combines the same previous prefix with *logia*, meaning study, to give the translation of study of secret coding.

Cryptography is the practice and study of techniques for secure communication in the presence of third parties. It is also a collection of techniques for construction and analysis of protocols to overcome the influence of jammers and which are related to various aspects of information security, such as data confidentiality, data integrity, authentication, and non-repudiation.

Along the centuries, governments used cryptography to cipher messages, supposed to remain in secrecy, while the spies tried to decipher them. During the wars, cryptography becomes more important, considering the nature of the operations.

Bletchley Park was the secret information and counter-information center in Great Britain during the Second World War. Is was so secret that remained as a legend after the end of the war, while England continued to break the codes of other countries, either enemies and friends (Haykin, 1999).

The first computer, the Collossus, was built in Bletchley Park, developed by Alan Mathison Turing (1912-1954), one of the greatest computer geniuses of the World. Destroyed after the end of the war, the Collossus was rebuilt from the original drawings.

The German Enigma code was broken there, with the help of Turing, which benefited from information passed by a Hungarian mathematician and

DOI: 10.1201/9788743813613-8

a German officer, which provided information to French spies in exchange for money. The French did not know how to decipher the code, and passed the information on the the British.

## 8.2 Cryptographic Aspects of Computer Networks

The Internet has revolutionized the ways in which companies do business, since the Internet Protocol (IP) is undeniably efficient, inexpensive and flexible (Alencar, 2012). This section presents the main cryptographic aspects of modern TCP/IP computer networks, which include digital signature technology based on asymmetrical cryptographic algorithms, data confidentiality by applying symmetrical cryptographic systems, and system Public Key Infrastructure (PKI) (Tanenbaum, 2003).

The possible vulnerabilities of TCP/IP computer networks, and possible techniques to eliminate them, are considered. It seem that only a general and multi-layered security infrastructure could cope with possible attacks to the computer network systems.

### 8.2.1 Potential Vulnerabilities of Computer Networks

The Internet Protocol (IP) is efficient, inexpensive and flexible. However, the existing methods used to route IP packets leave them vulnerable to security risks, such as spoofing, sniffing and session hijacking, and provide no form of non-repudiation for contractual or monetary transactions.

Organizations need to secure communications between remote offices, business partners, customers and travelling and telecommuting employees, besides securing the internal environment. The transmission of messages over the Internet or intranet poses a risk, given the lack of protection at the existing Internet backbone.

Control and management of security and access between the entities in a company's business environment is important. Without security, both public and private networks are susceptible to unauthorized monitoring and access. Internal attacks might be a result of minimal or nonexistent intranet security.

Risks from outside the private network originate from connections to the Internet and extranets. Password-based user access controls alone do not protect data transmitted across a network. Without security measures and controls in place, the data might be subjected to attack. Some attacks are passive, and the information is only monitored. Other attacks are active, and the information is altered to corrupt or destroy the data or the network itself.

## 8.3 Principles of Cryptography

The general model for an encryption system is shown in Figure 8.1. The original message, also called plaintext and denoted by the letter $X$, is converted to a to an apparently random sequence, called ciphertext and denoted by the letter $Y$. The encryption process consists of an encipherment algorithm that uses a key $K$, which is independent of the plaintext. The algorithm produces a different output depending on the key used (Stallings, 1999).

It is important to consider that a cryptanalyst, or hacker, could observe the encrypted message and try to decode it. The algorithm must, therefore, be powerful enough to resist the attack.

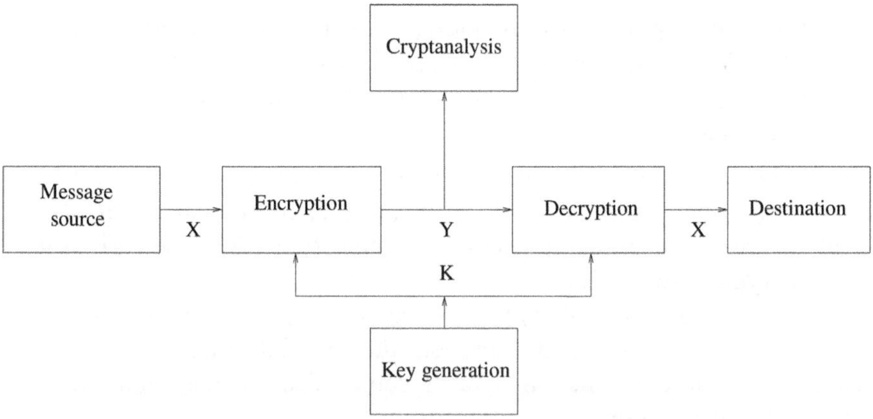


**Figure 8.1** General model for a cryptosystem.

Encryption can be seen as a transformation, parameterized by $K$,

$$Y = E(X, K), \tag{8.1}$$

which converts the original text $X$ to the ciphertext $Y$, to be transmitted.

At the reception side, the inverse transformation is performed on the ciphertext to produce the plaintext

$$X = D(Y, K). \tag{8.2}$$

Of course, the destination must possess the key to be able to invert the transformation. Therefore, the transmission of the key is an important part of the cryptobusiness.

The security of a cryptosystem depends on certain assumptions:

- The encryption algorithm must be robust enough that is difficult to decipher a message based only on the ciphertext.
- The key must be kept secret, and a secure channel should be provided for transmission.
- There is no need to keep the algorithm secret.

The application of cryptographic techniques depends on the knowledge of the security of the employed system. A cryptographic system can be classified as:

1. How to transform the plaintext to the ciphertext, as the encryption algorithms are based on two principles (Stallings, 1999):
   (a) Substitution, in which the individual symbols of the original text (bit, byte, letter, words) are mapped into other elements.
   (b) Transposition, in which the elements of the original text are rearranged.
2. How the original text is processed, which involves a block cipher, that processes a block of plaintext at a time, or a convolutional cipher, also called stream cipher, that processes the input symbols as they arrive at the encryption sub-system.
3. How the key is generated, which can lead to the production of a single, or symmetric, key to be used by both the transmitter and receiver, or use different keys for the sender and receiver, also called asymmetric or public key encryption.

## 8.4 Information Theoretical Aspects of Cryptography

It is possible to use the terminology of information theory to describe a secure encryption system. The measure of information, or entropy, of a plaintext, considered as a subset of symbols selected from the set of all possible messages, is given by (van der Lubbe, 1997)

$$H(X) = -\sum_{l=1}^{L} p(x_l) \log p(x_l), \tag{8.3}$$

in which $p(x_l), l = 1, 2, \ldots L$ represent the uncertainty of occurrence of the possible plaintexts, considering that the texts are mutually independent.

The entropy of the set of keys is given by

$$H(K) = -\sum_{m=1}^{M} p(k_m) \log p(k_m), \tag{8.4}$$

in which $k_m, m = 1, 2, \ldots M$ are the possible keys.

By the same token, it is possible to introduce a measure of information for the ciphertext

$$H(Y) = -\sum_{n=1}^{N} p(y_n) \log p(y_n), \tag{8.5}$$

in which $p(y_n), n = 1, 2, \ldots N$ represent the uncertainty of occurrence of the possible ciphertexts, considering that the texts are mutually independent. Usually, regarding the bijection from the plaintext into the ciphertext set, one considers $N = L$.

The conditional entropy, or key equivocation, is a measure of the uncertainty or information with respect to the key, when the ciphertext is available is defined as

$$H(K|Y) = \sum_{m=1}^{M} \sum_{n=1}^{N} p(k_m, y_n) \log p(k_m|y_m). \tag{8.6}$$

The uncertainty with respect to the plaintext, or conditional entropy when the ciphertext is available, also known as message equivocation, is defined as

$$H(X|Y) = \sum_{l=1}^{L} \sum_{n=1}^{N} p(x_l, y_n) \log p(x_l|y_m). \tag{8.7}$$

The conditional entropy, or uncertainty with respect to the key, for a given plaintext and corresponding ciphertext, is defined as

$$H(K|X,Y) = \sum_{m=1}^{M} \sum_{l=1}^{L} \sum_{n=1}^{N} p(k_m, x_l, y_n) \log p(k_m|x_l, y_m), \tag{8.8}$$

which is also known as key appearance equivocation.

Finally, the conditional entropy, or uncertainty with respect to the plaintext, when the key and the ciphertext are known, is defined as

$$H(X|Y,K) = \sum_{l=1}^{L} \sum_{n=1}^{N} \sum_{m=1}^{M} p(x_m, y_l, k_n) \log p(x_m|y_l, k_m). \tag{8.9}$$

Since there is a bijection between the plaintext and ciphertext sets, it is always true that

$$H(X|Y, K) = 0. \quad (8.10)$$

As expected, when the ciphertext and the key are available it is possible to retrieve the plaintext correctly, because the uncertainty with respect to $X$ is null. There is no loss of information whatsoever at the receiver, and the full original message is recovered.

### 8.4.1 Relations Between the Entropies

A cipher system user requires that the key appearance equivocation, which is represented as $H(K|X, Y)$, be as high as possible, because, if a cryptanalyst manages to obtain both the plaintext and the ciphertext, then the uncertainty with respect to the key must be as large as possible.

This can be seen by the following argument. From the previous results in information theory, the joint measure of information in the plaintext, ciphertext and key is

$$H(X, Y, K) = H(X|Y, K) + H(Y, K) = H(K|X, Y) + H(X, Y). \quad (8.11)$$

Also, consider the following relations

$$H(Y, K) = H(K|Y) + H(Y), \quad (8.12)$$

and

$$H(X, Y) = H(X|Y) + H(Y). \quad (8.13)$$

Combining the equations, one obtains

$$H(X|Y, K) + H(K|Y) = H(K|X, Y) + H(X|Y). \quad (8.14)$$

But, as discussed, $H(X|Y, K) = 0$, which results in

$$H(K|Y) = H(K|X, Y) + H(X|Y), \quad (8.15)$$

which leads to

$$H(K|X, Y) = H(K|Y) - H(X|Y). \quad (8.16)$$

Therefore, to obtain a large key appearance equivocation the message equivocation $H(X|Y)$ must be small. However, a small message equivocation implies that the uncertainty with respect to the plaintext, when the ciphertext is known, is small. But this is what must be avoided by the cryptosystem.

The uncertainty with respect to the key must be large to decrease the uncertainty with respect to the plaintext, and an increase in the uncertainty with respect to the plaintext decreases the uncertainty with respect to the key (van der Lubbe, 1997).

## 8.5 Mutual Information for Cryptosystems

The information theoretical approach provides additional results. The mutual information of the plaintext and the ciphertext is defined as

$$I(X;Y) = H(X) - H(X|Y) = H(Y) - H(Y|X). \tag{8.17}$$

As expected, the objective of the cryptodesigner is to minimize the mutual information $I(X;Y)$. If the ciphertext provides no information about the original message, then

$$H(X|Y) = H(X),$$

and the mutual information between the plaintext and the encoded message is zero, or $I(X;Y) = 0$. This the referred to as the absolutely secure cryptosystem.

It is possible to obtain a lower limit for the mutual information between the plaintext and the ciphertext. First, take into account Equation 8.16, and recall that $H(K|X,Y) \geq 0$, then it follows that

$$H(K|Y) \geq H(X|Y). \tag{8.18}$$

The use of one of the properties of entropy gives

$$H(K) \geq H(K|Y), \tag{8.19}$$

and therefore,

$$H(K) \geq H(X|Y). \tag{8.20}$$

Substituting this last inequality into Equation 8.17, gives

$$I(X;Y) \geq H(X) - H(K). \tag{8.21}$$

Inequality 8.21 implies that a decrease in the uncertainty of a set of keys improves, on average, the independence between the plaintext and the ciphertext.

It is implicit in the derivation that absolute security of a cryptosystem can only be achieved for

$$H(K) \geq H(X). \tag{8.22}$$

For uniformly distributed keys

$$H(K) = -\sum_{m=1}^{M} p(k_m) \log p(k_m) = \log(M), \tag{8.23}$$

and for uniformly distributed plaintexts

$$H(X) = -\sum_{l=1}^{L} p(y_l) \log p(y_l) = \log(L). \tag{8.24}$$

Therefore,

$$H(K) = \log(M) \geq H(X) = \log(L), \text{ or } M \geq L, \tag{8.25}$$

because of the monotonicity of the logarithm function.

The last condition implies that the key must be at least the same length as the message to be transmitted. However, the inequality can be avoided with the introduction of security events. When a security event happens the system can be considered absolutely secure. If the event does not occur, the cryptosystem may no be fully secure (Maurer, 1989) (Massey, 1990).

Even when there is a small chance of a security breach, an absolutely secure cipher is still feasible, for which $H(K) < H(X)$. A security event could be the transmission of a certain key $K$, followed by the plaintext, provided that the hacker does not type the secret key at the beginning. Without typing $K$, the sequence is obscure to the intruder, and the system is secure. If the hacker happens to type $K$, the ciphertext can be deciphered, and the system has become unreliable.

Therefore, the introduction of the concept of security event gives a new way of regarding the system security based on information theorems. Information security can be assured, even if the length of the key is smaller than the original sequence, given that a security event is defined for the system, and provided that the event actually occurs (van der Lubbe, 1997).

## 8.6 Introduction to Network Security

The Internet has changed the way in which people interact and companies do business, because the Internet Protocol (IP) is efficient, inexpensive and flexible. However, the existing methods used to route IP packets leave them vulnerable to several security risks, such as spoofing, sniffing and session hijacking, and do not provide the means of non-repudiation when dealing with contractual or monetary transactions.

Organizations need to secure communications between remote offices, business partners, customers and travelling and telecommuting employees, and also secure the internal environment against intruders.

The transmission of messages over the Internet, even by intranets, to different entities implies a risk, given the lack of protection provided by the existing Internet backbone.

The control and management of security and access between different entities in a company business environment is certainly important.

Public and private networks are susceptible to unauthorized monitoring and access, and some internal attacks might be a result of minimal or nonexistent intranet security.

Most risks to the private network originate from connections to the Internet, and password-based user access controls alone do not protect data transmitted across a network.

Some attacks are passive, that is, the information is only monitored, and other attacks are active, because the information is altered with the objective of corrupting or destroying the data or disrupting the network.

The network communications, as a rule, occur in a plaintext (unencrypted) format, which allows an attacker who has gained access to data paths in a network to monitor and interpret (read) the traffic. When an attacker is eavesdropping on communications, it is referred to as sniffing or snooping.

After an attacker has read data, the next logical step is often to modify it. This can be done without the knowledge of the sender or receiver.

In general, the most important security problem that administrators face in an enterprise is the ability of an eavesdropper to monitor the network. Without strong encryption services, that are based on cryptography, the information can be read by attackers, as it traverses the network.

## 8.7 Hash Functions

The hash of the data is used as a digital fingerprint to sign and verify the information content. To prevent a security problem, the hash function must satisfy the some criteria:

- The hash function must be collision-resistant, that is, it must be impractical to find a collision. No two different digital documents can be mapped onto the same hash format.

- The hash function must be a one-way function, that is, it must be difficult to find a pre-image for the function, for a given bit string, from the value range.

However, because the existence of collisions cannot be avoided, the requirements are of a theoretical nature.

A hash function maps a data file of arbitrary size onto a discrete sequence. The idea was introduced in cryptography, in 1976, by Diffie and Hellman, who identified the need for a one-way hash function as a building block of a digital signature scheme, as an algorithm to protect the authenticity of information. But, it is clear that the tool is useful to solve other security problems in communication and computer networks (Preneel, 1994).

The values returned by a hash function are called hash values, hash codes or digests. The hash function is usually used in combination with a hash table, a data structure used for rapid data lookup. The hash function permits to speed up a database lookup by detecting duplicated records in a large file.

In mathematics, engineering, computing and cryptography, universal hashing refers to the process of selecting a hash function at random, from a family of hash functions with a certain mathematical property. This guarantees a low number of collisions in average, even if the data is chosen by an adversary.

A family of functions $H = \{h : U \to [m]\}$ is called a universal family if, $\forall x, y \in U,\ x \neq y :\ \Pr_{h \in H}[h(x) = h(y)] \leq \frac{1}{m}$.

The privacy amplification permits the extraction of secret information, probably to be used as a cryptographic key, from a large data volume, that is only partially secret. The privacy amplification allows a large set of applications, according to the key (Maurer, 1995).

The next sections present a new derivation of the leftover hash lemma, based on the Rényi entropy of order two, also known as collision probability, to derive an upper bound on the statistical distance between the key and seed joint probability, and the hash bit sequence distribution.

### 8.7.1 Objectives of the Hash Function

A cryptographic hash function is used to verify whether a data file maps onto a certain hash value. On the other had, it is difficult to reconstruct the information based on the hash value. Therefore, it is used to assure data integrity, and is the building block of a Hash-based Message Authentication Code (HMAC), which provide message authentication.

The ideal cryptographic hash function has some desired properties. It is a deterministic function, that is, identical messages result in the same hash. It is fast to compute the hash value for a given message. It is impracticable to generate a message from its hash value, except by trying all possible messages, therefore the hash is a one-way function.

Additionally, a small change to a message should cause an avalanche effect, that is, it changes the digest so considerably, that the new hash value seems uncorrelated with the old hash value. It is collision resistant, that is, it is impractical to find two different messages with the same hash value. A cryptographic hash function should resist attacks on its pre-image.

The hash function creates a unidirectional process, that makes it impossible to guess the original contents of a file, based only on the message digest. In the following there is a short description of some known commercial algorithms (Wikipedia, 2019).

*Message-Digest algorithm* 4 (MD4), an algorithm developed between 1990 and 1991 by Ron Rivest. Is suffered several attacks, and has been considered an insecure algorithm. It is described in RFC 1320; MD5, described in RFC 1321.

The Message-Digest algorithm 5 (MD5) is a hash algorithm with 128 bits, developed by RSA Data Security, Inc. and described in RFC 1321. It is used in peer-to-peer protocols (P2P) for identity verification and logins. Attach methods have been published for the MD5. The algorithm produces a digest with 128 bits (16 bytes).

The Secure Hash Algorithm 1 (SHA-1) algorithm was jointly developed by the National Institute of Standards and Technology (NIST) and by the National Security Agency (NSA), in the United States. It presented problems, and the new versions SHA-2 and SHA-3 are in use. The program produces a digest with 160 bits (20 bytes).

The Secure Hash Algorithm 3 (SHA-3) was announced by NIST, in 2015. It is a subset of the Keccak cryptographic family, developed by Guido Bertoni, Joan Daemen, Michael Peeters and Gilles Van Assche. The algorithm produces digests with 224 bits, 256 bits, 384 bits and 512 bits. In the Bitcoin blockchain, the mining process is conducted by running SHA-256 hashing functions.

Whirlpool, is a cryptographic hash function developed by Paulo S. L. M. Barreto and by Vincent Rijmen, and adopted the International Organization for Standardization (ISO) and by the International Electrotechnical Commission (IEC) as part of the ISO 10118-3 standard. The algorithm produces a digest with 512 bits (64 bytes)

The RACE Integrity Primitives Evaluation Message Digest (RIPEMD-160) represents a family of cryptographic hash functions developed, in 1996, by Hans Dobbertin, Antoon Bosselaers and Bart Preneel, from the research group COSIC, Katholieke Universiteit Leuven. The software produces a digest with 160 bits (20 bytes).

BLAKE2 was created, in 2012, by Jean-Philippe Aumasson, Samuel Neves, Zooko Wilcox-O'Hearn, and Christian Winnerlein to replace algorithms MD5 and SHA-1.

### 8.7.2 Mathematical Preliminaries

Consider the random variable $X \in \mathcal{X}$, in a non-empty finite set, and two probability distributions, $P$ e $Q$, defined in this set. Define the statistical distance, a measure of distance between the referred probability distributions, as (Alencar and Assis, 2020)

$$\Delta[P,Q] = \frac{1}{2}\sum_{x\in\mathcal{X}} |P(x) - Q(x)| = \frac{1}{2}\sum_{l=1}^{L} |p(x_l) - q(x_l)|, \tag{8.26}$$

in which $L = |\mathcal{X}|$ is the number of distinct symbols in the message or file, $p(x_l)$ ans $q(x_l)$ represent the individual symbol probabilities, for the respective distributions $P$ and $Q$.

The collision probability is defined as,

$$P_C(X) = \sum_{x\in\mathcal{X}} p_X^2(x) = \sum_{l=1}^{L} p^2(x_l). \tag{8.27}$$

The uniform distribution has a small coincidence index, or collision probability, $P_C(X) = 1/L$, and any other distribution has a larger index.

The Rényi entropy of order $\alpha$ $(\alpha > 0, \alpha \neq 1)$ is defined as (Rényi, 1961)

$$H_\alpha(X) = \frac{1}{1-\alpha} \log \sum_{i=l}^{L} p^\alpha(x_l), \; \alpha \neq 1. \tag{8.28}$$

For the case $\alpha = 2$, one obtains the Rényi entropy of order two,

$$H_2(X) = -\log P_C(X) = -\log \sum_{i=l}^{L} p^2(x_l). \tag{8.29}$$

The following development demonstrates an inequality that involves the collision probability and the statistical distance. From Formula 8.27, it is possible to obtain

$$\sum_{x\in\mathcal{X}}\left[p_X(x)-\frac{1}{L}\right]^2=\sum_{1}^{L}\left[p_X^2(x)-2p_X(x)\frac{1}{L}+\frac{1}{L^2}\right] \tag{8.30}$$
$$=P_C(X)-\frac{1}{L}.$$

Considering that $Y\in\mathcal{Y}$ is a random variable defines as

$$Y=\left[p_X(x)-\frac{1}{L}\right], \tag{8.31}$$

its mean squared value is given by

$$\mathrm{E}[Y^2]=\frac{1}{L}\left[P_C(X)-\frac{1}{L}\right]=\frac{LP_C(X)-1}{L^2}. \tag{8.32}$$

Applying the inequality $\mathrm{E}^2[Y]\leq\mathrm{E}[Y^2]$, one obtains

$$\mathrm{E}[Y]\leq\sqrt{\mathrm{E}[Y^2]}=\frac{\sqrt{LP_C(X)-1}}{L}. \tag{8.33}$$

From the definition of statistical distance, from Formula 8.26,

$$\Delta[P,U]=\frac{1}{2}\sum_{x\in\mathcal{X}}\left|p_X(x)-\frac{1}{L}\right|=\frac{L\mathrm{E}[Y]}{2}, \tag{8.34}$$

in which $U\in\mathcal{U}$ represents the uniform distribution.

Substituting the result from 8.33, it is possible to obtain the main inequality

$$\Delta[P,U]\leq\frac{\sqrt{LP_C(X)-1}}{2}, \tag{8.35}$$

that relates the statistical distance and the collision probability.

### 8.7.3 Privacy Amplification

The privacy amplification theorem is related to the production of universal hash functions, as described in the following (Berens, 2013). First, assume that a sequence of $n$ bits has been generated, related to the random variable $X$, defined in the set $\mathcal{X}$ (Stinson, 1994a).

For non-empty finite sets, $\mathcal{X}$, $\mathcal{S}$ e $\mathcal{Z}$, consider that $X \in \mathcal{X}$ is a random variable that represents the transmitted message, that $S$ is a random variable uniformly distributed in the set of seeds $\mathcal{S}$, and that $Z \in \mathcal{Z}$ is the resulting random variable $f : \mathcal{X} \times \mathcal{S} \mapsto \mathcal{Z}$. Then, $f$ is called a universal hash function, if (Carter and Wegman, 1979)

$$P\left[f(x, S) = f(x', S)\right] \leq \frac{1}{|\mathcal{Z}|}, \tag{8.36}$$

in which $|\cdot|$ represents the cardinality, and the operation is valid for every choice of $x \neq x'$, that are elements of $\mathcal{X}$.

In other words, any two keys of the considered universal set may collide with probability at most $\frac{1}{|\mathcal{Z}|}$ when the hash function $f$ is drawn randomly from the set. This is exactly the expected probability of collision if the hash function assigned truly random hash codes to every key.

From a seed, represented by the random variable $S$, uniformity distributed in the set $\mathcal{S}$, it is possible to generate a safe key $K = f(X, S)$, of length $r$, with the application of a universal hash function $X$ and $S$, as follows, $f : \mathcal{X} \times \mathcal{S} \mapsto \{0, 1\}^r$, in which $1 \leq r \leq \infty$.

Given that the hash function $f$ and the random variable $S$ are public, the question is to know if the produced key is in fact safe.

The following result, known as the leftover hash lemma establishes that, given that the entropy of the sequence of $n$ bits of $X$ is superior to the sequence of the $r$ bits of the key, the key is supposed to have been uniformly generated (Stinson, 1994b).

$$\Delta\left[P_{K,S}, U_{\{0,1\}^r} \cdot P_S\right] \leq \frac{1}{2} \cdot \left[2^{-\frac{1}{2}[H_2(X)-r]}\right], \tag{8.37}$$

in which $P_{K,S}$ is the joint distribution of the key and seed, $P_S$ is the seed distribution, $U_{\{0,1\}^r}$ is the hash sequence uniform distribution, of length $r$ and $H_2(X)$ is the Rényi entropy of order two.

This result is also known as the privacy amplification theorem. In the following, there is a new derivation of the leftover hash lemma, that uses the collision probability.

In order to obtain Inequality 8.37, consider the following inequality, obtained from the Rényi entropy, for the case $\alpha = 2$,

$$H_2(X) = -\log P_C(X) = -\log \sum_{i=l}^{L} p^2(x_l). \tag{8.38}$$

This entropy is the negative of the logarithm of the coincidence index. It follows from the Jensen inequality (Alencar and Alencar, 2024), that the Rényi entropy of order two, or collision entropy, is limited by the Shannon entropy

$$H_2(X) \leq H(X), \tag{8.39}$$

with equality, if and only if, the probability distribution of $X$ is uniform.

Substituting the adequate parameters, one obtains

$$\Delta\left[P_{K,S}, U_{\{0,1\}^r} \cdot P_S\right] \leq \frac{\sqrt{|\mathcal{K}| P_C(K,S) - 1}}{2}. \tag{8.40}$$

Recalling that the probability distribution associated to the key is uniform, and that each key has length $r$, one has $|\mathcal{K}| = 2^r$. Also, substituting result 8.34 into 8.40, one obtains

$$\Delta\left[P_{K,S}, U_{\{0,1\}^r} \cdot P_S\right] \leq \frac{1}{2}\sqrt{2^r 2^{-H_2(K,S)} - 1}. \tag{8.41}$$

Considering that the mapping $f : \mathcal{X} \times \mathcal{S} \mapsto \{0,1\}^r$ cannot increase the entropy, then $H(K,S) \leq H(X)$, which, after substitution into 8.41 gives

$$\begin{aligned} \Delta\left[P_{K,S}, U_{\{0,1\}^r} \cdot P_S\right] &\leq \frac{1}{2} \cdot \left[2^{r - H_2(K,S)} - 1\right]^{1/2} \\ &\leq \frac{1}{2} \cdot \left[2^{r - H_2(K,S)}\right]^{1/2}, \end{aligned} \tag{8.42}$$

recalling that the probability is always positive or null.

Rewriting the inequality, exchanging the positions of the Rényi entropy, and the number of symbols $r$, with the resulting change in the signal, one obtains the result,

$$\Delta\left[P_{K,S}, U_{\{0,1\}^r} \cdot P_S\right] \leq \frac{1}{2} \cdot \left[2^{-\frac{1}{2}[H_2(K,S) - r]}\right]. \tag{8.43}$$

# Appendix A

## Probability Theory

*"The probability of apocalypse soon cannot be realistically estimated, but it is surely too high for any sane person to contemplate with equanimity."*
Noam Chomsky

### A.1 Set Theory and Measure

Georg Cantor (1845-1918) developed the modern theory of sets, in the end of the nineteenth century, established the mathematical and logical basis for the theory and demonstrated several important results. The concept of set cardinality, defined by Cantor, was fundamental to the theory. Cantor was born in Saint Petersburg, but lived most of his academic life in the city of Halle, Germany (Boyer, 1974). The basic ideas of universal set, empty set, set partition, discrete systems, continuous systems and infinity are as old as humanity itself.

Over the years, philosophers and mathematicians had tried to characterize the infinite, with no success. In 1872, J. W. R. Dedekind (1831-1916) indicated the universal property of infinite sets. He stated that a set is called infinite when it is similar to a part of itself, on the contrary the set is finite (Boyer, 1974).

Cantor also investigated the properties of infinite sets but, different from Dedekind, he noticed that the infinite sets are not the same. This led to the concept of cardinal numbers, to establish a hierarchy of infinite sets in accordance with their respective powers. Cantor ideas established the set theory as a complete subject. As a consequence of his published results on transfinite arithmetic, considered advanced for his time, Cantor suffered attacks from mathematicians like Leopold Kronecker (1823-1891), who barred him for a position at the University of Berlin.

Cantor found a position at the ancient and small University of Halle, in the medieval city of Halle in Germany, famous for its mines of rock salt, and died there in an institution for mental health treatment, following his attempts to apply his theory to justify religious paradigms in scientific events .

### A.1.1 Basic Set Theory

The notion of a set, as simple as it can be, is axiomatic, in a sense that a it does not admit a definition that does not resort to the original notion of a set. The mathematical concept of a set is fundamental for all known mathematics, and is used to build important concepts, such as relation, Cartesian product and function. It is also the basis for the modern measure theory, developed by Henry Lebesgue (1875-1941).

The set theory is based on a set of fundamental axioms: Axiom of Extension, Axiom of Specification, Peano's Axioms, Axiom of Choice, besides Zorn's Lemma and Schröder - Bernstein's Theorem (Halmos, 1960).

The objective of this section is to present the theory of sets in an informal manner, just quoting those fundamental axioms, since this theory is used as a basis to establish a probability measure. Some examples of common sets are given in the following.

- The binary set: $\mathbb{B} = \{0, 1\}$;
- The set of natural numbers, including zero: $\mathbb{N} = \{0, 1, 2, 3, \ldots\}$;
- The set of odd numbers: $\mathbb{O} = \{1, 3, 5, 7, 9, \ldots\}$;
- The set of integer numbers: $\mathbb{Z} = \{\ldots, -3, -2, -1, -2, 0, 1, 2, 3, \ldots\}$;
- The set of real numbers: $\mathbb{R} = (-\infty, \infty)$.

There are two really important relations in set theory: the belonging relation, denoted as $a \in A$, in which $a$ is an element of the set $A$, and the inclusion relation, $A \subset B$, which is read "$A$ is a subset of the set $B$", or $B$ is a super set of the set $A$. Sets may also be specified by propositions. For example, the empty set can be written as $\emptyset = \{a \,|\, a \neq a\}$, i.e., the set the elements of which are different from themselves.

A universal set contains all other sets of interest. An example of a universal set is provided by the sample space in probability theory, usually denoted as $S$ or $\Omega$. The empty set is that set which contains no element, usually denoted as $\emptyset$ or $\{\ \}$. It is implicit that the empty set is contained in any set, i.e., that $\emptyset \subset A$, for any given set $A$. However, the empty set is not in general an element of any other set.

A usual way to represent sets is by means of the Venn diagram, as illustrated in Figure A.1.

Sets are said to be *disjoint* if they have no element in common, as illustrated in Figure A.2. Thus, for example, the set of even natural numbers and the set of odd natural numbers are disjoint.

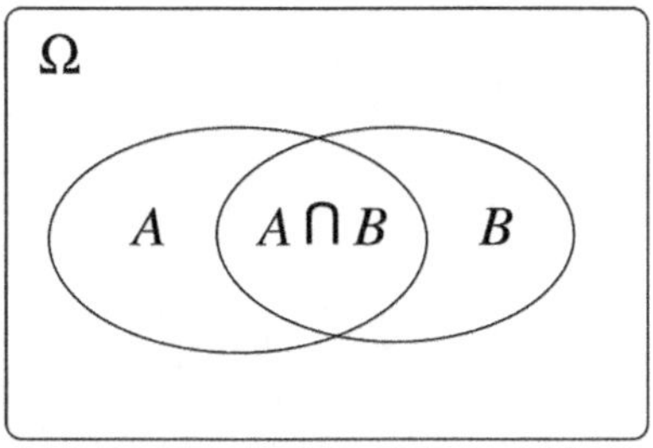


**Figure A.1** A Venn diagram that represents two intersecting sets.

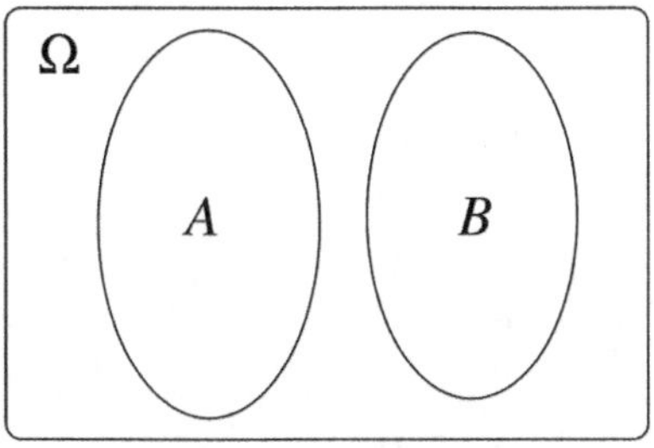


**Figure A.2** A Venn diagram representing disjoint sets.

### A.1.2 Some Operations on Sets

It is possible to operate on sets to produce new sets, or families of sets. The basic set operations are the complement, the union, the intersection, the subtraction and the symmetric difference.

- The operation $\overline{A}$ represents the complement of $A$ with respect to the sample space $\Omega$;
- The union of two sets is composed of elements that belong to $A$ or to $B$, and is written as $A \cup B$;
- The intersection of two sets is composed of elements that belong to $A$ and to $B$, and is written as $A \cap B$;
- The subtraction of sets, denoted $C = A - B$, gives as a result the set the elements of which belong to $A$ and do not belong to $B$.
  Note: If $B$ is completely contained in $A : A - B = A \cap \overline{B}$;
- The symmetric difference is defined as the set of elements that belong to $A$ and to $B$, but do not belong to $(A \cap B)$. It written commonly as $A \Delta B = A \cup B - A \cap B$.

The generalization of these concepts to families of sets, as for example $\cup_{i=1}^{N} A_i$ and $\cap_{i=1}^{N} A_i$, is immediate. The following properties are usually employed as axioms in developing the theory of sets (Lipschutz, 1968).

- **Idempotent**
  $A \cup A = A, \qquad A \cap A = A$
- **Associative**
  $(A \cup B) \cup C = A \cup (B \cup C), \qquad (A \cap B) \cap C = A \cap (B \cap C)$
- **Commutative**
  $A \cup B = B \cup A, \qquad A \cap B = B \cap A$
- **Distributive**
  $A \cup (B \cap C) = (A \cup B) \cap (A \cup C),$
  $A \cap (B \cup C) = (A \cap B) \cup (A \cap C)$
- **Identity**
  $A \cup \emptyset = A, \qquad A \cap U = A$
  $A \cup U = U, \qquad A \cap \emptyset = \emptyset$
- **Complementary**
  $A \cup \overline{A} = U, \qquad A \cap \overline{A} = \emptyset \qquad \overline{(\overline{A})} = A$
  $U = \emptyset, \qquad \overline{\emptyset} = U$
- **de Morgan laws**
  $\overline{A \cup B} = \overline{A} \cap \overline{B}, \qquad \overline{A \cap B} = \overline{A} \cup \overline{B}$

### A.1.3 Families of Sets

The concept of family is important to characterize finite or infinite combinations of sets. The increasing sequence of sets, such that $\lim_{i \to \infty} \cup A_i = A$, is one of the most useful families of sets. This sequence is used in proofs of limits over sets.

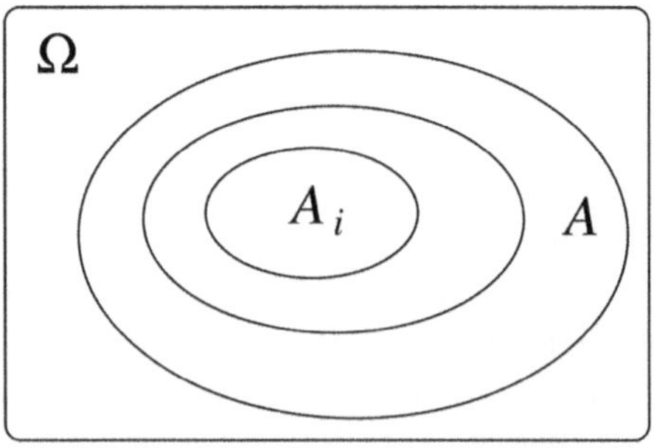


**Figure A.3** Increasing sequence of sets.

The decreasing sequence of sets is defined in a similar manner, as $\lim_{i \to \infty} \cap A_i = A$, and is also used in proofs of limits over sets.

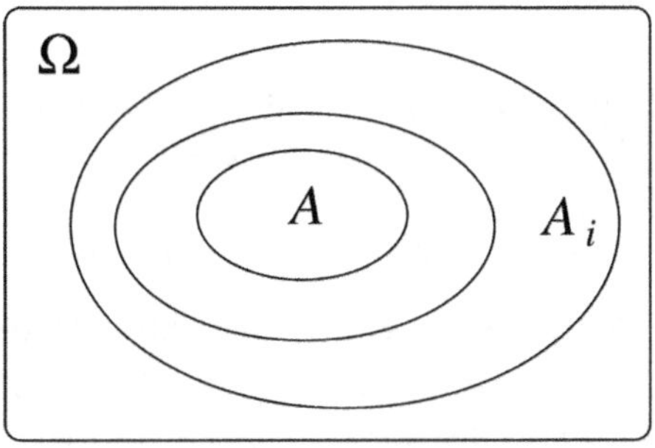


**Figure A.4** Decreasing sequence of sets.

### A.1.4 Indexing of Sets

The Cartesian product is useful to express the idea of indexing of sets. Indexing expands the possibilities for the use of sets, and permits to generate new entities, such as vectors and signals.

**Example**: Consider $A_i = \{0, 1\}$. Starting from this set it is possible to construct an indexed sequence of sets by defining its indexing: $\{A_{i \epsilon I}\}$, $I = \{0, \cdots, 7\}$. This family of indexed sets $A_i$ constitutes a finite discrete sequence, i.e., a vector.

**Example**: Again, let $A_i = \{0, 1\}$, but now use $I = \mathbb{Z}$, the set of positive and negative integers plus zero. It follows that $\{A_{i \epsilon Z}\}$, which represents an infinite series of 0's and 1's, i.e., it represents a binary digital signal. For example, $\cdots$ 0011111000 $\cdots$.

**Example**: Using the same set $A_i = \{0, 1\}$, but now indexing over the set of real numbers, $\{A_{i \epsilon I}\}$, in which $I = \mathbb{R}$, it is possible to form a signal which is discrete in amplitude but continuous in time.

**Example**: Considering $A = \mathbb{R}$ and $I = \mathbb{R}$, the resulting set represents an analog signal, this is, a signal that is continuous in time and in amplitude.

### A.1.5 An Algebra of Sets

For the construction of an algebra of sets or, equivalently, for the construction of a field over which operations involving sets make sense, a few properties have to be obeyed.

1. If $A \in \mathcal{F}$ then $\overline{A} \in \mathcal{F}$. $A$ is the set containing desired results, or over which one wants to operate;

2. If $A \in \mathcal{F}$ and $B \in \mathcal{F}$ then $A \cup B \in \mathcal{F}$.

The properties guarantee the closure of the algebra with respect to finite operations over sets. It is noticed that the universal set $\Omega$ always belongs to the algebra, i.e., $\Omega \in \mathcal{F}$, because $\Omega = A \cup \overline{A}$. The empty set also belongs to the algebra, i.e., $\emptyset \in \mathcal{F}$, since $\emptyset = \overline{\Omega}$, follows by property 1.

**Example:** The family $\{\emptyset, \Omega\}$ complies with the above properties and therefore represents an algebra. In this case $\emptyset = \{\}$ and $\overline{\emptyset} = \Omega$. The union is also represented, as can be easily checked.

**Example:** Given the sets $\{C_H\}$ and $\{C_T\}$, representing the faces of a coin, respectively, if $\{C_H\} \in \mathcal{F}$ then $\overline{\{C_H\}} = \{C_T\} \in \mathcal{F}$. It follows that $\{C_H, C_T\} \in \mathcal{F} \Rightarrow \Omega \in \mathcal{F} \Rightarrow \emptyset \in \mathcal{F}$.

The previous example can be explained by the following argument. If there a measure for heads then there must be also a measure for tails, if the algebra is to be properly defined. Whenever a probability is assigned to an event then a probability must also be assigned to the complementary event.

The cardinality of a finite set is defined as the number of elements belonging to this set. Sets with an infinite number of elements are said to have the same cardinality if they are equivalent, i.e., $A \sim B$ if $\sharp A = \sharp B$. Some examples of sets and their respective cardinals are presented next.

- $I = \{1, \cdots, k\} \Rightarrow C_I = k$;
- $\mathbb{N} = \{0, 1, \cdots\} \Rightarrow C_N$ or $\aleph_0$;
- $\mathbb{Z} = \{\cdots, -2, -1, 0, 1, 2, \cdots\} \Rightarrow C_Z$;
- $\mathbb{Q} = \{\cdots, -1/3, 0, 1/3, 1/2, \cdots\} \Rightarrow C_Q$;
- $\mathbb{R} = (-\infty, \infty) \Rightarrow C_R$ or $\aleph$;

For the above examples the following relations are verified: $C_{\mathbb{R}} > C_{\mathbb{Q}} = C_{\mathbb{Z}} = C_{\mathbb{N}} > C_I$. The notation $\aleph_0$, for the cardinality of the set of natural numbers was first employed by Cantor.

The cardinality of the power set, i.e., of the family of sets consisting of all subsets of a given set $I$, $\mathcal{F} = 2^I$, is $2^{C_I}$.

### A.1.6 The Borel Algebra

The Borel algebra, established by Félix Edouard Juston Émile Borel (1871-1956), and written as $\mathcal{B}$, or $\sigma$-algebra, is an extension of the algebra so far discussed to operate with limits at infinity. The following properties are required from a $\sigma$-algebra.

1. $A \in \mathcal{B} \Rightarrow \overline{A} \in \mathcal{B}$

2. $A_i \in \mathcal{B} \Rightarrow \bigcup_{i=1}^{\infty} A_i \in \mathcal{B}$

The properties guarantee the closure of the $\sigma$-algebra with respect to enumerable operations over sets. They allow the definition of limits in the Borel field.

**Example:** Considering the above properties it can be verified that $A_1 \cap A_2 \cap A_3 \cdots \in \mathcal{B}$. In effect, it is sufficient to notice that

$$A \in \mathcal{B} \text{ and } B \in \mathcal{B} \Rightarrow \mathcal{A} \cup \mathcal{B} \in \mathcal{B},$$

and

$$\overline{A} \in \mathcal{B} \text{ and } \overline{\mathcal{B}} \in \mathcal{B} \Rightarrow \overline{\mathcal{A}} \cup \overline{\mathcal{B}} \in \mathcal{B},$$

and finally

$$\overline{\overline{A} \cup \overline{B}} \in \mathcal{B} \Rightarrow \mathcal{A} \cap \mathcal{B} \in \mathcal{B}.$$

In summary, any combination of unions and intersections of sets belongs to the Borel algebra. In other words, operations of union or intersection of sets, or a combination of these operations, produce a set that belongs to the $\sigma$-algebra.

## A.2 Basic Probability Theory

The first known published book on probability is *De Ludo Aleae* (About Games of Chance), by the Italian medical doctor and mathematician Girolamo Cardano (1501-1576), which came out in 1663, almost 90 years after his death. This book was a handbook for players, containing some discussion on probability.

The first mathematical treatise about the Theory of Probability, published in 1657, was written by the Dutch scientist Christian Huygens (1629-1695), a folder titled *De Ratiociniis in Ludo Aleae* (About Reasoning in Games of Chance).

Abraham de Moivre (1667-1754) was an important mathematician who worked on the development of Probability Theory. He wrote a book of great influence in his time, called *Doctrine of Chances*. The law of large numbers was discussed by Jacques Bernoulli (1654-1705), Swiss mathematician, in his work Ars Conjectandi (The Art of Conjecturing).

The study of probability was improved in the $18^{th}$ and $19^{th}$ centuries, being worth of mentioning the works of French mathematicians Pierre-Simon de Laplace (1749-1827) and Siméon Poisson (1781-1840), as well as the German mathematician Karl Friedrich Gauss (1777-1855).

### A.2.1 The Axioms of Probability

The basic axioms of probability were established by Andrei Nikolaevich Kolmogorov (1903-1987), and allowed the development of the complete theory. The three statements are as follows (Papoulis, 1983):

1. Axiom 1 – $P(\Omega) = 1$, in which $\Omega$ denotes the sample space or universal set and $P(\cdot)$ denotes the associated probability;
2. Axiom 2 – $P(A) \geq 0$, in which $A$ denotes an event belonging to the sample space;
3. Axiom 3 – $P(A \cup B) = P(A) + P(B)$, in which $A$ and $B$ are mutually exclusive events and $A \cup B$ denotes the union of events $A$ and $B$.

Kolmogorov established a firm mathematical basis on which other theories rely, including the Theory of Stochastic Processes, the Communications Theory and the Information Theory, that use his axiomatic approach to Probability Theory.

Kolmogorov's fundamental work was published in 1933, in Russian, and soon afterwards was translated to German with the title *Grundbegriffe der Wahrscheinlichkeits Rechnung* (Fundamentals of Probability Theory) (James, 1981). In this work Kolmogorov managed to combine Advanced Set Theory, developed by Cantor, with Measure Theory, established by Lebesgue, to produce what to this date is the modern approach to Probability Theory.

The application of the axioms makes it possible to deduce all results relative to Probability Theory. For example, the probability of the empty set, $\emptyset = \{\}$, is easily calculated as follows. First it is noticed that

$$\emptyset \cup \Omega = \Omega,$$

since the sets $\emptyset$ and $\Omega$ are disjoint. Thus it follows that

$$P(\emptyset \cup \Omega) = P(\Omega) = P(\emptyset) + P(\Omega) = 1 \Rightarrow P(\emptyset) = 0.$$

In the case of sets $A$ and $B$ which are not disjoint it follows that

$$P(A \cup B) = P(A) + P(B) - P(A \cap B).$$

### A.2.2 Bayes' Rule

Bayes' rule, which is essential for the development of Information Theory, concerns the computation of conditional probabilities and can be expressed by the following definition,

$$P(A|B) = \frac{P(A \cap B)}{P(B)},$$

assuming $P(B) \neq 0$.

An equivalent manner of expressing the same result is the following,

$$P(A \cap B) = P(A|B) \cdot P(B) \ , \ \ P(B) \neq 0.$$

Some important properties of sets are presented next, in which $A$ and $B$ denote events from a given sample space.

- If A is independent of B, then $P(A|B) = P(A)$. It then follows that $P(B|A) = P(B)$ and that $B$ is independent of $A$.
- If $B \subset A$, then: $P(A|B) = 1$.
- If $A \subset B$, then: $P(A|B) = \frac{P(A)}{P(B)} \geq P(A)$.
- If $A$ and $B$ are independent events then $P(A \cap B) = P(A) \cdot P(B)$.
- If $P(A) = 0$ or $P(A) = 1$, then event $A$ is independent of itself.
- If $P(B) = 0$, then $P(A|B)$ can assume any arbitrary value. Usually in this case one assumes $P(A|B) = P(A)$.
- If events $A$ and $B$ are disjoint, and non-empty, then they are dependent.

A partition is a possible splitting of the sample space into a family of subsets, in a manner that the subsets in this family are disjoint and their union coincides with the sample space. It follows that any set in the sample space can be expressed by using a partition of that sample space, and thus be written as a union of disjoint events.

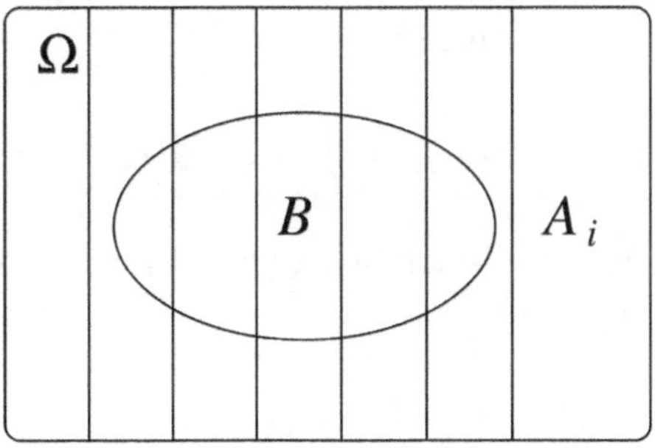


**Figure A.5** Partition of set $B$ by a family of sets $\{A_i\}$.

The following property can be illustrated by means of the Venn diagram, as illustrated in Figure A.5.

$$B = B \cap \Omega = B \cap \cup_{i=1}^{M} A_i = \cup_{i=1}^{N} B \cap A_i.$$

It now follows that

$$P(B) = P(\cup_{i=1}^{N} B \cap A_i) = \sum_{i=1}^{N} P(B \cap A_i),$$

$$P(A_i|B) = \frac{P(A_i \cap B)}{P(B)} = \frac{P(B|A_i) \cdot P(A_i)}{\sum_{i=1}^{N} P(B \cap A_i)} = \frac{P(B|A_i) \cdot P(A_i)}{\sum_{i=1}^{N} P(B|A_i) \cdot P(A_i)}.$$

## A.3 Random Variables

A random variable (r.v.) $X$ represents a mapping of the sample space on the line, that is, the set of real numbers. A random variable is usually characterized by a cumulative probability function (CPF) $P_X(x)$, or by a probability density function (pdf) $p_X(x)$.

**Example:** A random variable with a uniform probability density function, in the interval $[0, 1]$, is described by the formula

$$p_X(x) = u(x) - u(x-1).$$

It follows, by Axiom 1, that

$$\int_{-\infty}^{+\infty} p_X(x)dx = 1. \tag{A.1}$$

In general, for a given probability distribution, the probability that $X$ belongs to the interval $(a, b]$ is given by

$$P(a < x \leq b) = \int_a^b p_X(x)dx. \tag{A.2}$$

The cumulative probability function $P_X(x)$, of a random variable $X$, is defined as the integral of $p_X(x)$,

$$P_X(x) = \int_{-\infty}^{x} p_X(t)dt. \tag{A.3}$$

### A.3.1 Expected Value of a Random Variable

Let $f(X)$ denote a function of a random variable $X$. The average value, or expected value, of the function $f(X)$ with respect to $X$ is defined as

$$E[f(X)] = \int_{-\infty}^{+\infty} f(x)p_X(x)dx. \tag{A.4}$$

The following properties of the expected value follow from (A.4).

$$E[\alpha X] = \alpha E[X], \tag{A.5}$$

$$E[X + Y] = E[X] + E[Y] \tag{A.6}$$

and if $X$ and $Y$ are independent random variables then

$$E[XY] = E[X] \cdot E[Y]. \tag{A.7}$$

### A.3.2 Moments of a Random Variable

The $k^{th}$ moment of a random variable $X$ is defined as

$$m_k = E[X^k] = \int_{-\infty}^{+\infty} x^k p_X(x) dx. \tag{A.8}$$

Various moments of $X$ have special importance and physical interpretation, as defined in the following:

- $E[X]$, arithmetic mean, average value, average voltage, statistical mean;
- $E[X^2]$, quadratic mean, total power;
- $E[X^3]$, measure of asymmetry of the probability density function;
- $E[X^4]$, measure of flatness of the probability density function.

### A.3.3 Variance of a Random Variable

The variance of a random variable $X$ is an important quantity in communication theory, usually meaning AC power, defined as follows,

$$V[X] = \sigma_X^2 = E\left[(X - E[X])^2\right]. \tag{A.9}$$

The standard deviation $\sigma_X$ is defined as the square root of the variance of $X$.

### A.3.4 Characteristic Function

The characteristic function $P_X(w)$, also called moment generating function, of a random variable $X$ is usually defined based on the Fourier transform of the probability density function (pdf) of $X$, which is equivalent to substitute $f(x) = e^{-j\omega x}$ in (A.4), that is,

$$P_X(w) = E[e^{-j\omega x}] = \int_{-\infty}^{+\infty} e^{-j\omega x} p_X(x) dx, \text{ in which } j = \sqrt{-1}. \tag{A.10}$$

The statistical moments of a random variable $X$ can also be obtained directly from then characteristic function, as follows,

$$m_i = \frac{1}{(-j)^i} \frac{\partial^i P_X(w)}{\partial w^i} |_{w=0} \,. \tag{A.11}$$

Given that $X$ is a random variable, it follows that $Y = f(X)$ is also a random variable, obtained by the application of the transformation $f(\cdot)$. The probability density function of $Y$ is related to that of $X$ by the formula (Blake, 1987)

$$p_Y(y) = \frac{p_X(x)}{|dy/dx|} |_{x=f^{-1}(y)} \,, \tag{A.12}$$

in which $f^{-1}(\cdot)$ denotes the inverse function of $f(\cdot)$. This formula assumes the existence of the inverse function of $f(\cdot)$ as well as its derivative in all points.

#### A.3.4.1 Two Important Distributions

Two important distributions, which appear frequently in engineering problems, are presented in the following, the Gaussian and the sinusoidal random variables.

1. **Gaussian random variable**
   The random variable $X$ with pdf

   $$p_X(x) = \frac{1}{\sigma_X \sqrt{2\pi}} e^{-\frac{(x-m_X)^2}{2\sigma_X^2}} \tag{A.13}$$

   is called a Gaussian (or Normal) random variable.
   The Gaussian random variable plays an important role in engineering, considering that many well known processes can be described or approximated by this pdf. The noise present in either analog or digital communications systems usually can be considered Gaussian as a consequence of the influence of many factors (Leon-Garcia, 1989).
   Note that, in Formula A.13, $m_X$ represents the average value and $\sigma_X^2$ represents the variance of $X$.
2. **Sinusoidal random variable**

   A sinusoidal tone $X(t) = V\cos(\omega_0 t + \phi)$, in which $V$ represents a constant amplitude, $\omega_0$ is a constant frequency, and $\phi$ is a uniformly distributed random variable, has the following pdf

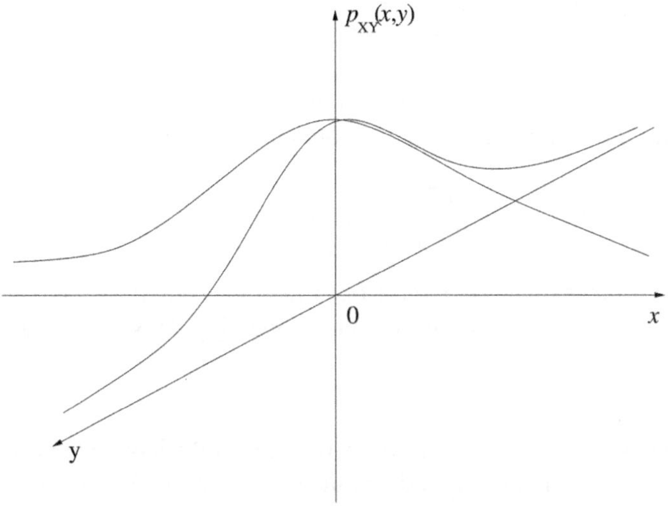


**Figure A.6** Joint probability density function.

$$p_X(x) = \frac{1}{\pi\sqrt{V^2 - x^2}}, \ |x| < V. \tag{A.14}$$

### A.3.5 Joint Random Variables

Consider that $X$ and $Y$ represent a pair of real random variables, with joint pdf $p_{XY}(x, y)$, as illustrated in Figure A.6. The probability of $x$ and $y$ being simultaneously in the region defined by the polygon [abcd] is given by the expression (Alencar and Alencar, 2024).

$$\text{Prob}(a < x < b, c < y < d) = \int_a^b \int_c^d p_{XY}(x, y)dxdy. \tag{A.15}$$

The individual pdf's of $X$ and $Y$, also called marginal distributions, result from the integration of the joint pdf as follows,

$$p_X(x) = \int_{-\infty}^{+\infty} p_{XY}(x, y)dy, \tag{A.16}$$

and

$$p_Y(y) = \int_{-\infty}^{+\infty} p_{XY}(x, y)dx. \tag{A.17}$$

The joint average $E[f(X, Y)]$ is calculated as

$$E[f(X,Y)] = \int_{-\infty}^{+\infty}\int_{-\infty}^{+\infty} f(x,y)p_{XY}(x,y)dxdy, \tag{A.18}$$

for an arbitrary function $f(X,Y)$ of $X$ and $Y$.

The joint moments $m_{ik}$, of order $ik$, are calculated as

$$m_{ik} = E[X^i, Y^k] = \int_{-\infty}^{+\infty}\int_{-\infty}^{+\infty} x^i y^k p_{XY}(xy)dxdy. \tag{A.19}$$

The two-dimensional characteristic function is defined as the two-dimensional Fourier transform of the joint probability density $p_{XY}(x,y)$

$$P_{XY}(\omega,\nu) = E[e^{-j\omega X - j\nu Y}]. \tag{A.20}$$

When the sum $Z = X + Y$ of two statistically independent random variables is considered, it is noticed that the characteristic function of $Z$ turns out to be

$$P_Z(\omega) = E[e^{-j\omega Z}] = E[e^{-j\omega(X+Y)}] = P_X(\omega)\cdot P_Y(\omega). \tag{A.21}$$

As far as the probability density function of $Z$ is concerned, it can be said that

$$p_Z(z) = \int_{-\infty}^{\infty} p_X(\rho)p_Y(z-\rho)d\rho, \tag{A.22}$$

or

$$p_Z(z) = \int_{-\infty}^{\infty} p_X(z-\rho)p_Y(\rho)d\rho. \tag{A.23}$$

Equivalently, the sum of two statistically independent random variables has a probability density function given by the convolution of the respective pdf's of the random variables involved in the sum.

The random variables $X$ and $Y$ are said to be uncorrelated if the expected value of their product is the product of their expectations, that is,

$$E[XY] = E[X]\cdot E[Y]. \tag{A.24}$$

The criterion of statistical independence of random variables, which is stronger than correlation, is satisfied if the joint probability density function can be expressed as the product of the marginal distributions,

$$p_{XY}(x,y) = p_X(x)\cdot p_Y(y). \tag{A.25}$$

# Glossary of Information and Coding Theory Terms

*"Data is not information, information is not knowledge, knowledge is not understanding, understanding is not wisdom."*
Clifford Stoll

This glossary presents the fundamental definitions of information theory, communications, network security and includes the acronyms most used by engineers and computer network specialists (Stallings, 1999) (Alencar and da Rocha Jr., 2022) (Furiati, 1998) (Design, 2001) (Skycell, 2001) (MobileWord, 2001) (TIAB2B.com, 2001) (Alencar, 2002) (Alencar, 2022). It is also based on the parameters established by the Center for Studies, Response and Security Incident Handling in Brazil (CERT.br), which is part of the Management Committee of Internet in Brazil (CERT.br, 2019).

**Adware** – Advertising Software. Specific type of spyware. Program designed specifically to display advertisements. It can be used legitimately, when incorporated into programs and services, as a form of sponsorship or financial return for those who develop free programs or provide free services. It can also be used for malicious purposes when the advertisements shown are targeted, according to the user's navigation and without the user knowing that such monitoring is being carried out.

**ANSI** – American National Standards Institute. US-based organization that, among other activities, develops standards for telecommunications.

**Antimalware** – Tool that seeks to detect and then cancel or remove malicious code from a computer. Antivirus, antispyware, antirootkit and antitrojan programs are examples of antimalware tools.

**Anti-spam filter** – Program that allows you to separate emails according to predefined rules. Used both for the management of mailboxes and for the selection of valid e-mails from the various spam received.

**Antivirus** – Type of antimalware tool developed to detect, cancel and eliminate viruses and other types of malicious code from a computer. It can also include personal firewall functionality.

**AP** – Access Point. Device that acts as a bridge between a wireless network and a traditional network.

**ARP** – Address Resolution Protocol. Enables the packaging of IP data into Ethernet packets, being used to find an Ethernet network through a specific IP number.

**ARQ** – Automatic ReQuest for retransmission or automatic request for retransmission. Elementary protection scheme against transmission errors in which the receiver detects errors and automatically requests the retransmission of information c c a o.

**Artifact** – Any information left by an attacker on a compromised system, such as programs, scripts, tools, logs and files.

**ASCII** – American Standard Code for Information Interchange or code for information exchange. Each ASCII character is formed by a seven-bit code plus a parity bit.

**ATM** – Asynchronous transfer mode. Data transfer pattern using a total of 53 bytes packets, with 5 bytes for addressing and 48 bytes of information.

**Attack** – Any attempt, successful or unsuccessful, to access or unauthorized use of a service, computer or network.

**Attacker** – Person responsible for an attack, an attempted access or unauthorized use of a program/computer.

**AT&T** – American Telephone and Telegraph. Long distance operator in the USA.

**AWGN** – Additive white Gaussian noise or channel. Channel with broadband noise with flat power spectral density.

**Backdoor** – Type of malicious code. A program that allows an attacker to return to a compromised computer, by including services created or modified for this purpose. Usually this program is placed in such a way that it is not noticed.

**Bandwidth** – Amount of data that can be transmitted on a communication channel, in a given time interval.

**BCH** – Bose-Chaudhuri-Hocquenghem. Family of linear block codes used for error correction.

**BER** – Bit error rate. Ratio between the number of bits received in error and the total number of bits transmitted. It is also known as error probability.

**Berlekamp-Massey algorithm** – An algorithm to find the shortest linear-feedback shift register (LFSR) for a given binary output sequence. The algorithm searches the minimal polynomial of a linearly recurrent sequence in an arbitrary field.

**Blacklist** – List of e-mails, domains or IP addresses, known sources of spam. Resource used, both on servers and in e-mail reader programs, to block messages suspected of being spam.

**Block Code** – Block codes are used for error correction. The term refers to any error-correcting code that acts on a block of $k$ bits of input data to produce $n$ bits of output data $(n, k)$.

**Bluetooth** – Standard for data and voice communication technology, based on radio frequency and intended for the connection of devices over short distances, allowing the formation of personal wireless networks.

**BOOTP** The Bootstrap protocol assigns an IP address to computers that do not have a hard disk. The server provides a file with the operating system to run it.

**Botnet** – Network formed by hundreds or thousands of computers infected with bots. It allows to enhance the harmful actions performed by bots and be used in denial of service attacks, fraud schemes, sending spam, among others.

**Bot** – Type of malicious code. Program that, in addition to including functionality of worms, has communication mechanisms with the attacker that allow it to be controlled remotely. The process of infection and propagation of the bot is similar to that of the worm, that is, the bot is able to propagate automatically, exploiting existing vulnerabilities in programs installed on computers.

**Broadband** – Type of connection to the network with capacity above that achieved, usually in dial-up connection via telephone system. There is no definition of broadband metrics that is accepted by everyone, but it is common for broadband connections to be permanent and not switched, such as dial-up connections.

**Brute force** – Type of attack that consists of guessing, by trial and error, a username and password and, thus, executing processes and accessing websites, computers and services in the name and with the same privileges of that user.

**Cardinality** – A measure of the number of elements in a set.

**CCITT** – Former name of ITU-R, ITU committee responsible for technical recommendations for telephone and data transmission systems.

**CD** – Compact Disk.

**Certification authority** – Entity responsible for issuing and managing digital certificates. These certificates can be issued to different types of entities, such as: person, computer, department of an institution, institution etc.

**Code distance** – The minimum distance between two distinct code words. It indicates the number of errors a code can correct.

**CODEC** – COder/DECoder. Device that converts analog signals into digital signals and vice versa.

**Code Signing** – A certificate for software developers to digitally sign the source code of applications created by them.

**Coding theory** – The study of the properties of codes and their respective suitability for specific applications.

**Convolutional Code** – Convolutional code is a type of error-correcting code in which the output bits are obtained as a result of logical operation on a current bitstream, along with considering some bits of the previous stream.

**Cookie** – Small file that is saved on the computer when the user accesses a website and sent back to the same website when accessed again. It is used to maintain information about the user, such as shopping cart, product list and browsing preferences.

**Coset** – In algebra, a coset is a subset of mathematical group consisting of all the products obtained by multiplying fixed element of group by each of elements of given subgroup. Given a group $G$ and a subgroup $H$ of $G$, a left coset of $H$ in $G$ is formed by multiplying each element of $H$ by a fixed element $g$ from $G$ on the left side.

**Coset leader** – A coset leader is one of the vectors of minimum weight in the coset.

**COST** – European Commission for Cooperation in Technical and Scientific Research.

**CRC** – Cyclic Redundancy Check. Method for detecting errors in serial transmissions.

**Cryptoanalysis** – The process of identifying or tracking failures or loopholes in a cryptographic system.

**Cryptographic Algorithm** – The computational procedure used to encrypt and decrypt messages.

**Cryptography** – Science and art of writing messages in encrypted form or in code. It is part of a field of study that deals with secret communications. It is used, among other purposes, to: authenticate the identity of users; authenticate bank transactions; protect the integrity of electronic funds transfers; and protect the confidentiality of personal and commercial communications.

**Cryptology** – The study of cryptography and cryptanalysis.

**CSLIP** Compressed SLIP is the data compression for the SLIP protocol, which uses the Van Jacobson algorithm to reduce the packet size. It is also used with PPP, being called CPPP.

**CSR Key** – Text file containing information for requesting the digital certificate and which is generated by the web server.

**Cyclic code** – A block code, for which the circular shifts of each codeword produces another word that belongs to the code.

**DDos** – Distributed Denial of Service. Denial attack that occurs when a set of computers tries to take service out of other computers, networks or programs.

**Decoding** – The process of translating received messages into codewords of a given code.

**Decryption** – The process of converting an encrypted message to the original intelligible message.

**Denial of service** – Malicious activity by which an attacker uses a computer or mobile device to take a service, computer or network connected to the Internet out of operation.

**DHCP** Dynamic Host Configuration Protocol – Designates IP addresses for computers connected to the network. It is a server-based service that automatically assigns IP addresses to each computer that joins the network. DHCP can perform all BOOTP functions.

**Dial-up connection** – Switched connection to the Internet, that is transmitted through an analog modem and a fixed telephone network line, which requires the modem to dial a phone number to access it.

**Digital certificate** – Electronic record consisting of a set of data that distinguishes an entity and associates it with a public key. It can be issued to people, companies, equipment or services on the network (for example, a website) and can be approved for different uses, such as confidentiality and digital signature.

**Digital signature** – Code used to prove the authenticity and integrity of an information, that is, that it was actually generated by those who claim to have done so and that it has not been altered.

**Distance of a code** – The minimum distance between two distinct code words.

**Distributed Denial of Service** – Malicious, coordinated and distributed activity by which a set of computers or mobile devices is used to shut down a service, a computer or a network connected to the Internet.

**DNS** – Domain Name System, responsible for the translation, among other types, of machine/domain names to the corresponding IP address and vice versa.

**DS-SS** – Direct Sequence Spread Spectrum or spectral spread by a direct sequence.

**Eb/No** – Energy-per-bit to noise power density ratio. Figure of merit for digital communication systems.

**E-commerce scam** – Type of fraud in which a scammer, in order to obtain financial advantages, exploits the relationship of trust between the parties involved in a commercial transaction.

**EGP** – Exterior Gateway Protocol. Protocol used between routers of different systems.

**E-mail spoofing** – Technique that consists of altering the header fields of an e-mail, in order to make it appear that it was sent from a certain source when, in fact, it was sent from another source. .

**Encryption** – Conversion of an intelligible message, clear text, to an encrypted message.

**Entropy** – The average amount of information conveyed by an event, when considering all possible outcomes.

**Error Correction Code** – An Error Correction Code (ECC) checks transmitted data for errors and corrects them as soon as they are found.

**Error Correction** – The process of detecting errors in transmitted messages and reconstructing the original error-free data. Error correction ensures that corrected and error-free messages are obtained at the receiver.

**Error trapping** – Consists of cyclically shifting, bit by bit, the syndrome of the received word, always observing its Hamming weight.

**Ethernet** – It is an interconnection architecture for local networks, a set of layers that provides the encapsulation of frames, before being sent to the network.

**ETSI** – European Telecommunications Standards Institute.

**Euclid's algorithm** – An algorithm for finding the greatest common divisor (GCD) between two numbers. The GCD is the largest number that divides two numbers without a remainder. It is also known as Euclidean algorithm.

**EV SSL** – Extended Validation Secure Socket Layer. Advanced or extended validation SSL certificate.

**Exploit** – Malicious program designed to exploit a computer or program's vulnerability.

**FCC** – Federal Communications Commission. US government agency responsible for regulatory issues in the telecommunications area.

**FEC** – Forward Error Correction. Technique in which data is modified to increase its robustness to channel errors, with the aim of improving the probability of system error.

**FFT** – Fast Fourier Transform.

**Firewall** – Security device used to divide and control access between computer networks.

**FTP** File Transfer Protocol – Allows the transfer of files between two computers using a login and password.

**GnuPG** – Set of free and open source programs, which implements symmetric key encryption, asymmetric keys and digital signature.

**Greylisting** – Filtering method for spam, implemented directly on the email server, which temporarily refuses an email and receives it only when it is resent. Legitimate e-mail servers, which behave correctly and in accordance with the specifications of the protocols, always forward messages. This method assumes that spammers rarely use legitimate servers and therefore do not resend their messages.

**Hamming distance** – The Hamming distance between two vectors, with same number of components, is the number of differing positions. The Hamming distance is a metric to evaluate the proximity of the information vectors.

**Hamming weight** – The Hamming weight of a vector is the number of null positions in it.

**Harvesting** – Technique used by spammers, which consists of scanning web pages, mailing list files, among others, in search of e-mail addresses.

**Hash function** – Cryptographic method that, when applied to information, regardless of its size, generates a single, fixed-size result, called a hash.

**Hoax** – Message that has alarming or false content and that usually has as its sender, or points as the author, some institution, important company or government agency. Through a thorough reading of its content, it is usually possible to identify meaningless information and attempted strikes, such as chains and pyramids.

**Hot fix** – Security fix.

**HTML** – HyperText Markup Language is a protocol used for transferring web pages between the server and the client. It works as a kind of universal language that is used to create pages on the Internet.

**HTPPS** – Specifies the usefulness of HTTP, through a security mechanism.

**HTTP** Hypertext Transfer Protocol is used to transport HTML pages from network servers to browsers. The protocol performs communication between servers and browsers installed on client computers.

**HTTP** – in HyperText Transfer Protocol. Protocol used to transfer web pages between a server and a client (for example, the browser).

**HTTPS** – HyperText Transfer Protocol Secure over SSL. Protocol that combines the use of HTTP with security mechanisms, such as SSL and TLS, in order to provide secure connections.

**ICMP** Internet Control Message Protocol (ICMP) manages and produces the error report for transporting data during communication between computers.

**Identity theft** – An act by which a person tries to impersonate another person, by assigning himself or herself a false identity, in order to obtain undue advantages. Some cases of identity theft can be considered a crime against the public faith, typified as false identity.

**IDS** – Intrusion Detection System. Program, or a set of programs, whose function is to detect malicious or anomalous activities.

**IDS** – Intrusion Detection System. Program with the function of detecting unauthorized activities on the computer.

**IEEE** – Institute of Electrical and Electronic Engineers. US organization responsible for publications and standards in several areas of electrical engineering.

**IFFT** – Inverse fast Fourier transform.

**IGMP** Internet Group Management Protocol is used to support multicasting messages and to track groups of users on the computer network.

**IGP** Interior Gateway Protocol – Each system on the Internet can choose its own routing protocol. RIP and OSPF are examples of IGP protocols.

**IN** – Intelligent network. Structure built on the telephone network for the provision of additional services such as virtual private network, personal DDG , service 0800, 0900, connection with the Internet and a single number for users.

**Information Theory** – A branch of mathematics that defines and analyzes the concept of information. Information theory involves the application of statistics and probability theory, and include the design of systems for data transmission, encryption, compression, and other information processing.

**Inmarsat** – International Maritime Satellite Corporation.

**Invader** – Person responsible for carrying out an invasion (compromise).

**Invasion** – Successful attack that results in accessing, manipulating or destroying information on a computer.

**IP Address** – Sequence of numbers associated with each computer connected to the Internet. In the case of IPv4, the IP address is divided into four groups, separated by periods and composed of numbers between 0 and 255, for example, "193.0.3.3". In the case of IPv6, the IP address is divided into up to eight groups, separated by colons and composed of hexadecimal numbers, between 0 and FFFF, for example, "2019:DB9:C011:901D:DA28:126B::3".

**IP** Internet Protocol. Except for ARP and RARP, all data from all protocols is packaged in an IP data packet, which addresses and manages data packets sent between computers.

**ISDN** – Integrated services digital network or integrated services digital network. Digital telephone service with speed between 57.6 kbit/s and 128 kbit/s.

**ISI** – Intersymbol interference. Problem in digital communication system in which adjacent symbols in a sequence are distorted due to non-ideal frequency response , causing dispersion that interferes with the time domain in neighboring symbols.

**IS** – Interim Standard.

**ITU** – International Telecommunications Union.

**ITU** – International Telecommunication Union. Organism associated to the UN that regulates telecommunications worldwide .

**ITU-R** – ITU Radio Standardization Sector.

**ITU-T** – ITU Telecommunications Standards Sector.

**JPEG** – Joint Photographic Experts Group. Organization that, among other things, sets standards for images.

**kbit/s** – kilobits per second. Thousands of bits per second. It is recommended to use the shannon [Sh] unit, corresponding to bits per second (bits/s).

**Keylogger** – Specific type of spyware. Program capable of capturing and storing the keys typed by the user on the computer keyboard. Usually the activation of the keylogger is conditioned to a previous action of the user, such as access to a specific e-commerce site or Internet Banking.

**kHz** – Kilohertz. Frequency unit that equates to $10^3$ Hz.

**LAN** – Local Area Network or local computer network.

**LBG** – Linde-Buzo-Gray. Algorithm proposed by Linde, Buzo and Gray in 1980, constituting the most widely used technique for dictionary design (vector quantization).

**Linear code** – A linear code is an algebraic code over a finite field, in which the addition of two codewords is a codeword and the multiplication of a codeword by a field element is also a codeword.

**LMDS** – Local Multipoint Distribution System. Fixed wireless system used for voice and data transmission.

**Majority logic decoding** – Majority logic decoding (MLD) codes are powerful due to the simplicity of the decoder. It is a method of decoding by voting that is simple to implement and is extremely fast. Is also a method to decode repetition codes, based on the assumption that the largest number of occurrences of a symbol was the transmitted symbol.

**Malicious code** – Generic term used to refer to programs designed to perform harmful actions and malicious activities on a computer or mobile device. Specific types of malicious code are: viruses, worm, bot, spyware, backdoor, Trojan horse and rootkit.

**Malvertising** – Malicious advertising. Type of scam that consists of creating malicious ads and, through advertising services, displaying them on various web pages. Generally, the advertising service is tricked into believing that it is a legitimate ad and, by accepting it, it intermediates the presentation and makes it appear on several pages.

**Malware** – Malicious software. Malicious program or code.

**Master key** – Unique password used to protect (encrypt) other passwords.

**Master password** – Master key.

**Maximum likelihood decoding** – A technique used to determine the most likely transmitted message in a digital communication system, based on the received signal and statistical models of noise and interference.

**Mbit/s** – Mega-bits per second. Millions of bits per second. it is recommended to use the shannon unit [Sh] to imply bit per second.

**Meggitt decoder** – A decoder that computes the error syndromes of all correctable error patterns from a small number of error syndromes ans avoids the need for a syndrome table.

**MHz** – Megahertz. Frequency unit that equates to $10^6$ Hz.

**MIPS** – Millions of instructions per second.

**MMS** – Multimedia Message Service. Technology used in cellular telephony for the transmission of data, such as text, image, audio and video.

**Mobile broadband** – Type of broadband connection. Wireless long distance access technology through a mobile phone network, especially 3G and 4G (respectively the third and fourth generation of mobile telephone standards defined by the International Telecommunication Union (ITU).

**Mobile code** – Type of code used by Web developers to incorporate greater functionality and improve the appearance of Web pages. Some types of mobile code are: Java programs and applets, JavaScripts and ActiveX components (or controls).

**Mobile device** – Equipment with computational resources that, due to its small size, offers great mobility of use and can be easily carried by its owner. Examples: notebooks, netbooks, tablets, PDAs, smartphones and cell phones.

**Modem** – MOdulator and DEModulator. Equipment that converts digital signals from a computer into analogue signals that can be transmitted by physical means, such as telephone lines, pay-TV cable or fiber optics.

**MPEG** – Motion Picture Experts Group. Organizations which, among other things, define standards for video signals.

**MSB** – Most Significant Bit. Binary digit in the most significant position of the binary word.

**MSE** – Mean Square Error or average error.

**Multiple domains (MDC)** – Certificate for companies that have multiple addresses and want to encrypt all of them.

**MUX** – Multiplexer. Equipment that combines several signals to be transmitted on a single transmission channel.

**Network Scanning** – Technique that consists of performing thorough searches on networks, with the objective of identifying active computers and collecting information about them, such as available services and installed programs.

**NEXT** – Near-End Crosstalk. Crosstalk or interference between local transmitter and receiver, usually associated with a pair cable.

**NFS** – Network File System. It is a networking protocol for distributed file sharing.

**NTP** – Network Time Protocol. Type of protocol that allows the synchronization of the clocks of devices on a network, such as servers, workstations, routers and other equipment, from reliable time references (Source: http://ntp.br/).

**NTT** – Nippon Telephone and Telegraph Co.

**OFDM** – Orthogonal frequency division multiplexing.

**Open Proxy** – Poorly configured proxy that can be abused by attackers and used as a way to make certain actions on the Internet anonymous, such as attacking other networks or sending spam.

**Opt-in** – Message sending rule that defines that it is prohibited to send commercial emails or spam, unless there is a prior agreement by the recipient.

**Opt-out** – Rule for sending messages that defines that it is allowed to send commercial e-mails, but a mechanism must be provided so that the recipient can stop receiving the messages.

**OSPF** Open Shortest Path First. A type of dynamic routing protocol.

**P2P** – Acronym for peer-to-peer. Network architecture where each computer has equivalent functionalities and responsibilities. It differs from the client/server architecture, in which some devices are dedicated to serving others. This type of network is usually implemented via P2P programs, which allow [connecting one user's computer to another to share or transfer data, such as MP3, games, videos and images.

**Page Defacement** – Also known as graffiti, is a technique that consists of altering the content of the web page of a website.

**Password** – Character set, unique to the user, used in the process of verifying his identity, ensuring that he is really who he claims to be and that he has the right to access the resource in question.

**Patch** – Security fix.

**PCI** – Standards established by global financial institutions to ensure security in credit card payment transactions.

**PenTest** – Test that simulates an invasion on the website in order to find and correct the identified security flaws.

**Personal firewall** – Specific type of firewall. Program used to protect a computer from unauthorized access from the Internet.

**PGP** – Pretty Good Privacy. Program that implements symmetric key cryptography, asymmetric keys and digital signature. It has commercial and free versions.

**Pharming** – Specific type of phishing that involves redirecting the user's navigation to fake websites, through changes to the DNS service.

**Phishing** – Type of scam through which a scammer tries to obtain a user's personal and financial data, through the combined use of technical means and social engineering.

**Plug-in** – Program generally developed by third parties and which can be installed in the web browser or e-mails programs to provide extra functionality.

**PMD** – Principle of Majority Decision. When receiving a digital signal, the principle guarantees the choice of the most frequent symbol.

**PN** – Pseudorandom noise. Digital noise generated by the displacement recorder widely used in systems with spectral spreading by direct sequence.

**POP3** Post Office Protocol version 3 is used by client users to access an email account on a server to get the message.

**Pop-up window** – Type of window that appears automatically and without permission, overlapping the Web browser window, after the user accesses a website.

**PPP** Point to Point Protocol is a form of serial data encapsulation that represents an improvement over SLIP, capable of providing bidirectional serial communication similar to SLIP, but supports AppleTalk, IPX, TCP/IP and NetBEUI along with TCP/IP.

**Prepayment Fraud** – Type of fraud in which a scammer tries to trick a person into providing confidential information or making an advance payment, with the promise of receiving some kind of benefit in the future.

**Probabilistic decoding** – An iterative decoding technique used to decode codes efficiently.

**Proxy** – Server that acts as an intermediary between a client and another server. It is usually used in companies to increase the performance of access to certain services or to allow more than one machine to connect to the Internet. When badly configured (open proxy) it can be abused by attackers and used to make certain actions on the Internet anonymous, such as attacking other networks or sending spam.

**PSTN** – Public switched telephone network.

**QoS** – Quality of service. Parameter used to measure the quality of various functions of a communication network.

**RACE** – Research and Development for Advanced Communications. European committee for the creation of advanced communication networks.

**RAM** – Random access memory.

**RARP** Reverse Address Resolution. This protocol is to allow a permanent memory computer to have an IP address starting from its Ethernet address.

**RIP** Routing Information Protocol dynamically updates routing tables over WANs and the Internet. The distance vector algorithm is used to calculate the best route for the packet.

**ROM** – Read-Only Memory.

**Rootkit** – Type of malicious code. Set of programs and techniques that allows you to hide and ensure the presence of an attacker or other malicious code on a compromised computer. It is important to note that the name rootkit does not indicate that the tools that comprise it are used to obtain privileged access (root or Administrator) on a computer, but rather to maintain privileged access on a previously compromised computer.

**RS** – Reed–Solomon. One of the classes of error correction codes.

**RZ** – Return-to-Zero. Coding system in which part of a symbol takes the zero level.

**SAN** – Small Area Network or small computer network, usually limited to a few tens of meters.

**San UCC** – Certified for Microsoft Exchange applications.

**SA** – Simulated Annealing. Algorithm used in optimization problems. It relates optimization problems of a combinatorial nature with the physical process of cooling molten metals.

**Scam** – Misleading or fraudulent schemes or actions. Usually, they aim to obtain financial advantages.

**Scanner** – Program used to scan computer networks, in order to identify which computers are active and which services are being made available by them. Widely used by attackers to identify potential targets, as it allows to associate possible vulnerabilities to services enabled on a computer.

**Scan/Scanner** – Technique for scanning networks and computers, in order to find viruses or unauthorized modifications.

**Screenlogger** – Specific type of spyware. Program similar to keylogger, capable of storing the position of the cursor and the screen displayed on the monitor, when the mouse is clicked, or the region surrounding the position where the mouse is clicked. It is widely used by attackers to capture the keys typed by users on virtual keyboards, available mainly on Internet Banking sites.

**Secure connection** – Connection that uses an encryption protocol for data transmission, such as HTTPS or SSH.

**Security fix** – Fix designed to eliminate security holes in a program or operating system.

**Security incident** – Any adverse event, confirmed or suspected, related to the security of computer systems or computer networks.

**Security Policy** – Document that defines the rights and responsibilities of each person in relation to the security of the computational resources he uses and the penalties to which he is subject, in case he does not comply with it.

**Systematic search** – A method that involves searching through a large set of search results where necessary.

**Site** – Internet site identified by a domain name, consisting of one or more hypertext pages, which may contain text, graphics and multimedia information.

**Site Shielding** – Service package that identifies and corrects website vulnerabilities.

**SLIP** Serial Line Internet Protocol – This protocol places data packets in frames in preparation for transport by network equipment. It sends data over serial lines, without error correction, addressing or packet identification and without authentication. SLIP only supports the transport of IP packets.

**S/MIME** – Secure/Multipurpose Internet Mail Extensions. Standard for signing and encrypting e-mails.

**SMS** – Short Message Service is a technology used in telephony to send and receive short text messages. Unlike MMS, it only allows text data and each message is limited to 160 alphanumeric characters.

**SMTP** – Simple Mail Transfer Protocol. Protocol responsible for transporting e-mail messages on the Internet.

**Sniffer** – Computer device or program used to capture and store data traveling over a computer network. It can be used by an attacker to capture sensitive information (such as user passwords), in cases where insecure connections are being used, that is, without encryption.

**Sniffing** – Traffic interception.

**SNMP** Simple Network Management Protocol is used to manage network elements based on sending and receiving data.

**SNRseg** – Segmental Signal-to-Noise Ratio.

**SNR** – Signal-to-Noise Ratio.

**Social engineering** – Technique by which one person seeks to persuade another to perform certain actions. Used by scammers to try to exploit greed, vanity and good faith or to abuse the ingenuity and trust of others, in order to scam, deceive or obtain confidential and important information.

**Social Network** – Type of social network that allows users to create profiles and use them to connect with other users, share information and group according to common interests. Some examples are: Facebook, Orkut, Twitter, Linkedin, Google+ and foursquare.

**Soft opt-in** – Rule similar to opt-in, but in this case it provides for an exception when there is already a business relationship between sender and recipient. Thus, the recipient's explicit permission is not required to receive e-mails from that sender.

**SONET** – Synchronous Optical NETworkNorth American standard for high-speed digital optical networks.

**Spam Bots** – Automated programs that generate excessive traffic to a web-site through robots.

**Spamcop** – Institution that offers several anti-spam services, the most well-known being the one that allows you to automatically complain about incoming spam.

**Spammer** – Individual who sends the spam.

**Spam** – Term used to refer to unsolicited e-mails, which are usually sent to a large number of people.

**Spam zombie** – Computer infected by malicious code (bot), capable of transforming the user's system into an email server for sending spam. In many cases, the user of the infected computer takes time to realize that his computer is being used by an attacker for this purpose.

**Sponsored link** – Type of link displayed prominently on a search site when specific words are searched by the user. When the user clicks on a sponsored link, the search engine receives a previously agreed value from the advertiser.

**Spyware** – Specific type of malicious code. Program designed to monitor the activities of a system and send the collected information to third parties. Keylogger, screenlogger and adware are some specific types of spyware.

**SQNR** – Signal-to-quantization noise ratio.

**SSH** – Secure Shell is a protocol for accessing a remote computer using encryption, which allows actions such as executing commands and transferring files.

**SSID** – Service Set Identifier is a unique set of characters that identifies a wireless network. The SSID differentiates one wireless network from another, and a client can normally connect to a wireless network only if it can provide the correct SSID.

**SSL EV** – Extended validation cryptography, which in addition to protecting information trafficked on the website, validates the company's corporate name and CNPJ.

**SSL** – Secure Sockets Layer. Like TLS, it is a protocol that, through encryption, provides confidentiality and integrity in communications between a client and a server, and can also be used to provide authentication. SSL is a basic encryption for any e-commerce that aims to protect information trafficked on the website. It was developed by the Netscape team in the 1990s, and later replaced by TLS.

**SWIFT** – Society for Worldwide Interbank Financial Telecommunications. Network developed to support the exchange of information from banks and financial institutions.

**TCP/IP** – Transmission Control Protocol/Internet Protocol This term is widely used in Internet protocols.

**TCP** – Reliable connection used to control the management of applications at the service level between computers. It does both the sequential transport of data and the verification of its integrity.

**Telnet** – Command used to open a remote session on another computer. It is based on TCP for transport and is defined by RFC854.

**TFTP** Trivial File Transfer Protocol – Allows the transfer of files between two computers without the need for a login and password. More limited sense is little used.

**TIA** – Telecommunications Industry Association.

**TLS** – Transport Layer Security. Like SSL, it is a protocol that, through encryption, provides confidentiality and integrity in communications between a client and a server, and can also be used to provide authentication.

**Traffic interception** – Technique that consists of inspecting data trafficked on computer networks, through the use of specific programs called sniffers.

**Trellis decoding** – Trellis decoding is a popular method to recover encoded information corrupted during transmission over a noisy channel. A trellis for a code establishes a one-to-one correspondence between codewords and paths.

**Threshold decoding** – Also known as majority logic decoding.

**Trojan horse** – Type of malicious code. Program normally received as a gift (for example, virtual card, photo album, screen saver, game) that, in addition to performing the functions for which it was apparently designed, also performs other functions, usually malicious and without the user's knowledge.

**UBE** – Unsolicited Bulk E-mail. Term used to refer to unsolicited emails sent in large quantities.

**UCE** – Unsolicited Commercial E-mail. Term used to refer to unsolicited commercial e-mails.

**UDP** – Unreliable connection used to control the management of applications at the service level between computers.

**UHF** – Ultra-high frequency. Frequency range from 300 MHz to 3 GHz.

**URL** – Universal Resource Locator. String of characters that indicates the location of a resource on the Internet.

**User account** – Also called ' username" and "login name." Corresponds to the unique identification of a user on a computer or service.

**Virus** – Program or part of a computer program, usually malicious, that spreads by inserting copies of itself, becoming part of other programs and files. The virus depends on the execution of the host program or file so that it can become active and continue the infection process.

**Viterbi decoder** – A decoder that uses the Viterbi algorithm for decoding a bitstream that has been encoded using a convolutional code or trellis code.

**VPN** – Virtual Private Network. Term used to refer to the construction of a private network using public networks (for example, the Internet) as infrastructure. These systems use encryption and other security mechanisms to ensure that only authorized users can access the private network and that no data will be intercepted while passing through the public network.

**Vulnerability Exploitation** – A program or part of a malicious program designed to exploit an existing vulnerability in a computer program.

**Vulnerability** – Security holes that can be exploited by attackers.

**WAF** – Security Firewall that protects web applications from attacks and invasions.

**WAN** – Wide area network. Computer network covering a wide area.

**WAP** – Wireless Application Protocol. Global protocol used on many wireless systems, for users to view and interact with data services.

**Web bug** – Image, usually very small and invisible, that is part of a web page or an e-mail message, and that is designed to monitor who is accessing that page or e-mail message.

**Weldon algorithm** – A majority decoding algorithm for block codes associated with finite geometries.

**WEP** – Wired Equivalent Privacy. Security protocol for wireless networks that implements encryption for data transmission.

**Whitelist** – List of e-mails, domains or IP addresses, previously approved and that, normally, are not submitted to the configured antispam filters.

**Wi-Fi** – Wireless Fidelity. Trademark, generically used to refer to wireless networks that use any of the 802.11 standards.

**Wildcard** – Encryption for those who want to protect several subdomains under a specific address.

**Wireless network** – Network that allows the connection between computers and other devices through the transmission and reception of radio signals.

**Wireless Network** – Wireless network.

**WLAN** – Wireless Local-Area Network. Type of network that uses high frequency radio waves, instead of cables, for communication between computers.

**WLL** – in Wireless Local Loop or wireless LAN. Broadband system that uses RF to transmit voice and data.

**Worm** – Type of malicious code. Program capable of automatically propagating through networks, sending copies of itself from computer to computer. Unlike the virus, the worm does not include its own copies in other programs or files and does not need to be run to spread. Its spread occurs through the exploitation of existing vulnerabilities or flaws in the configuration of programs installed on computers.

**WPA** – Wi-Fi Protected Access. Security protocol for wireless networks designed to replace the WEP protocol. Designed to operate with Wi-Fi products that only offer WEP technology, through program updates. It includes two improvements over WEP: better encryption for data transmission and user authentication.

**X.25** – Standard of data transmission in packets.

**Zombie computer** – Name given to a computer infected by bot, as it can be controlled remotely, without the knowledge of its owner.

# References

Abbe, E., Shpilka, A., and Ye, M. (2020). Reed–Muller codes: Theory and algorithms.

Abramson, N. (1963). *Information Theory and Coding*. McGraw-Hill, New York.

Aczél, J. and Daróczy, Z. (1975). *On Measures of Information and their Caracterizations*. Academic Press, New York.

Alencar, M. S. (2002). *Telefonia Digital, Quarta Edição*. Editora Érica Ltda., ISBN 978-85-365-0364-6, São Paulo, Brasil.

Alencar, M. S. (2007). The Information is Relative – Second Part (in Portuguese). Article for an electronic journal in the Internet, Jornal do Commercio *On Line*, Recife, Brazil.

Alencar, M. S. (2012). *Engineering of Computer Networks (in Portuguese)*. Publisher Editora Érica Ltda., ISBN 978-85-365-0411-7, São Paulo, Brazil.

Alencar, M. S. (2022). *Cryptography and Network Security*. River Publishers, Delft, The Netherlands.

Alencar, M. S. and Alencar, R. T. (2024). *Set, Measure, and Probability Theory*. River Publishers, Delft, The Netherlands.

Alencar, M. S. and Assis, K. D. R. (2020). A New Derivation of the Leftover Hash Lemma. *The ISC International Journal of Information Security*, 12(3):55–58.

Alencar, M. S. and da Rocha Jr., V. C. (2022). *Communication Systems, 3rd Edition*. Springer Nature, Cham, Switzerland.

Ash, R. B. (1965). *Information Theory*. Dover Publications, Inc., New York.

Berens, S. (2013). Conditional RÃl'nyi Entropy. Master's thesis, Mathematisch Institute, Universiteit Leiden.

Berlekamp, E. R. (1968a). *Algebraic Coding Theory*. McGraw-Hill.

Berlekamp, E. R. (1968b). *Algebraic coding theory*. McGraw-Hill.

Berrou, C., Glavieux, A., and Thitimajshima, P. (1993). Near Shannon limit error-correcting coding and decoding: Turbo Codes. In *Proceedings of the*

*1993 IEEE International Conference on Communications (ICC'93)*, pages 1064–1070.

Blahut, R. (1983). *Theory and Practice of Error Control Codes.* Addison Wesley.

Blake, I. F. (1987). *An Introduction to Applied Probability.* Robert E. Krieger Publishing Co., Malabar, Florida.

Boyer, C. (1974). *História da Matemática.* Editora Edgard Blucher Ltda., São Paulo, Brasil.

Carter, J. L. and Wegman, M. N. (1979). Universal Classes of hash Functions. *Journal of Computer and System Sciences*, 18:143–154.

CERT.br (2019). GlossÃąrio. Cartilha de SeguranÃğa para Internet, Centro de Estudos, Resposta e Tratamento de Incidentes de SeguranÃğa no Brasil, São Paulo, Brasil.

Chase, D. (1972). "A Class of Algorithms for Decoding Block Codes with Channel Measurement Information". *IEEE Transactions on Information Theory*, 18:170–182.

Clark, G. C. and Cain, J. B. (1981). *Error-Correction Coding for Digital Communications.* Plenum Press.

Csiszár, I. and Kórner, J. (1981). *Information Theory: Coding Theorems for Discrete Memoryless Systems.* Academic Press, New York, USA.

da Rocha Jr. & J.L. Massey, V. (1993). "A New Approach to the Design of Codes for the Binary Adder Channel". *Cryptography and Coding III (Editor M.J. Ganley), IMA Conf. Series, New Series.*, (No. 45):179–185.

da Rocha Jr. & R. Palazzo Jr., V. (1987). *Códigos Corretores de Erros.* International Symposium on Information and Coding Theory, ISICT'87, Campinas, São Paulo.

da Rocha Jr., V. C. (2001). "CÃşdigos Corretores de Erros". Course notes, Federal University of Pernambuco.

da Rocha Jr, V. C. (2014). *Elements of Algebraic Coding Systems.* Momentum Press, New York, USA.

Design, C. S. (2001). Communication systems design – reference library: Glossary. Internet site, www.csdmag.com/glo- ssary.

Dorsch, B. G. (1974). A decoding algorithm for binary block codes and $j$-ary output channels. *IEEE Transactions on Information Theory*, 20(3):391–394.

Elia, M. (1987). Algebraic decoding of the (23,12,7) golay code (corresp.). *IEEE Transactions on Information Theory*, 33(1):150–151.

Elias, P. (1954). Error-Free Coding. *IRE Transactions on Information Theory*, IT-4:29–37.

Elias, P. (1955). Coding for Noisy Channels. *IRE Convention Record – Part 4*, pages 37–46.

et al., M. E. M. (1963). Coding and Decoding Operations Research. Final report on contract (afcrl)af 19(604)-6183, General Electric Co.

Fano, R. M. (1963). A heuristic discussion of probabilistic decoding. *IEEE Transactions on Information Theory*, pages 64–74.

Feinstein, A. (1954). *"A New Basic Theorem of Information Theory"*. PhD thesis, Research Laboratory of Electronics, Massachusetts Institute of Technology.

Feinstein, A. (1958). *Foundations of Information Theory*. McGraw-Hill Book Company, Inc., New York, USA.

Forney Jr., G. D. (1973). The viterbi algorithm. *Proceedings of the IEEE*, 61:268–278.

Furiati, G. (1998). "Serviços são Reclassificados". *Revista Nacional de Telecomunicações*, (227):32–35.

Halmos, P. R. (1960). *Naive Set Theory*. D. Van Nostrand Company, Inc., Princeton, USA.

Hamming, R. W. (1950). "Error Detecting and Error Correcting Codes". *Bell Systems Technical Journal*, 29:147–160.

Hartley, R. V. L. (1928). "Transmission of Information". *Bell Systems Technical Journal*, page 535.

Hartmann, C. R. P. and Rudolph, L. D. (1976). An Optimum Symbol-by-Symbol Decoding Rule for Linear Codes. *IEEE Transactions on Information Theory*, 22:514–517.

Haykin, S. (1988). *Digital Communications*. John Wiley and Sons, New York.

Haykin, S. (1999). *The Code Book – The Science of Secrecy from Ancient Egypt to Quantum Cryptography*. Doubleday, New York, USA.

Helgert, H. J. (1974). Alternant codes. *Information and Control*, (26):369.

Hsiao, C. C. . M. (1984). Error-Correcting Codes for Semiconductor Memory Applications: A State of the Art Review. *IBM Jour. Res. and Dev.*, 28:124–134.

James, B. R. (1981). *Probabilidade: Um Curso em Nível Intermediário*. Instituto de Matemática Pura e Aplicada – CNPq, Rio de Janeiro, Brasil.

Jelinek, F. (1969). A fast sequential decoding algorithm using a stack. *IBM Journal of Research and Development*, 13:675–685.

John E. Meggitt (1961). Error correcting codes and their implementation for data transmission systems. *IEEE Transactions on Information Theory*, (7):234.

Jr., E. J. W. (1968). Some Results on Majority Logic Decoding. In *Proceedings of Symposium on Error Correcting Codes, University of Wisconsin*.

Jr., E. J. W. (1971). "Decoding Binary Block Codes on Q-ary Output Channels". *IEEE Transactions on Information Theory*, 17:713–718.

Khinchin, A. I. (1957). *Mathematical Foundations of Information Theory*. Dover Publications, Inc., New York, USA.

Konheim, A. (1981). *Cryptography a Primer*. John Wiley & Sons.

Leon-Garcia, A. (1989). *Probability and Random Processes for Electrical Engineering*. Addison-Wesley Publishing Co., Reading, Massachusetts.

Lin, S. and Costello, D. (1983). *Error Control Coding: Fundamentals and Applications*. Prentice-Hall.

Lipschutz, S. (1968). *Teoria de Conjuntos*. Ao Livro Técnico S.A., Rio de Janeiro, Brasil.

MacKay, D. J. C. (2003). *Information Theory, Inference, and Learning Algorithms*. Cambridge University Press, Cambridge, United Kingdom.

MacWilliams, F. J. C. and Sloane, N. J. A. (1977). *The Theory of Error-Correcting Codes*. North-Holland.

Markman, I. (1987). *Introdução à Codificação Corretora de Erros*. Grupo de Comunicações por Satélite, TelebrÃąs, Campinas, São Paulo.

Massey, J. (1969a). "Shift Register Synthesis and BCH Decoding". *IEEE Transactions on Information Theory*, 15:122–127.

Massey, J. L. (1963a). *Threshold Decoding*. MIT Press, Cambridge, Massachussets.

Massey, J. L. (1963b). Threshold Decoding. Technical report, Massachussets Institute of Technology, Cambridge, USA.

Massey, J. L. (1969b). Shift-register synthesis and BCH decoding. *IEEE Trans. on Info. Theory*, 15(1):122–127.

Massey, J. L. (1990). The Relevance of Information Theory to Modern Cryptography. In *Proceedings of the Bilkent International Conference on New Trends in Communications, Control and Signal Processing (NILCON'90)*, pages 176–182, Ankara, Turkey. Elsevier Science Publisher.

Maurer, U. M. (1989). A Provably-Secure Strongly-Randomized Cipher. In *Proceedings of the Monte Verita Seminar On Future Directions in Cryptography*, Ascona, Switzerland.

Maurer, U. M. (1995). Generalized Privacy Amplification. *IEEE Transactions on Information Theory*, 41(6):122–127.

MobileWord (2001). Mobileword's glossary. Internet site, www.mobileworld.org.

Nenno, R. B. (1987). An introduction of the theory of nonlinear error-correcting codes. Master's thesis, Rochester Institute of Technology.

Nyquist, H. (1924). "Certain Facts Affecting Telegraph Speed". *Bell Systems Technical Journal*, page 324.

Omura, A. V. . J. (1979). *Principles of Digital Communications and Coding*. McGraw-Hill.

Omura, J. K. (1969). On the viterbi decoding algorithm. *IEEE Transactions on Information Theory*, 15:6–12.

Papoulis, A. (1983). Random Modularion: a Review. *IEEE Transactions on Accoustics, Speech and Signal Processing*, 31(1):96–105.

Papoulis, A. (1984). *Probability, Random Variables, and Stochastic Processes*. McGraw-Hill, New York.

Pickholtz, R.L., Schilling D.L., Milstein L.B. (1982). "Theory of Spread–Spectrum Communications – A Tutorial". *IEEE Transactions on Communications*, COM. 30(5):855–884.

Pierce, J. R. (1980). *An Introduction to Information Theory – Symbols, Signals & Noise, Second Edition*. Dover Publications, Inc., New York, USA.

Pless, V. (1982). *An Introduction to the Theory of Error-Correcting Codes*. John Wiley & Sons., Inc.

Preneel, B. (1994). "Cryptographic Hash Functions". *European Transactions on Telecommunications*, 5(4):431–448.

Reed, I. S. (1954). A class of multiple-error-correcting codes and the decoding scheme. *IRE Transactions Information Theory*, IT-4:38–44.

Reed, I. S., Truong, T.-K., Chen, X., and Yin, X. (1992). The algebraic decoding of the (41, 21, 9) quadratic residue code. *IEEE Transactions Information Theory*, 38:974–986.

Reed, I. S., Yin, X., and Truong, T.-K. (1990). Algebraic decoding of the (32, 16, 8) quadratic residue code. *IEEE Transactions Information Theory*, 36:876–880.

Rényi, A. (1961). "On Measures of Entropy and Information". In *Proceedings of the 4th Berkeley Symposium on Mathematics, Statistics and Probability*, volume 1, pages 547–561, Berkeley, USA. University of California Press.

Reza, F. M. (1961). *An Introduction to Information Theory*. McGraw-Hill Book Co., New York.

Rhee, M. Y. (1998). *CDMA – Celular Mobile Comunication & Network Security*. Prentice Hall PTR. Korea.

Ricciardi, L. M. (1990). *Lectures in Applied Mathematics and Informatics.* Manchester University Press, Manchester, United Kingdom.

Rudolph, L. D. (1964). Geometric Configurations and Majority Logic Decodable Codes. M. e. e. thesis, University of Oklahoma.

Rudolph, L. D. (1969a). *"Generalized Threshold Decoding of Convolutional Codes".* PhD thesis, Department of Electrical Engineering, Syracuse University.

Rudolph, L. D. (1969b). Threshold decoding of cyclic codes. *IEEE Transactions Information Theory*, IT-15:414–418.

Sayood, K. (2006). *Introduction to Data Compression.* Morgan Kaufmann, San Francisco.

Scholtz, R. A. (1982). "The Origins of Spread-Spectrum Communications". *IEEE Transactions on Communications*, COM. 30(5):822–854.

Shannon, C. E. (1948a). "A Mathematical Theory of Communication". *The Bell System Technical Journal*, 27:379–423.

Shannon, C. E. (1948b). A mathematical theory of communication. *Bell System Technical*, 28:379–423.

Skycell (2001). Glossary of satellite terminology. Internet site, www.satellitetelephone.com.

Stallings, W. (1999). *"Cryptography and Network Security – Principles and Practice.* Prentice Hall, Upper Saddle River, USA.

Stinson, D. R. (1994a). Combinatorial Techniques for Universal Hashing. *Journal of Computer and System Sciences*, 48:337–346.

Stinson, D. R. (1994b). Universal Hashing and Authentication Codes. *Designs, Codes and Cryptography*, 4:369–380.

Tanenbaum, A. S. (2003). *Computer Networks.* Prentice-Hall, PTR, Englewood Cliffs, USA.

TIAB2B.com (2001). Everything communications. Internet site, www.-tiab2b.com/glossary.

Tomlinson, M., Tjhai, C. J., Ambroze, M. A., Ahmed, M., and Jibril, M. (2017). *The Modified Dorsch Decoder*, pages 399–419. Springer International Publishing, Cham, Switzerland.

van der Lubbe, J. C. A. (1997). *Information Theory.* Cambridge University Press, Cambridge, United Kingdom.

van Lint, J. (1982). *Introduction to Coding Theory.* Springer Verlag.

Viterbi, A. J. (1967). Errors bounds for convolutional codes and asymptotically optimum decoding algorithm. *IEEE Transactions on Communications Technology*, 19:260–269.

Viterbi, A. J. (1971). Convolutional codes and their performance in communication systems. *IEEE Transactions on Communication Technology*, 19(5):751–772.

Viterbi, A. J. (1985). "When Not to Spread Spectrum – A Sequel". *IEEE Communications Magazine*, 23(4):12–17.

Wicker, S. B. (1995). *Error Control Systems for Digital Communication and Storage*. Prentice Hall, New Jersey.

Wikipedia (2019). Cryptographic Hash Function — Wikipedia, The Free Encyclopedia. [Online; acesso em 16 de julho de 2019].

Wikipedia (2023). Reed–Muller Code – Wikipedia, The Free Encyclopedia. [Online; accessed July 2, 2024].

Wikipedia (2024). Albert Girard — Wikipedia, The Free Encyclopedia. [Online; accessed 4-July-2024].

Willems, F. M. J. (2009). "Introduction to Convolutional Codes". Course notes, Eindhoven University of Technology.

Wolf, J. (1978). "Efficient Maximum Likelihood Decoding of Linear Block Codes Using a Trellis". *IEEE Transactions on Information Theory*, 24:76–80.

Wolf, J. K. (2008). "An Introduction to Error Correcting Codes". Course notes, University of California, San Diego.

Wolf, J. K. (2021). "An Introduction to Reed–Solomon Codes". Course notes, University of California, San Diego.

Wozencraft, J. M. and Reiffen, B. (1961). *Sequential Decoding*. MIT Press, Cambridge, USA.

Y. Sugiyama, M. Kasahara, S. H. and Namekawa, T. (1975). "A method for solving a key equation for decoding Goppa codes". *Information and Control*, 27:87–99.

Zadeh, L. A. (1965). Fuzzy Sets. *Information and Control*, 8(3):338–353.

# Index

# About the Author

**Figure A.7** Marcelo Sampaio de Alencar.

**Marcelo Sampaio de Alencar** was born in Serrita, Brazil, in 1957. He received his bachelor degree in electrical engineering, from the Federal University of Pernambuco (UFPE), Brazil, 1980, his master degree in electrical engineering, from the Federal University of Paraiba (UFPB), Brazil, 1988 and his Ph.D. from the University of Waterloo, Department of Electrical and Computer Engineering, Canada, 1993. He has 47 years of engineering experience, and 37 years as an IEEE Member, currently as a life senior member. Marcelo Alencar has supervised 7 post-doctoral researchers, 23 doctoral thesis, 36 master dissertations, two graduate monographies and several undergraduate students.

He is the founder and president of the Institute for Advanced Studies in Communications (Iecom). He has published over 560 engineering and scientific papers, and 31 books. He has also written chapters for 14 books.

Marcelo S. Alencar has contributed in different capacities to the several international scientific journals and he has been involved as a volunteer with several IEEE and SBrT activities, including being a member of the Advisory or Technical Program Committee for several events. He was a columnist of the traditional Brazilian newspaper Jornal do Commercio for two decades, and he was vice-president external relations of SBrT. He is a member of the IEEE, IEICE, in Japan, SBrT, SBMO, SBPC, ABJC and SBEB, in Brazil. He studied acoustic guitar at the Federal University of Paraiba, and keyboard and bass at the music school Musidom. He is composer and percussionist of the famous carnival club Bola de Ferro, in Recife, Brazil.

For Product Safety Concerns and Information please contact our EU representative GPSR@taylorandfrancis.com Taylor & Francis Verlag GmbH, Kaufingerstraße 24, 80331 München, Germany

**Batch number: 10824168**

Printed by Printforce, the Netherlands